'An extraordinarily vivid and compelling memoir of a painful and impoverished childhood . . . What makes this a great book is the sheer skill of a writer who, from earliest days, was "a sensitive plant with a memory like a packet of razor blades" . . . It's quite a trick to write about such stuff without self pity, but Galloway manages triumphantly' *Sunday Times*

'It is a model of how to write out of, rather than about, yourself, and a concentrated account of how the world acts upon us when we are too young to take action against it . . . Few writers can match Galloway's grasp of quite how differently life operates when you are that young and why' *Guardian*

'The writing, like all of her writing, is pared down, chisel-perfect' *Sunday Herald*

'Galloway's sublime prose and fierce honesty set [this memoir] apart . . . she keeps a child's sense of bewilderment and secret understanding' *Daily Telegraph*

'As contemplative as it is funny, as talented as it appears to disbelieve the worth of its telling . . . On reluctantly closing the boards of this unforgettable memoir, the words "first volume" are strangely comforting – a combination of Galloway's power and the fact that the wee girl done good make it so' *Scotland on Sunday*

'The finely realized book is rich with texture, poignant minutiae and flashes of dark humour' *Time Out*

'Utterly convincing and compelling. Her writing beautifully evokes the nature of childhood memories' *Books Quarterly*

'Galloway's evocation of life on the west coast of Scotland in the late 1950s is entrancing. With a sniper's precision, she conjures the minutiae of working-class Scottish life' *Guardian*

'Galloway is brilliant on the minute detail of childhood perception. She is also brave, funny, resilient and in spite of everything full of emotional generosity' *Daily Mail*

'An extraordinarily detailed, beautiful book' *List*

'A funny, touching, and beautifully written tale' *Big Issue*

'Amazingly vivid . . . Galloway perfectly captures the solace an unhappy child can find in domesticity: she knows that a neat, ordered house is "like being held"' *Observer*

This is Not About Me

Janice Galloway

GRANTA

Granta Publications, 12 Addison Avenue, London W11 4QR

First published in Great Britain by Granta Books, 2008
This paperback edition published by Granta Books, 2009

A CIP catalogue record for this book
is available from the British Library.

1 3 5 7 9 10 8 6 4 2

ISBN 978 1 84708 099 8

Typeset in Palatino by M Rules

Printed and bound in Great Britain by
CPI Bookmarque, Croydon

To my mother, for then;
my husband, for now.

Acknowledgements

I owe many thanks. First to Jonathan, James and Alison for their support and patience; to Derek Johns, Juliet Pickering, Pru Rowlandson and David Graham for their encouragement, enthusiasm and tact; to Bella Shand for her terrific commitment and hard work; to Andrew O'Hagan; to White and McKay for time at Jura Whisky Lodge and to Catriona Mack and Willie Cochrane for my comfort there; to Bernadette Plissart, Fiona Morrison and the trustees of Hotel Chevillon, Grez-sur-Loing, who let me stay there and write; to The Scottish Arts Council, the Scottish Book Trust and the National Library of Scotland, without whom, nae money. Thanks also to Grant Wilkie, Robin Robertson and Dan Franklin.

1

This is my family.

We're ranged on a sofa and too close because the sofa is meant for two. The photographer's idea. My mother is on the left side, my sister on the right. I'm in the middle, emerging from between the adults' knees, the only one who's five. Maths renders my mother forty-five but she looks older. Everybody did then. Her body is angled towards the centre of the picture but her face is full-on, eager, lipstick so red it's black. Cora's the opposite book-end, and is full-on all over. I can't account for the bruising on her ankles, but the shoes were from Corner Duncan's in the sale, proper stilettos with V-shaped toes, lino-puncturing heels. She wears no stockings so her legs are pale grey, cloudy as marble. The hair, however, is black. It's the blackest thing in a picture with lots of black. It was black to start with but she dyed it with blue stuff, stuff someone told her Elvis used, so it came out very black indeed, no flecks of light and sprayed to within an inch of freeze-dried. Her face is chalky and square, but her hands are lovely. They're a spare set of hands for somebody indolent, somebody like Zsa Zsa Gabor, till you look close and see the tops of her

fingers are darker than the rest, like Sobranie Filter Tips. No rings
though. For a number of reasons, rings weren't Cora's thing. Her
arm-rest has two fag-burns and an ashtray with a full-strength on
the lip, threading wispy ectoplasm across her knees. There was
always a fag, always a fag-burn, so these details make the com-
position evocative. There is a photographer present and we're not
at ease, not really, but if every picture tells a story we want this
story to suggest we amount to something, that we are, at the least,
getting by. In our best duds, our bravest faces, we're trying our
damndest to look right at home.

Home itself, or at least the front room that makes our context,
is less carefully composed. The clock over the mantel reads ten
past four but the window says it's dark outside, winter. Brass
urns, like funerary ornaments, clutter the sill alongside a cut-
glass bowl, a stag's head in brass and two porcelain dancers.
The curtains have oval patterns of flowers, the wallpaper has
tiny hanging baskets in falling rows separated by stripes, the
carpet is speckled and the sofa has a swirly jungle design with
interlocking palm fronds. Each sofa arm has floral covers and the
rug sports stripes and roses. There are three chairs, a wicker
rocker with embroidered cushions and a pair of short bare legs
poke into the picture from the right, suspended by unknown
means. It's a doll all right, and if it's a doll, it's mine. I am impli-
cated in these surroundings by this evidence alone. We must
have looked at this room, with its no space and nothing matching, every day, and not turned a hair. We made it. This was
normal. Ours.

Even the clothes, our hand-picked choices, shout: my mother in a pallid suit with a black fern pattern, Cora in a dark dirndl dress spattered with vast white lotus flowers and a collar that capes the shoulders of her otherwise bare arms. She has big gypsy hoops and enough mascara to block strong sunlight. I am mostly party frock and ankle socks, things sent all the way from America. From the look on my face, I'm trying to hide something. All the same, my mother is smiling. My sister is not. Her shoulders are high, chin forward like a boxer, her half-shut eyes wondering who the hell you think you're looking at; her bone-china wrists are crossed just *so*. She looks within an ace of spontaneous combustion. She looks exactly like Cora. But we share the sofa. We look at the lens. We, I say. *We.* Our hipbones must be touching.

The fireside rug, the fire surround.
A poker with a thistle top, set within hand's reach.
Six transparent wrists.

My mother thought I was the menopause. She came to terms with the fact that I wasn't in Buckreddan Maternity Home in Kilwinning because that was where women in labour went. Local doctors gave out the impression of no choice. Pregnant meant Buckreddan, no question. Perhaps the words suggested duress and distress, or perhaps because it was in an age when pregnant women were kept mostly out of sight, but most people missed off the Maternity Home part and called the hospital simply Buckreddan. Told I was born in Buckreddan, I pictured a country village, not a building. I was sixteen before I caught sight of the word on a sign as I shot by on a bus, and turned in time to see a small red sandstone house, a late-Victorian edifice with the look of a once-posh hotel. Buckreddan Maternity Home the sign said, to the sound of pennies dropping. All the way to Ayr on the worn-shiny double seat of a Scottish Motor Transport single-decker, I tried to imagine it inside. I pictured artillery ranks of bloated women, thin sheets, the occasional nurse with an origami hat like Florence Nightingale. Using garbled notions from the telly, I pictured babies in another room, each cased in its own box, howling under strong electric lights. I had to be among them somewhere, but that was as far as the picturing went. I couldn't picture the absurdly named delivery suites, since I had no idea what delivery was or what such a suite might contain, but I could imagine bottles all right. Bottles and nappies, the standard shorthand for newborns. I knew they were wet and troublesome and noisy. They were easy to spoil and got powdered milk – *formula* – in bottles. That was all I knew about babies.

They tried to make us breast-feed, my mother said once in a rare burst of revelation. It was horrible. I told them I was too old, but the Sister didn't care. It's for baby, she said. *Baby*. As though a baby would know any different.

For fear of the Ward Sister, however, she had a go but it hurt. It was only when her attempts led to my throwing up blood, twice, that she was let stop.

I told them, she said, but you've no dignity in these places.

You canny do that sort of thing when you're forty, I said. Anyway, you did fine on the bottle.

I could picture the insipid green wards and the Big Ward Sister not taking no for an answer. I could picture my mother, or someone like her, a small head afloat on a sea of white cotton as a red tide of blood oozed towards her like lava. I could picture bottles clanking and rattling down the corridors on metal trolleys, fresh, white and full of reconstituted powder that had once been the milk of larger, abler animals. What I couldn't picture was me, the little vampire in the midst of the melodrama, the source of worry and unease.

That's how come you've a delicate stomach, she said, hauling me out of imagining. They made me breast-feed. You had a Bad Start.

Every time she said this, there was a pause. I knew what was next. So did she.

If I'd known you were coming, she'd say eventually, if I'd found out. *Things would have been different.*

I had no reason to doubt her meaning or that her meaning was less than sincere. Things would have been different. Decades on, when my mother was delirious and thinking she was going to die, she let slip she'd miscarried at least twice after me. There should have been, god help us, more. Maybe I'd put her on her guard, seized all the chances and left my found-out, flushed-out little siblings with none. Maybe, on the other hand, her body had made those decisions alone. It was never clear, never clarified, never referred to again. I was, as my sister reminded me

every day of my childhood, bloody lucky to be there at all. If she'd
kent you were coming, she'd say. Nobody needed to say the rest.

———————

Sannox Drive was nowhere near Buckreddan and nowhere near
the shore. To get there from the sea, the defining force that gave
Saltcoats its name, meant walking from Windmill to Chapelwell
Street, past the station to Raise Street, then up Sharphill to Dalry
Road, which led, if let, to somewhere else. It took twenty minutes
on foot, all uphill, and because there were cows not far off, it was
arguably *up the country*. Sannox Drive was the one house we lived
in where the smell of seaweed was not discernible. There was no
heavy traffic and no pub. There was a shop and a bus stop, a
wood with swing ropes, good neighbours and a driveway. We
had no car because my father smashed it, but the house having
such a thing as a *driveway* must have lent a sense of possibility. All
her life my mother referred to this place as *the Sannox House*, as
though it was paved with rhinestones, had its own grounds and
adjacent funfair. It was the place she hoped to grow old in. What
I remember of it is nothing at all. We moved when I was one year
old because the walk back from town with the pram was impossible for a woman with asthma. All I know for sure about this
house, then, rests in two snaps.

In both, there is a pebble-dashed concrete block, four oblong
windows with flaky sills, a front door, a coal shed and grass. The
foreground of one has a face over the side of a pram the size and

colour of a hearse; the second shows the same baby and a man, both sitting on a tartan rug as though it's sunny. We are father and daughter. Dad is seated, three inches of leg pale above the tops of his socks before the turn-ups begin. His arm, outstretched behind to keep me from falling, disappears into a white froth of dress. Under a thick coxcomb that must have been fashioned around my mother's finger that morning, my face has no more definition than a snowman's. Post-war, fed what my sister never knew. That sister is not in evidence, having not long married an unsuitable Glasgow chap and fled the nest, pregnant, with barely a goodbye, but there's her bike, saved *in case*, hanging like the sword of Damocles on somebody else's alcove roof. So much for snaps. Whatever was special about this dwelling doesn't show here. It looks just like every other 1950s Scottish housing estate, exactly like Aunty Kitty's two streets up.

I can deduce, of course: the sense, quite literally, of going up in the world, two bedrooms and a driveway, a garden, a cat called Tiger. By the time I was four we'd notched up three new addresses, but Sannox Drive was the best one. In later years, my mother's recalled fondness for the place made me jealous, peeved I couldn't conjure the best thing I'd never really had. It turned into carping for a cat, a dog, anything with fur that would be mine too.

I've asthma, she'd say, wheezing. I canny be doing with animals at my age. I don't even like them. They just die. Anyway, you'd a goldfish.

This was a cheat. Goldfish you won at the fair died. It was a rule of nature. But real pets were different.

How would you know? she said. Of course they died. What did I think had happened to Tiger? I didn't know. It had never occurred to me to ask, just want. Tiger – she said, she always used his name – got old and he couldn't manage properly any more. So he got himself up the Sannox Woods and never came back. They know what's coming, she said, her eyes filling up so alarmingly that mine did too. They go and find somewhere quiet and just wait. They leave and don't come back. They die. It's what they do.

She wanted to be clear and this was crystal. They died. They upped and died and nothing anybody could do would stop it. Pets, every last one of them, *died*. It was horrible and noble and hideously embarrassing at the same time. My mother, a woman who had blind-eyed a pregnancy, had seen the cat saunter off into the night and had read the cards straight off. She had never forgiven him.

So there'll be no cats, no dogs, nothing. Never. You can just forget it.

And that was that. Even so, she tempted fate. I watched her dicing bread for birds and talking to strange mutts in the street. She cooed like a pigeon near kittens and consorted with people's budgies. Animals are more bother than they're worth, she'd say, sloughing off the top of the milk for a back-door stray, convincing no one. I drew no attention to the contradictions, just watched. It's the only thing to do when you're not sure what you're learning. I shut up and watched.

Despite her helpless fondness, we had no pictures of Tiger. We had no pictures of my sister in the Sannox House and none of my mother and father inside it either. I do not mean there was a shortage of material. We had hundreds of photographs, hidden in an oilcloth bag under the double bed, but few that seemed much to count. We had black and whites and sepias, hand-tinted colour. We had ends of legs and thumbs and heads beneath a mile of sky and studio groups where whole persons might emerge in odd surroundings; we had friends and long-since nameless acquaintances, children in groups and duets, pictures of shorn, stocky men playing accordions and pictures of women with rouge-blossom cheeks, cheering them on. We had women with pinnies of varying floral design and elderly women in matching sets with specs; women under washing lines and shopping, getting on buses and showing off their nicest clothes; pictures of girls with pigtails and school ties, ribbon-haired toddlers and small groups of men on corners with varying lengths of fags. Every face has something of the ethereal, the gift of old techniques and preferences, mixes of chemicals, the quality and grain of age on paper, silver, fluid. As though what courses through the veins is light, not blood at all. But few of them, beyond this accidental beauty, gave much away. There are gaps and curious omissions, more hidden than revealed. There are no old men, a mere handful of domestic interiors, none of Christmases or birthdays, parties or pets. None of funerals or trembling thresholds, no bearing aloft of newborns or moments of mundane family calm, no wedding photographs. Not for years, at least, and certainly none of *their* wedding, not even one. What we held as our own was brickwork and best frocks and prams in scraps of garden, faces with the features blotted out by sun. These, we led ourselves to believe, were the real story, and I believed it too. This man in the picture was my father, the puffball with the screwed-on hands was me, learning by habit and usage, rote. I knew I had a blood sister even if she wasn't there. I knew I had a dead brother and an absent cat that had melted into the Sannox Woods and never come home again. I had aunties who were real aunties and aunties who were cousins and aunties who were my mother's friends and these legions of aunties had husbands I hardly clapped eyes on and there was no getting away from any of it. These were my people. After the initial panic, a flurry before surrender, no doubts at all.

My father had hair the colour of Lyle's golden syrup. His stubble looked like glitter on a sunny day but he didn't smile much, at least not at home. We know he smiled outside sometimes because there's a snap of him taken during the war doing it. He's in some kind of army uniform with his socks on display next to three other men dressed the same. They wear an equal quantity of Brylcreem. My father is the tallest.

He wasn't tall, my mother used to say, he just picked short friends. That's him trying to look as if he fought, but he never fought. He got invalided out with flat feet and drove a lorry. He never left the bloody country.

The lorry carried heavy water and he smoked while he was driving, the whole journey from Inverness, roads fit only for sheep, cratered with potholes.

He had no idea, she said, shaking her head at his monstrous good fortune. Could have blown himself up at any minute and I'd have got an army pension. But he didn't. He was always lucky. Lucky and bloody useless.

Before all that, though, he'd had a different uniform and was doubtless a different man. Back then, he was a bus driver. His father had been a bus driver and he was a bus driver too. My mother had run from being a domestic servant and a cotton worker to the as near as dammit white-collar embrace of Scottish Motor Transport, who assigned her as a clippie to Eddie's depot. That was how they met. There's a photo of them with the bus, the pair of them just about to set off on shift. My dad, looking natty, poses near the radiator with his hat tilted at a rakish angle. He's not smiling but he doesn't look too upset with life either. She, however, is radiant. In Cuban heels, her corporation uniform filled out like a coke bottle, she's a clippie to be reckoned with. Another driver, not my dad at all, is looking over like she's Carmen Miranda, and you can't help thinking he's right. That's my mother before much of her life had happened to her and she looks a million dollars. She looks competent, confident, *good*. She was. She sold bus tickets and told off drunks and ejected spitters and helped elderly men and women on with shopping bags no bother. She lifted up babies while mothers got settled, folded carrycots and kept a running tab of who needed to know where their stop was, if it was now or nearer the shore road flats. She put up with vomit and urine, the frail and the foul-mouthed, being touched up and insulted and threatened. Even if she went home at night with her hands reeking of stale nickel and her shoulder bruised from the weight of pennies the size of Ritz crackers, she liked her work just fine. Drivers smiled when they teamed with Beth McBride. Yet there's my father, leaning on the radiator grille of a wee cream-coloured bus, not even looking in her direction. Maybe he was nervous in front of the lens. Maybe he's too cool for his own good. It's impossible to tell from this frozen moment whether he's aware of the prize right there beside him or not and one should not judge. Given that not long enough after they met, they ran away together to dodge her mother and get married, it's safe to say he noticed something. She was pregnant, of course, and just nineteen. He was nearly thirty. Between an entirely everyday rock and a hard place, my mother married my father and he married her back. 1937. It was what you did then. They promised to live with the consequences for life.

What the happy couple thought in their heart of hearts, whether they would have dared to think at all given the pressure of expected procedure, is anyone's guess. The Galloways, his side, could not have been thrilled. Beth, his chosen McBride, could only have been a comedown. Her family were a long line of miners and labourers while his could boast a glove-maker, a chauffeur, two cart-drivers and a chap who had, at least on one occasion, owned a van. That Eddie was in charge of a big, important vehicle was in keeping: Beth, however, had raised her prospects and knew it. Then she gave it all up to have her baby and the baby died. Robert. The name of her first child was Robert. He died, depending on who did the telling, two days to a matter of months after the birth but they were married now. Whatever else occurred, they had made promises. They were, it seems, the kind who thought it fair to try and keep them.

Less than two years later, the result of this trying was Cora. My big sister, their first durable child, their only child for years. For Cora Doreen Galloway my mother hung up her uniform for good and stayed home. She watched her husband going off in the mornings with the baby in the crook of her arm, knowing the pay packets were all his now, that he would decide the housekeeping, that there was no money for extras. She kept the high heels for seldom, bought split peas for soup and her asthma got worse. That was something she came to rely on, something she repeated often so I wouldn't have to find out the hard way. *Things can always get worse.*

They did. Through the war and everyone's iron railings being taken away for munitions and Hess flying over Scotland to surrender and the heavy water and the blowing away of three of my father's fingers for ever and ever and the booze becoming more than medicine; through house moves and shifts of expectation and the raising of the daughter born after the dead son, a daughter who never sat at peace and tried everyone's patience by being, amongst other things, a smart cookie and a cheeky bitch, they arrived, ten years after the war, survivors along with all the rest, at Sannox Drive.

That's where I will join them, fresh from hospital, smelling of boiled cotton and curdled milk. Not yet, but soon. It is still the enchanted house, the best house, a house with prospects. The nightmare of getting their daughter to focus on schoolwork is past, her erratic boyfriends are no longer at the door. Newly married, baby on the way and glad of the escape thus far, Cora's in Glasgow and settled. A word for a mother's tongue to roll over, test for satisfactory texture: *settled*. Sannox Drive has the promise of peace. Tiger is chasing birds and coming home from the woods when his name is called. There's a front green right beneath the window frame with wallflowers and dahlias and Cora's old bike drapes over their alcove space at the front door. Eddie has a tiny shop with the compensation money he got from a car crash with a local bus. It's a newsagent and tobacconist, the Cabinette, selling what you'd expect alongside sweeties on penny trays and squibs and sparklers and the odd baby's dummy. They own a television and a washing machine. He has sisters and a brother still living; she has brothers and sisters and nieces and nephews and a one-eyed mother who lives not far from a salt-water rusted iron bridge and the wildest part of the shore. The Cabinette is near the train station, wild with rose bay willow herb, the fast track to Glasgow wherein are work, the shops, a liberal dusting of industrial soot and hundreds of thousands of starlings that gather every evening to deafen George Square. And beyond that, and beyond that, is the sea. The sea carries away the odd clueless Glasgow boy who doesn't know that tides come in but we do. We are friends with the waves, our town named after the bay they have cut out on the sand. Eddie never goes near the sea, but Beth walks there sometimes, out by the pier that goes nowhere. Eddie owns a complete set of hardwood bowls with his name on the hubs, his own jack.

He plays at the local green with his sister Rose, her husband Angus. It's a trim green with dahlias and blowsy chrysanths. They take their bowling seriously at Saltcoats Bowling Club and Eddie plays like a champion. Beth goes to the bowling green too, but not to play. Beth plays no games but she sings. Her brothers play accordions in the local pubs and despite the smoke and the smell of alcohol that bleeds from the bar, she goes there too sometimes just to hear them. Tommy looks like Clark Gable. Allan had a twin that died at birth. Saul and Jack live in England. Jack was the mayor of Darton once and Saul was a singer of psalms. Willy was captured by Italians during the war and suffers from malaria and a long memory. He will not set foot in an Italian café. Kitty, the oldest, lives just up the road. Beth talks about these people all the time.

Sometimes, enjoying the freedom allowed by her absent daughter, Beth works in the newsagent. She likes to meet people and if he sleeps off the drink in the afternoons he might not go out again at night. She had thought she would miss Cora and so she does, but she doesn't miss the fights. Now there is only him to deal with and she's had plenty of practice there. Sometimes, drunk beyond caring, Eddie claims he's better than all of this. He lived a previous life at the court of one of the Bourbon sorts in Fontainebleau, he says, stumbling, and Beth, who knows Bourbons only as biscuits, rolls her eyes and says nothing. For once, things are more predictable, almost calm. But things of which she knows nothing yet are shifting and multiplying, and it's all about to change. Everything. Lock, stock and for good.

She's in the kitchen when it starts. There's a wooden sideboard, a walk-in larder and a big Ulster sink. The smaller sink is up and running too because washing takes up lots of sinks. It needs lots of sinks, too many buckets of water and that bloody leaky hose that's perished down one side. And the whole of Friday. That's what washing takes. She's been on her feet in the shop three days this week and the smell of booze from Massie's two doors down made her woozy even over all that distance. Women aren't allowed in Massie's and it makes her seethe. It's not as though she wants to go in, it's the *prohibition*. She goes to the Labour Club and the Bowling Club and it's warm. There's music and company. Massie's isn't company. It's about making Davie Massie rich and fleecing families of money. Even thinking about it now is making her queasy. But there's the washing to do. All day. Outside it's snowing, but that's neither here nor there. Needs must and the devil is always bloody driving.

The heartburn isn't getting better. Heartburn, sciatica and this other indigestion pain somewhere near her kidneys. Her head hurts under the scarf she tied like a turban to keep the perm crisp, and the steam in the kitchen is already stifling. She puts one hand on her temple and remembers last night's dinner. Stewing steak. They had stewing steak with bread for the gravy and carrots and a quarter pound of Milk Tray listening to the radio: Ruby Murray, Rosemary Clooney, Jimmy Young. She can't be arsed with Jimmy Young but *Unchained Melody* was on this particular day and she listened anyway. Singing makes things better. *Lonely rivers flow to the sea, to the sea.* Crooning it now makes her perkier. Under the lid of the tub, everything's twisting together nicely, getting clean. *I'll be coming home, wait for me.* She pokes a towel with a wooden stick she's been told not to use because it might catch in the drum but old habits die hard. A rush of steam comes up and flushes her face and all the way to the base of her neck, chasing a sudden trail of sweat down her back. She can feel it, snaking. Then the pain that's been dogging her all morning comes back, sudden this time, like a fist. Maybe a disk is slipping down there, a trapped nerve. She closes her eyes, looks down as the flush of warmth drives right down past her belly and opens them again to see the HOOVER sign wavering. And water.

Her feet, now she moves her toes in the slippers, are wet. Something told her they would be, but she hadn't wanted to know. Now it has to be acknowledged. Her skirt is wet too and there's a brownish puddle on the lino, now she looks, seeping between the joins of tile. This bloody machine. Again. There was something wrong with the damn thing from the first day, him and that waste of space he hung about with at Massie's bumping it in through the front door, a big grin on their faces like they'd done her a favour because they'd turned up with a second-hand washing machine. That wasn't fair and she knew it. At least he'd brought the damn thing. They had a washing machine, he said, she should remember that when she was casting up; they were the only ones in the street. Her eyes are watering now, the way they do more often these days. *It's the Change,* her mother said. *Change of Life. That'll bloody sort you out.* The thickening at her waistline, the weight in her chest. This is what happened. You turned into an older woman and nobody wanted to know. But it wasn't the Change. Maybe she knew damn well what it was, just couldn't bring herself to admit it.

She can't admit it now either. The water keeping coming makes her not want to think any more. She bends to the pile of dirty stuff to fish out a towel, leans into wiping up the puddle, squelching in her stocking soles and feels dizzy, helpless. The *Change.* Twinges in her knees and ankles, flushing in her face, varicose veins and restless legs. Restless legs sound like just the kind of thing she would get. Snow changes to hail behind the window, makes a noise like rattling and she can deny it no longer. This water, this flood. It's her. Dull-getting-worse pain rocks her back and belly, echoing around her like the rings of Saturn, a big stone thrown in slow motion into a deep, deep well. The water is, she confesses now, whether she wants to or not, the water is all hers.

It was too late. Everybody knew that. She was pushing forty, had a daughter who was pregnant herself. She had a nice house, a cat and a washing machine of sorts to care for. But it happened. Maybe I was small and didn't kick, or not much. Not so you'd force yourself to buckle under, admit I was there. Maybe denial of the bleeding obvious was better than making a choice. She cast me as inevitable – *the Change* – and let it run its course. Whatever was true, this was the story. My mother thought I was the menopause. Whatever plans she had before her waters broke were off with the tide. Not giving up till the last, through the rage of an unexpected, unpremeditated, unplanned and unwished-for labour, she was a mother all over again.

Late baby, winter baby. Mistake.
At least their sex lives were in decent fettle.

She must have mopped up the puddle, taking her time. Nobody else would. Maybe she cried. Maybe none of it happened that way at all. The washing machine worked fine for another three years, no hitches. After that, we were somewhere else and she was back to wooden poles and boiling water, a scrubbing board, a brush.

If I'd kent, she'd say, her eyes narrowing. If I'd just bloody known.

2

My mother said it was him that went to the registry office. Not her.

It was my father, she said, who fetched up my name.

He had express instructions to call me Eleanor or Louise. My mother's name, Elizabeth, had been rejected out of hand. She'll only get Lizzie, my mother said. Saying it made her shiver, as though she had touched a spider. *Lizzie.* I hate that bloody name.

My mother had more names than anyone I knew. Friends, acquaintances and colleagues called her, variously, Bess, Bette, Beattie, Liza, Eliza, Ella, Lili, Liesel, Lulu, Blossom and Pearl. Blood family called her Beth and that was the name she liked. Not for me, though. I was to be Eleanor or Louise, she said, names held by no other member of the family, something special. Then he got to the Register Office and said the first thing that came into his head, and the first thing was Janice.

Janice, my mother said in absent moments, addressing no one in particular. Godknows where he got *that* from. Mind you, it could have been worse.

I've had Jan, Janet, Jinty, Jeanny and on rare occasion, my name in cod French, the stress on the second vowel: Jan-*neice*. My mother's alternatives and transformations sounded fashioned, affectionate, chosen; mine, much fewer in number, sounded only like mistakes. It was a dull name, plain as a bucket. If I hated it, my mother's subtext ran, it was *his* fault. *He* had gone to the registry office and pulled this travesty from thin air. That's the kind of father I had – a father who didn't care enough to choose something nice.

I was in my forties and to terms with my forename before I saw a copy of my own birth certificate, and it's there like a thud, two syllables, no middle names or initials to sound different, splendid or mysterious with. The signature on the foot of the document, however, is my mother's. *Hers*, not his. I read it several times, grasping the implications, the meaning of this shift. It meant that what I'd been told, what I'd moreover believed, the legend of my naming in the history of our family and its dereliction of care wasn't true. The birth date was all right, at least, right down to the correct year: a little life-raft of provable fact. And the name. The name was not open to dispute. Out of the blue, unaccounted for, unclaimed as anyone's responsibility, I was *Janice*. No one, apparently, chose it.

In my second year of life, we shifted, to a new council block apartment that was no smaller or bigger than Sannox Drive but which was, however, different. The block had been designed by an *architect,* my mother said, as though houses were ever designed by anyone else. It was nearer the registry office, Granny McBride and the Cabinette. It was nearer the shops and shore, and with no steep uphill journey home, would make life easier with a toddler at your heels. It was also nearer Massie's. *He* liked it, she said. Brand new: we were first in. Not even a mark on the skirting. He *loved* that house.

If you opened the windows on stormy days you could hear the sea. If you stood on a chair and looked over the roofs of the maisonettes opposite, you could even see it. In a seaside town, that signified. It was official now, indisputable. We belonged.

———

Saltcoats meant seaside. The air its residents breathed was thick and saline. The shop windows in Hamilton Street were crazed with sodium chloride crystals, like frost all year round. Spray might slap you in the eye as you wheeled by in a pram or stumbled along the prom wall, making a brackish taste on the tongue. Gulls settled on lamp-posts, telegraph poles, car roofs and chimneys, on ice-cream vans, fences, railings, bus-stop shelters, benches, the bandstand and the church. They stole bread put out for sparrows and thrushes and wrens and blackbirds. They fought pigeons and dive-bombed tourists to snatch their chips on the wing. Behind everything else was the reek of seaweed, rotting seaweed and completely rotted seaweed, a scent that was never less than bracing. On stormy days, enough brine and thick marine ozone filtered the atmosphere to pickle live herring. Nobody fished at the shore, but we had eels and cockles and dogfish that sucked your legs in the summer as you strode the waves. We had three cinemas, six chip restaurants, three amusement arcades, six Italian ice-creameries and a pub every two hundred yards. The shore-front ranged guest houses and hotels, the kinds of places you could take women to drink, places with snooker tables, not darts. Courting couples could sit in the promenade pagodas or wait for music at the bandstand and children gambled pennies away at the amusement arcade. Mostly people sat on the shore and headed for the open-air pool, a death trap ringed by broken stone and skin-shredding barnacles. My Granny McBride, near-blind and unable to swim, had been the pool attendant for three summers by the time I was two. They gave her a pole to hold out for anyone drowning, but there was no call. It was only for one fortnight of summer, after all, the fortnight of Glasgow Fair. Every July, she watched pallid Glaswegians arrive for the sand, the wind and the algae-scented air; every July she warned me to keep away from them.

They're on their holidays, she'd explain. Anything might happen.

More often than not, the Glasgow visitors sat on the sand in the thick of genuine Saltcoats drizzle, crazed with freedom, eating dry bread straight from the packet while their kids sliced their fingers to slivers on dune rushes and broken glass. They mistook rafts of bladderwrack for sharks or submarines, and harmless jellyfish were pounded to pieces with rocks, sticks and penknives because they had no defences. Dead sea urchins were collected in buckets while baby crabs scrambled sideways from scream-green netting. Marine anemones waved rubbery red arms from rock pools, withdrawing at every shadow. There were queues round the block for the Regal irrespective of what was showing and the Melbourne Café ran out of raspberry sauce for cones. For two weeks, we lived in a place meant for other people. We laid on special stuff, stalls selling buckets and nets, pink peppermint rock with our name right through in red, wavy lines. *Saltcoats, Saltcoats, Saltcoats.* The Cabinette sold ashtrays with *Haste ye Back* in wavy letters under a scrubby painting of a Scottie dog and what's more, people bought them. And when the fag packets were fished out of the water and the part-time landladies were just ladies again, we returned to ourselves. The watchers gone, we returned to real life. To the overwhelming sensation of waiting, of stasis. Of being on hold.

There was mother, there was father. There was me.

There was Granny McBride's freezing kitchen, Aunty Kitty's electric fire and walks to Dockhead Street in pink leather reins, their tight hold over my chest if I tried to run. The reins had a cartoon of a horse on the bib, cantering. There was a drawer with talcum powder, scraps of towelling, yellow fish oil in a bottle and a veiny enamel cup. There was the dark and the streetlamps furred in fog. These things were the world, what counted.

This is my earliest memory.

I am on the floor with my arms stretched out, trestle-style, trying to stand. And out of nowhere, the blue, there is nothing but fingers. They are my fingers, buckling and searing like burning. When I turn towards the pain, I see half my hand. The rest disappears under my father's shoe. My father is standing on my hand. There is a sensation of rushing in my head then my mother's voice, crying out; the rustle of cloth too loud and too near. And someone says *shhhh* like the sea. *Shhhhh. Shhhhh.* Awful screaming that must be me.

I have other memories of my fingers under my father's shoes, the bursting sensation that goes with them. But this is the earliest. I will add the surprise of random cigarette burns, sudden dips and falls, a pepper of shocks with no remembered cause. I have one very clear recollection of hurrying under a table and the flat wood overhead, the whole thing shaking like Samson's pillars as something heavy falls on top. And sunlight. Someone in a dress opening a curtain to let brightness come streaming, blinding, in.

Shhhhh.

I have a recollection of waking up next to Eddie Galloway, once. He's warm, almost hot, and there are dark shapes on the ceiling with the curtains shut. I'm behind him, my arm trying to reach round his waist and not managing and he looks round over my shoulder with his eyes big and calls me sexy. It was only a noise to me, the word, but I remember it. *Sexy.* Said with a smile in his voice, something reassuring and cosy and very rare indeed. Maybe men had less fraught relationships with daughters then. I

could see his eyes creased at the side, knew he was smiling. I
don't know where I usually slept, but next to him wouldn't have
been it. Even so, the memory of being warm next to him, warm
and impossibly welcome, does not shift.

Almost all my memories of my mother's physical closeness
from those first years are cheats by comparison. They involve the
smell of spit on hankies and the feelings of choking (top buttons,
the attaching of scarves or ties under pixie hoods or bonnets) and
scrubbing (the removal of chocolate, soup-stains, ice-cream from
the mouth, fingers or cardigan chest). Sometimes a singing voice,
and sometimes staring at the ceiling with the mattress under my
back listening to her whistle in her sleep. Everything else from
that first time at Wellpark is blurry, none of it showing our home.
Three other memories, of different places entirely, are very clear
indeed.

One is outdoors, my feet on an unsteady surface while sunlight
stripes the front of a white dress. The white dress is on me and
almost too bright to see at all. The sunshine in my eyes is like needles but I know someone is there. I can't move out of the dazzle.

The second is a wide-open field with a pole cutting through it
like a false horizon. There are big buttons down my chest and it's
cold. My soles push against a foot-plate and there are no people
here, only grass, a field with edges so far away I might be lost in
its depths. I am not on a boat, but there's a distinct sensation of
floating. I am hoping, shivering, that someone will come.

The third is being in a small room that goes suddenly dark. I'm
alone in the dark in a dress that feels crushy and scared to death

in case something is sneaking up. I remember standing very still trying to work out if I'm being watched, my eyes straining into blackness. Then someone coughs and there is a too-close flash, spots before the eyes, and people sighing. My lip is bleeding.

I swear I can hear my own heartbeat in every one. Maybe that's what made them stick. So much for feeling. What they are in terms of fact, location, pack-drill, the stuff that would stand up in a court of law, is more questionable. What something is and what it feels like are two different things. I know because my mother told me. These were not recollections to her: they were events evidenced by photographs, and she'd been there every time.

That's you at Granny McBride's, she said, hauling out the box of snaps to prove it. Look. You're nearly two and it's the gravel path at the side of the house in Guthrie Brae.

She shows a six-inch-wide pebble track to the front steps, the sun coming through a one-foot section of fence and on to my frock. Uncle Tommy is taking the shot. Behind him is my Granny McBride, the mask of Agamemnon in a bun. She is wearing a pinny and so am I.

That dress, my mother said. It was yellow. It's maybe the sun-shine made you think it was white. But it was yellow.

The truth about the endless field is it's only my granny's front grass, a pocket-hanky of a lawn. The insistence on the hugeness of the green in my memory made my mother furious. She called me a bigger liar than Tom Pep, whoever he was. Finally, the dark-room mystery is only me having my picture taken at Aunty Rose's wedding when I was three and a bit. Some photographer had wanted the light out to make the shot arty – a girl in white surrounded by black – and everyone in the room was in on the lights going out except me, which explains the sighing. I am scoring high on adorability by being clueless. My mother had no recollection of anything being wrong with my lip so maybe that's embroidery. The memory, however, includes a taste. Salt and brackish. Blood.

Your Aunty Doreen sent that frock from America, my mother said, gazing at the flower girl with no flowers, her eyes searching surreptitiously for a door, a way to run. It was pink. You were up all night because I'd put your hair in papers to make ringlets and they kept you awake. That's underslept, that face. You took a huff then fell asleep at the top table and never ate your dinner. There used to be a picture of that as well, you sleeping and the cake beside you, only somebody stole it.

Somebody stole it. As though our family snaps were *bona fide* treasure, not just slips of paper with no relevance to anyone at all but us. They were not slips of paper to her, however. They were not even a perspective. They were absolute reality. If I continued to know that the garden was a field and what a torn lip tasted like, I was on my own. Collusion or loneliness: without knowing the words, one is aware of the choice. I was, she said, a born storyteller, a drama queen and a bigger liar than Tom Pep. A child's memory bears no more relationship to reality than a cartoon, surely: a scramble of imperfect synaptic snaps put together any old how. An adult, on the other hand, is in possession of the whole picture. This understanding throws us all sooner or later. Unquestioned, it will throw you entirely away.

———————

Every day was different, every day the same. Changes, shifts, dissolving sands. We went to Granny McBride's in Guthrie Brae, Aunty Kitty's, the shops, the shore. We went to the Cabinette and back home again. Every so often she needed to leave me with someone and the choices were few.

Guthrie Brae was painted in leftover paint colours the council must have acquired on the cheap. Granny McBride's pride and joy were her whitewashed front steps and her weeded gravel pathway. She liked a tidy house and had no toys. Even so, she got me to contend with. Only now and then, but still.

See you're not longer than an hour, Beth, she'd say when my mother left, always running. And bring back milk.

I liked my Granny McBride. She fed me. She teased me with her glass eye, holding out the matchbox she kept it in to see me open it and find myself watched by a disembodied ocular prosthetic from its nest of cotton wool. She hid behind doors and shuffled out whispering *boo* and told me about the time she had tried to drown a cat in the boiler. More often than not she'd let me sit, bending the legs of a teddy bear backwards and forwards while she listened to the radio and sang in a tremulous falsetto. But she was seventy-two when I was born and had thought her days of this kind of thing were done and my mother didn't blame her. Not at all. Leaving me with Granny McBride was a last-ditch measure and one my mother did not abuse. There was a Granny Galloway as well, but by the time I was walking, she was not much more than a wraith in a nightie, getting out of her bed only to allow her sheets to be changed. Her speech had gone by then and she was well-nigh demented, but there was a calm about her that Granny McBride did not possess. Granny Galloway, however, was in no shape to offer respite from a toddler. She had no real idea of who I was. Granddads were out on the grounds there were none. Killed down pits or by coal dust, drink and drowning at sea, I didn't know enough to miss them. What a grandfather might do or say or add to the general texture of life was beyond me. Granddads, like pets and baby sons, didn't last.

Aunty Kitty should have been a source of help because she was an aunty, but it didn't work out. She scared me and I seemed to scare her back.

Canny be easy at your age was her commonest greeting. She'd look right at me when she said it. Christ, she's the spitting image of Eddie. I know I shouldny say it, but she is.

Don't ask for nothing, my mother always warned when we rolled up at the door, finger poised over the buzzer. I didn't. Kitty's two kids were adults with children of their own. Her grandchildren, every last one, were older than me.

It can play with our Alma, Kitty said. Outside. I suppose it can catch a ball?

It was me. I could catch a ball but I wasn't good at it, and Alma felt imposed upon. We had the same Celtic skin: so pale we looked powdered, tearable as tissue. We had the same look in much the way my mother and Kitty had, but less in common. I did not belong with children, even older ones like Alma. I belonged with middle-aged couples in Bowling Clubs, discussing dahlias while my mother insisted she couldn't stop, she'd just popped in to fetch Eddie's kit. I belonged in the social rooms of bars with my uncles playing accordions while my mother sang. I belonged behind the skirts of her coat at the butcher's, the telly rentals shop, the Co and the doctor's where she seemed to need to go all the time. I belonged with her and felt keenly out of place anywhere else. She could not have bargained for this. The second-youngest of seven, all her siblings save Tommy, my lovely uncle Tommy that laughed so readily and had run away to London at least once. Everyone but her had, as the phrase ran, *got their lives back*. Their kids had left the looking-after stage, and they weren't keen to babysit anybody else's. My mother needed time, not least for shifts in the Cabinette, but she had made her own bed and knew who was supposed to lie in it. Grasping straws, she tried Rosebuds.

Rosebuds was a social club in the church hall for nursery tots of both sexes, like Brownies but with smaller people. Being there meant milling about trying to get used to the idea your mother had disappeared, some confusing games involving *being quiet*, and cod liver oil with a compulsory lie down afterward. Some gagged and cried all the way through the castor oil, including me. Some bit. The finale was lying on our backs riding imaginary bicycles then running in circles changing direction when someone waved a hanky. Before long, Top Rosebud complained I was short on comprehension. I did not sleep and refused castor oil, I often sat down in one place during the running-about session, and I had wet myself in Quiet Corner and not told anyone. I did not, she explained, *fit in*.

It was all true. I'd rather have been at Kitty's. At least Kitty left me to my own devices when I was at her place. I clung next time I was taken to the church hall and pined when my mother left anyway. If she didn't do the afternoon shift in the shop, nobody would. But she never took me back. Rosebuds was gone. In its place came Gloria.

Gloria lived round the ancient Springvale tenements. She had red frizz instead of hair and a chalk-white face, her skin so transparent you could see the veins in her neck working. I remember a wee fold-up mattress in a curtained-off recess. She had had a baby in that bed, she said, and the doctor refused to get in it to help. She cried very suddenly, stopped very suddenly and asked if I wanted a biscuit. Adults being inexplicable was just part of the drill, and I had no worries about Gloria. She had pictures on the windowsill of three children, smiling. I've forgotten the names, but their faces were black. Black foster kids were easier come by, but they always moved on. Her eyes filled up again. How long I went to Gloria's, how often, I have no idea. Given my mother's softness and sense of duty, it would not have been much. It do remember Gloria's face, and that she held me as I left her house on at least one occasion. It was unfamiliar and lung-squeezing and too close for comfort, but I did not draw back. Gloria, her breasts like car bumpers and her face powder drizzling on my duffle-coat like dandelion seeds, embraced me without stint whether I liked it or not. How it ended is a mystery, though the words *midnight flit* enter my head when I think of her. Whatever happened, my mother was high and dry. Gloria disappeared suddenly and there was no one to take me on any regular basis, no way to work. *You've nobody but yourself to blame,* Kitty said, sitting at our fireside with tea dregs in her cup like a gypsy. It was part of their cryptic, grown-up talk, but it stopped me fiddling with crayons long enough to look up, listen. Whatever it meant, it was to do with me.

She'd given it her best shot, we both had. But all roads led back to where they started. We were thrown back on each other, the closed space of Wellpark Road, Eddie. If he went out increasingly, it was easy to see why. The house, he said it more than once, this two-bedroom catch of architect design, was always bloody full of women.

———

We spent nearly four years at Wellpark Road. During this time, my parents accumulated few photos. They had other things to do, were middle-aged, less camera-prone. They did, however, pay good money to a local studio for snaps of me, two sessions, one year apart. I have no memory of either being taken, no one left to tell me what they signify, but the snaps are there. They show things clearly.

The first is an Alpine landscape with fir trees and distant mountain tops, snow on a rickety log fence. Two doves are perched on the handlebars of a little silver scooter in the foreground, sitting near the headlights as though they're preparing to fly. Right behind the doves is the child, two and a half years old and not one of her duffle-coat toggles sitting flush. Her trews are too short and the scooter, perched up on a purpose-built stand, is too big for her feet to reach the rests. Her face is white, the hair wavy, the baby coxcomb turned into a curl. The mouth, like a rabbit's, does not smile, probably because the surroundings are so queer. The sky is painted, the rocks are card and the doves are stuffed. This is a studio, a set-up, a deliberate fabrication, but the game is to pretend it's not. This is giving her some difficulty. Her eyes aren't focused on the feathers, the scooter with no engine, the sketched-in pines, but on something off-stage. Maybe it's the door, a window showing the trees and cars in the street beyond. Maybe it's mother, smiling, coaxing, egging her on.

The second is in Harris's department store, a whole year on. This time, nearly four, she's sitting on a stranger's knee in a cardboard sledge surrounded by cardboard presents and a plastic 2D snowman. Santa looks bored to the point of faint and his beard's elastic tie is cutting his face. But there she is, on his lap, braving the situation no bother at all. She wears hand-knitted Fair Isle mittens and a wee pixie hood, her cheeks are Dutch doll circles from wool-induced heat. Despite the scuff on her shoes, she looks just the way people would like their toddlers to look in such photographs: healthy as a pug and smiling for Scotland. Her feet are on the ground, showing all the appearance of firmness, of being centred, of growing. Whatever she thinks, and it seems to be nothing, she knows how she is meant to look and, eyes dead on the lens, she's showing it fit to bust. Things are coming into focus, being watched for all they're worth. And something, she knows, is watching back.

Between these two pictures, the world turned.

3

Things never stay the same. They get worse, they get better or they get different. My mother was keen for at least the last. Stuck at home with me and Eddie, knowing the shop was running at a loss, she turned, reckless, to logic. She'd work and take me with her. It was *their* shop, for crying out loud: other people's rules did not apply. The Cabinette, choking with fags and magazines, could be as good a nursery as any. It was the wider world, a fine solution, a chance to get free sweeties. The shop and everything in it suited me right down to the ground.

Beth cleaned, served, sorted stock and beetled about in the store-room, complaining. You can't get the staff these days, she'd say, meaning me. Joke. She assigned me to fags because it was easy, and I fancied I was good at it. If slippery packets of single boxes needed straightening into neatness, polished on a sleeve so they glittered under the shop bulb; if matches had to be raked into rows, rough side down, I was your girl. You could grate your knuckles on the strikers of Swan Vesta boxes, scrape your nose sucking up the cordite scent. Higher on the wall, out of reach, were the sweetie jars; penny trays with cheap pocket money chews lay open to dust and flies below the counter. Penny white mice and liquorice pipes, Drumsticks, Everlasting Strips. Blackjacks and Fruit Salad, Love Hearts, little dots of Parma Violets rolled in clear purple tubes to sniff, not even eat, to rub on the wrist for perfume. The penny trays were my favourites. When it got too busy, I'd be put in the shop window with the open display boxes of sweeties and fireworks, the local rags, *Ardrossan and Saltcoats Herald* and *Glasgow Evening Times*, folded with the picture headlines on top. The breadth of the window space was no more than a larder shelf, the whole shop not much bigger than a bathroom. If I sat in the window with my legs full out, I'd have fallen off the back and on to the tiny strip of floor space behind the counter. So I sat in a corner, legs folded under my frock, a living shop display for any who cared to look in. I had a cloth picture book with a printed kitten in it, paper, crayons. Now and then, somebody would knock the glass, as though I was a goldfish. It was public but not onerous. I ate a lot of halfpenny caramels, littering the window space with wrappers. Sooner or later I'd be airlifted back, flying past the green- and gold-wrapped boxes of Gold Leaf and, if it was very quiet, she'd set me on top of a cardboard box and let me serve. She'd find the stuff, hand it to me to deliver to the customer, then the money would travel the reverse route. Two hands on the till, pressing the buttons. We pretended the cash register was a piano and played duets. Mr Dixon, an elderly chap who came in every day, as though cigarettes were vegetables and best bought fresh, used to ask for me by name.

I wouldn't buy my fags from anybody else, he said. I want Miss Fags or no one. It has to be my girlfriend or don't bother.

He gave me a Christmas card with *Miss Fags* on the front and I knew it was me. His usual was Woodbines and Capstan Full Strength as singles, the number depending on whether he'd won any bets that week, and he looked back over his shoulder and winked on the way out. I had friends, a place in the window, something to do; through the narrow display glass, a view of the outside world. People came and went at the station, the steam billowing up the street when the train had left them behind. Near closing time, men walked along the street holding bundles from Piacentini's chippy, searing their fingers on hot newsprint. I could see it all and it saw me. If I turned around, there was the inside of the shop, with its colours and shiny cellophane and people in ones and twos, waiting. It was orderly and it was cheery. People knew who I was. Then it was the time of night to pull down the shutters and begin fishing for keys. The fat set for the shop doors and the outside shed's splay of locks, the window shutter and the doors barely fitted inside her bag. But it was the other set, the tinny tinkle of the house keys emerging, that made my spine shiver. We were shutting up shop and going home. And home was another thing entirely.

———

You knew he was in because of the way the air sat in the house, the displacement of dust. It was something animal that gave him away, something animal that picked him up, sent the message for the chest to tighten, the ears to prick. In the right mood, I could feel him through walls. It was the sensation of being in an open field, losing the hand you thought you were holding, the ground beginning to sink underfoot.

My father was clumsy. It was a family legend. He dropped things, crashed things and fell off pavements. Books fell off shelves and pens burst at his touch. He lost three fingers in a wartime cock-up with some heavy water that had his name on. By the time we'd been at Wellpark Road a year, the neighbours must have known it too. Eddie Galloway was a whole series of accidents waiting to happen. Indoors, between ourselves, his accidents took on a different quality. As though we were haunted, our house was full of cracks and breakages, grazes, burns. These things seemed to happen despite us. They were often unobserved, at least by me, and their origins were seldom attributed or admitted. But they happened. The evidences were round us all the time. I began to work out that they happened most often when he came home with a stumble in his step, his voice awkward, his hands not able for his shoelaces. When he was *in no fit state*, and my mother told me to go to bed – *off you pop* – even if it wasn't time. Lying awake in the dark and waiting for her to come through, as she always did eventually, you'd hear sounds like someone clearing a cupboard. Soft thuds, the odd, muffled exclamation of surprise, annoyance, growling in the throat. And sooner or later, if not that day, the next, something falling, smashing, tearing apart.

In the mornings, there would be another scuff on the skirting or a dunt on the door, the chipboard panel with a peep-hole through to its brown insides. Now and then, I'd find a piece of something, an unherded fragment that had shot beneath the settee. It broke, she'd say, if she said anything at all. Watch you don't cut your fingers.

It was the stuff's fault. It just broke. *Butterfingers.*

Shhh, she'd say, one finger up to her mouth. Don't go in the living room, hen. You'll wake him up. *Shhh* and we'll get some peace.

That was the important thing to bear in mind. *Shhh.*

Peace was achievable through silence. Something we did, something as incidental as waking him up, triggered things that every instinct said were best avoided. I learned to stay by doors and windows when he got up, shoeless, kept my eyes keen and my head down, watching sidelong for clues. But our chairs broke and our picture frames cracked all the same. Once, I watched him throw my trike against our outside wall. The whole thing bounced, ricocheting off the concrete bin store, buckling and splitting to a stop. And my mother sat down next to it, its twisted mudguard and fallen-off trailer, and stared, not at him, but at the pieces. He stared at her but she did not stare back. She stared at the pieces, her mouth open but speechless, as though the trike had exploded of its own accord. It broke, she said later. Knowing I'd seen, she said it anyway. Anyway, you're too big for a trike now. Never mind. He said nothing. Of course not. It was *things* that did it. They exploded around him, a mean conspiracy of objects and fate. My father was simply accident-prone.

He lost money. He had a nosebleed that ruined two hankies. He got vomit on his tie, his trousers, his socks.

Sometimes, he'd come home bright as a steel button. Oh yes, my mother said, in the right mood and with enough drink, dad was the life and soul. He'd find strangers and bring them in after closing time, ruthlessly jovial in his own kitchen; men you never saw again yet who sat down with their feet under the table as though they belonged here and asked me my name, my age, if I knew I was Eddie's spit. Conversation exhausted, they'd tell me to fetch them a glass, a cigarette, matches. They'd want to know if my mother was in and call my father *Eddie* as though they had a perfect right. And dad would set me on his knee and show me off, bounce me on his precarious lap and tell me to sing. I was, at least, entertaining. It didn't last. Beth would appear, fully dressed because there was a guest of sorts whether she knew who they were or not, ready to scoop me back to bed as though the thought just occurred and she happened to be passing. But everyone knew it hadn't. He'd got me out of bed on purpose. I knew and she knew and he knew. Even the men knew. They'd look sheepish, briefly, but they didn't shift. Who shifted was her. And it was then, when he'd won, she turned to go with me under one arm and no questions asked, that he'd lose the bright mood, opt for the dark.

We didny get you out your bed eh? Me and my friends here? She kept walking. You'll be keen to show some hospitality to the company then eh? Give us something to eat? Give us a song?

The life and soul. Things, it was understood as we left the

room, the laughter, the slink of glass, might get broken. Most times, though, he'd come home alone and spend ages sitting on the hall carpet till my mother came to coax him to bed. *Take your shoes off, Eddie, let me loosen the laces. Come on, let's get you right.* I'd fall asleep to his name, my mother's voice soft from the hallway. *You sit down and I'll help you with these shoes. Eddie, Eddie, Eddie.*

That he tried now and then to be someone else, slipping his fingers behind my ears to find pennies, or stringing a little paper Charlie Chaplin doll between two chair backs to make it dance, only made me nervous. *Dance, Charlie, dance*, he'd say in a voice more like one of his sisters, and the cane would turn, Charlie's barely unfolded legs jerking. It was a paper puppet being tugged on a string he held behind his back. I could see how it worked, but he'd look at me and wait for a smile. I was supposed to smile. I was meant to show him pleasure and delight, reassure him I saw nothing and that life was all right after five minutes of fun. But it wasn't trustworthy and it wasn't true. I hated these times because they did not last. I hated the cheat of it. But I did not hate him. I did not hate her. I did not hate anybody. I just wished it was different. Soon enough, it was.

Things turned one Friday night. I was in pyjamas, and outside was dark enough to make the windows into mirrors. I held a spoon up to hide the reflection of my face in the glass, then went down the hallway, following the smell of cooking to the kitchen. It was late, but she was making stew.

It takes a long time, she said. I'll shout you. Now on you go and play.

But there was nobody to play with and anyway, I wanted to be with her, in with the steam and the magic, the mess of different bits turning into something good. When it was ready, she said, she would blow on it till it cooled and we'd eat together, up late just the two of us in our night things, conniving. She had a floral housecoat on, no curlers.

You'll not make it any quicker by looking at it, she said. Shoo. Away and play.

I must have gone back to the living room eventually, because that's where I was when the front door opened. And in he came.

Maybe it was foggy, maybe it was his breath coming in from the cold, but he seemed to appear in a cloud, stumbling so the door thudded on its hinges behind him, dark and the mist outside rushing in like water. I was aware of standing in my night things, holding a spoon, staring.

What are you looking at? he said. He said it just the once, but the tone of his voice made me turn away. He swayed for a moment, leaving the door open behind him, and began down the hallway. There was something more alluring elsewhere. He could smell it. His shoulder hit against the hallstand tipping it side-ways, but it did not fall. Sweating, slack-skinned, he made the four and a half yards to the kitchen without further incident, almost quietly. It dawned on me then, watching him advance, that she maybe didn't know he was coming. He started moaning, as though a word was stuck in his mouth and he couldn't manage to let it out. Even so, I chose not to shout. Making any kind of noise when things were this volatile was a risk, one I was not prepared to run. She must have turned and seen him then. I heard her *O* of surprise. There was the dry scuffle of hands, rubbing. And he started.

Why was she cooking at this time of night? Who was it for? The questions were stuff I'd heard before, not necessarily a sign things would worsen. They were just the kinds of questions he asked when he was in this mood, the kind that had no right answers. Who told her to cook stew anyway? he said, warming up now. She knew full well he didn't *want* stew. So if it wasn't for him, who was it for? He knew how much stewing steak cost and it was a bloody fortune. So who – he was going like a train now, his voice filling out, finding his chest – who was it supposed to be *for*?

Most times, she'd have let him run till he exhausted himself. Till he'd spat up the whole lot and become bored, distracted or just lost his thread. I'd heard her often enough through the bedroom wall. Not tonight. Tonight, she interrupted.

Jesus Eddie, she said, don't start. Don't start.

Even I knew this was a serious gamble. It would work or it wouldn't. Her voice hung alone for a moment before he made up his mind. She lost.

It was me, not her, that altered what happened next. If her voice had not cracked, if he had not roared back, I might have done nothing at all. Beyond all sense, I ran towards the kitchen light and my father inside it, filling the space. Not knowing what to do, I did something anyway. I spoke.

Mum. One word, clean, like a triangle. My voice. Not his name, hers. *Mum.*

He looked over his shoulder, tilting off beam just enough for me to see her face, for her to see mine. Seizing the chance, she pointed at me.

Look what you're doing, she said. She was shaking. It's for her. Who do you bloody think it's for?

Something shadowed his face, so brief it was almost not there at all. Then, light-switch sober and without staggering once, he crossed to the back door and clicked the latch. Night sucked into the warm room, a draught skirling through the house and banging the front door shut. Slowly, he crossed the kitchen and reached for the pot on the cooker, lifting it in one hand. It stayed there, balanced, as though he was trying to guess its weight. Then he walked to the door with it, reached back, swung and opened his hand. The pot lifted on the air like a seagull and kept going, out of sight over the washing lines. And we watched it, the time it had taken to make and the money it cost to buy, the good thing it should have been, as it disappeared into space. There was a soft clank as it landed out somewhere in the tangle of weeds beyond the garden wall and a whistling noise in my ears. I knew the whistling noise was the one that wasn't really there.

That was for us, she said. *Us*. Her voice was stuck in her throat. Not just you.

There was a long silence, dead slow, while things chose which way they would fall.

Well, he said. It's not for fucking anybody now. Is it?

He didn't smile but he looked OK. Calmer. Business concluded, he left the kitchen to the sound of his own feet on the lino and she tidied up. Nobody cried. I waited on at the open door, my toes freezing, looking out beyond next-door's garden. The stars were showing over the pigeon loft and our window made light-filled boxes on the grass. I was working something out as I stood there, for once nobody telling me shift or go and play, something important. He had done it on purpose. I thought about the pot, the food inside, the way it hurtled out of sight. He knew it was ours and he'd thrown it away, not by accident, or mistake, or because he couldn't help it. He'd done it *on purpose*. The spoon was still in my hand. I couldn't let it go. Shivering in the draft, grasping something unbearable, I looked up and wondered where the moon had gone. *Butterfingers. No fit state.* He had known full well.

———

Set in motion, things slide fast. I did not like what I knew about my father now, but he wasn't finished. He had no idea how to try. The tiniest of realisations, after some crucial fact occurs, can tilt life over, carry the weight of a last straw. I was not quite four, but have a very clear memory indeed of ours.

It's still chilly outside, but past the weather for stew. We have all, apparently, moved on. My mother is in front of the mirror, singing *If I were the only girl in the world and you were the only boy*, and fetching stuff from the hall cupboard one piece at a time: a cardigan, a rain-mate, a scarf. Going out takes time if it's to be done right. And she does things right. Spare rain-mate, purse, black nylon gloves. I'm put together already in a navy coat, small enough to make my arms stick out stiff while I'm waiting, as though I have no elbows. The inside of my gloves is wavy knitting, a fingertip picture of the sea, and beyond the window is mist, the kind of weather that shows breath. *A Garden of Eden just made for two.* She snips up the lock and hums the rest. Only one more thing to fetch now and we're off. Stay, she says. Just you wait right there and we'll away. She starts to tell me we're taking something but I don't hear what it is. She's out of earshot already, veering into the kitchen to fetch it. *Nothing to change our joy.* Out of earshot for speaking, anyway. Wherever she is in the house, you can hear her singing.

I'm in a line of shut doors. A dark hump moves in the bottom corner of the mirror and I know it's me, that what I see is the top of my own head. So I reach up on the tips of my shoes to try and see a whole face, and I do. The thing is, it's not mine. Right behind me, the energy of him suddenly everywhere, my father comes through the front door and I'm tipping sideways through a rip of door seals. Before I know how it happened, I'm not in the hall any more, I'm in the living room and the key is turning, shutting me in.

Eddie, she says. I can hear her in the hallway. The handle rattles and stops suddenly. Eddie, for goodness sake. We're just going to my mother's. Open this door.

Then the whole thing goes too fast. There's thudding, which means he is out there with her, and my mother raising her voice, saying *no*. The handle slips against the wool of my glove when I try it from my side, but it doesn't budge. Only two things are clear: I am not leaving and she is not getting in. Her voice rises but he is silent. He says nothing at all. The gloves are tied at the cuff and tight, so hard to shift I hardly try, and there's nothing to do but watch the shutness, listen to the noises behind it, things I can't see, changing. A few dull thumps and her saying *no*, and a single rumble of rage. His. The front door thunders shut and there's silence for a whole moment. Then he comes in, alone. He's in a suit, the tie squint and crushed, his eyes not fixed on any one thing. He glances out of the window, shuts the living-room door behind him and locks us both inside. I watch the key turn, the string through its eye slipping inside the blackness of his pocket, and wait.

Mummy's away out, he says.

Her footsteps, the points of her heels, like running or walking on the spot, click over outside.

You've to stay in with me. I watch the place where the key went. You've to stay with me and play a game. He takes his jacket off, straightening the tie, pulling himself, piece by piece, together. Sit, he says. He says it the way you talk to a dog you didn't trust. We're playing a game while she's away.

My coat is still buttoned to the neck. We were going out and now we're not and these clothes are not right for inside. His face isn't right either. I only know my eyes have drifted to the door when he catches it, snaps his fingers.

There's nothing out there, he says. Now sit. Sit there when I tell you. He points at the settee. Just bloody sit.

So I sit. I sit right on the edge and my feet leave the floor and nothing feels solid. Nothing feels safe. He waits staring right at me till he's sure, then walks slowly to the tallboy and rummages in the bottom drawer just as the noise starts. Like a wall falling down, the suddenness of it a shock right down to the bone. It takes a moment to realise it's the window, shuddering fit to break. Over the top edge of the settee, her hands come into view, making marks on the glass. My mother is outside her own home, battering her fists against the window so hard the frame flakes paint. But he doesn't turn round. He doesn't even look up, just goes on fishing in the drawer. I look at her face, at his.

Open the door. She's just a wean, Eddie. Open the door.

It's as much a howl as anything, her eyes melted into black creases and that's all I see because he snaps his fingers again, knowing I'll turn away from her, that I'll turn towards him. And there he is, my father, laying out a chequer-board on the side-table. He picks up a stack of counters in one hand, letting them fit snug. Then slowly, one after another, he sets them down in their rightful places. The set of his body and face says nothing unusual is happening in the room or the space around us at all. But she's still behind me, getting louder. It makes no sense he can't see. Whether he can or not, he doesn't. And for now, for this moment, I know something. There is what is real and what people can force you to pretend is real, and pretending is wrong. I don't know that in as many words, but I know it in my fingers. They're stiff, rusted up with refusal. Not for long, though, nothing that can't be undone. And he knows how. He looks up, puts one last red button dead centre on its square, and stares. The window rattles and she shouts his name, his name like nails down a blackboard. He doesn't even flicker, just keeps looking. And what he's looking at is me. We have the same eyes. Everybody says so. Just the same. They lock now, point to point and the look wants to break me clean down the middle.

Me first, he says. He slides the playing piece back and forth, playing, while she shouts one last time. Then there's a slithering noise, something heavy slumping hard down on to the path. We both hear it but what he does is he makes his move. One square. And pushes the board towards me.

Now you, he says, calm, clear. I do nothing. We're playing, he says, you and me. See? Now it's you.

He lifts the hand I know is mine, pulls the ties and slips off my glove in one easy move. Carefully, he places my fingertips firmly on the nearest piece, a dead ivory circle.

Now, he says. Play.

Outside, my mother moans like a seal. His eyes rivet on the board so he can't see mine filling up, making the whole room quiver. Even so, the piece starts to shift.

I'm warning you, he says. His jaw clicks.

And I choose. Knowing this is the wrong thing, that this is all the wrong thing, I play.

I don't remember what happened after that. She must have given up and walked to her mother's with no bag, no key, not sure if she'd get back in the same night, the next, ever. But she did. She would have needed to knock, but he would have let her in. Eventually. Three days later, all the stock in the outhouse behind the Cabinette burned down. The shop nearly went up with it. He'd gone in drunk and dropped a fag on the floor. He'd been stock-taking and the place was full of fireworks. Only little boxes, but still. My mother saw the display it made, pretty golden sparks over the roofs of other houses, not knowing what it was as she came back home off a bus from Kitty's.

Every bloody penny, she said, snapping her fingers, *bang*.

Nothing was insured. He didn't believe in insurance. He said insurance was for mugs. Instead, he took what was left of the housekeeping from the tin in the pantry and consoled himself as he saw best fit. She had to go to Massie's to get him, put him to bed and farm me out to Aunty Marie, who had two kids already and a drunk man of her own. At least it wasn't Kitty. Given time to herself, Beth made a decision. We all found out what it was soon enough.

I have no memory of the move, its hanging in the air. It occurred to me years later that maybe he had sensed it coming, that fear was why he had shut us together. That he was clinging, trying to terrify one or other of us into stasis, obedience, god-helpus, affection. On the other hand, maybe not. Whatever the intention, if there was any at all, all he had done was make things pressing. She might have gone to her mother's, her sister's, to all sorts of places if it hadn't been for me. There was nowhere to take us, but we had to be together. There was nowhere to take us, but we had to go.

She must have done the rounds asking. Maybe she went to the doctor to ask for pills *for nerves* as people did then, and her situation had emerged. Maybe she cried. More likely she didn't. She did not cry easily or for effect and couldn't turn it on as a device and still look fetching, the way women do in films. But however the conversation had progressed, Dr Hart, a man my mother had always despised as a snob, said the surgery had a boxroom. It was over the very building in which they sat and it would keep the rain off. It cost next to nothing, which was more than she had, but she could, he supposed, clean the surgery instead. Work, thank god. *Work.* She'd been a domestic and a cotton-carder, a clippie and a shop-keeper's assistant. She'd had a washing machine of her own. Now she got a boxroom and tuppence to get by on and she took it with open arms. If she wept at all, it would have been then, but she'd have waited till she was outside. She'd have held her back stiff and got out with her face intact as far as she could. The revelation of weakness, in her experience, could do terrible, terrible things.

Over the heads of Doctor Hart, Doctor Caroll and Doctor Deans, then; over the heads of the sniffing, spitting, gurgling, limping, seeping hordes downstairs in the dungeon of the waiting room, we waited too. And when they were gone, when the big outside door was shut over, she came into her own. Fag ash, fallen hair and cast-off tissues, kidney bowls and carpets and big glass jars. Racks of jars. She had to promise to keep me quiet, of course, especially during surgery hours. But I was good at being quiet. It was something at which I excelled. We could get by.

In some ways the move was easy: just clothes and toys enough for one case. Not so much as a kettle. Rose said Eddie wasn't well and needed looking after and she was a bad wife for letting him down, but she knew that already. It was a horrible choice, certainly, but not a hard one. She'd put in twenty-two years already. After all that time, it must have seemed unlikely that more would make anything any better. Rose was his sister, doing what a sister would. Or maybe she just resented being dumped with his care.

Maybe she can do a better job, my mother said. Maybe she can just do the bloody looking after herself.

Nobody got the address to begin with, just in case, and even I knew why. We left the architect-built house at Wellpark Road, a woman in her early forties with a wean, no man, no national assistance and no prospects because all these nothings were better than being with Eddie. We lost the trike, or what was left of it. Some time between Christmas and the New Year, we lost a lot of things. What we acquired was a boxroom above the doctor's surgery, a two-ring hob and a sink behind a curtain, a divan settee, no toilet. My mother stood at the window of the attic and wept, then chose to look on the bright side.

Oh well, she said. Things can always get worse. We're not dead yet.

I remember her stretching her neck, her hand lifting to cross her chest as though testing for a heartbeat. Just to check.

4

You can knock me down, steppa my face
Slanty my name all over the place
Do anything that you wanna do
But uh-uh honey lay offa my shoe

I'm singing under the table.

You can do anything but lay offa my blue sway shoe.

It's not a real table, just a chipboard circle balanced on legs, but under here I'm Elvis.

Look at this lovely new radio, my mother says in a chirpy voice, I'll just test it.

She pretends to turn up the volume of thin air and that's when I sing. I can do *Hound Dog, Love Me Tender* and *Heartbreak Hotel*. I can roll out a passable Doris Day, Connie Francis and Perry Como and warble the refrains of *Que Sera Sera, Magic Moments* and *This Old House* with whole sentences intact. I know heaps of songs and a stack of singers, but none are a patch on Elvis. Elvis is The King.

That's a great radio, my mother says. Jings, the reception is terrific. You only get the best programmes on this radio. I'll have to keep this.

And that's my cue. Doesn't matter if someone else is there, this is the moment that counts. It's me! I yell, bursting out from under the table, hopping, demented with excitement. She does a stage look of astonishment, so good I tell her the same thing again, again. It's me, I roar. A full confession. *Me*.

You came in through the surgery entrance on the main street, past the plate with the doctors' names in brass, then along the corridor and up the stairs. It was dark all year because the door at the back of the close was latched, but the corridor howled a gale anyway. The back close door was green, the latch brown and fat under the fingers with decades of layered gloss. Chips in the paintwork made it clear those who had been before us liked brown. They liked all kinds of brown. Chocolate close walls, tan stairwell, terracotta on the sides of the steps. My god, Beth, Kitty said on her one and only visit, it's like an explosion in a shit factory in here. And she was right. There was no stone or metal surface that hadn't been smothered in coffee, ochre, treacle, mud or manure. When the eyes became used to the fudgy gloom, our stairs, their concrete edges pitted as millstones, emerged in a half-spiral leading up to the rooms above. They were *rooms* not because we had more than one, but because we had neighbours.

We were on the left; the Misses May on the right. I knew they were sisters because my mother told me; they may even have been twins, but knowing anything for sure about the Mays wasn't easy. They kept themselves fastidiously to themselves and neither responded to questions. They had round specs and elderly musquash coveralls and went everywhere as a pair till the elder Miss May had a stroke. Younger Miss May went out even less after that and my mother got their messages. What they needed never amounted to much and would be written on a note pushed under our door. They sometimes answered when she brought the stuff back, sometimes didn't; if not it was simply left on their mat and she'd say *That's me away*, so they knew to reach out a hand and fetch it. Occasionally, a cloud of cooking smells, usually mince, said the door had been opened moments before, though whether anyone had come out or gone in was anybody's guess. We were never inside their attic, they were never inside ours. I think my mother would have liked to know them better but they were *nervous*. Something to be said in a whisper: they suffered from *nerves*.

Mind you, my mother said, polishing their letter-box because, like Everest, it was there, don't we all? Poor old souls. Godknows what'll happen when one of them goes.

It took a while to work out she meant when one of them *died*, that *to go* was *to die* said another way. Realising this made things clearer but much more disturbing. For no reason other than that they were silent, I liked the sisters. But liking people didn't stop them dying, leaving, vanishing away. I kept an eye on their door, listening for tell-tale scuffling sounds that meant they were still there, all present and correct.

If they can hang on at their age, so can I, my mother said. She dabbed more Brasso on a blackened cloth. I can give it a try.

I watched the reflection of her face as she polished, hoped they didn't let her down.

What have we got? my mother would say, and look at me, expectant. We've got – she'd clap her hands together, say it loud – plenty! Cue Gershwin, garbled singing, another morning.

We had one sofa bed, one telly, one comfy chair, one fireplace, one fireside rug, one sink, one mantelpiece complete with ornaments. It was the size of storage for a mad aunt, somewhere for boxes, not people. But there we were, behind a doorway so low my mother, all five foot three of her, had to stoop to get in. We also had a tin bath, a radio, a hot water bottle, a chip-board plant table, a skinny tallboy and odd bits of bedding. We had a green brocade curtain that smelled of old to hide the kitchenette, itself a tiny space the size of six floor tiles which housed a one-ring Baby Belling, a sink, a bathroom wall cabinet and three shelves. Pots and bleach and tins of mysterious cleaning stuff lived under the sink behind a dishrag suspended on a wire. The potty lived in there too, pink plastic and rough as cracked heels. Near the potty, an omelette pan wherein lurked onions. She didn't fry much because frying lingers and the skylight didn't open. Plates, mugs and saucers, towels, soap, washing powder, Dettol, Vim, washing-up liquid, the tea caddy and sugar tin were stacked on the shelves like a skyline of Glasgow. No vent. The wallpaper peeled up in bubbles when subjected to steam and since we valued the cheapness of all foodstuffs boilable, the wallpaper was never at ease.

It's the inside of the Wooden Horse, this, my mother said, her hands in the kitchen and her feet on the living room rug. You'd think we were bloody Munchkins.

The living room had at least some room for manoeuvre. The ceiling was low enough for an adult to touch, but it had windows and a fire, the way a living room should. Its heart was the divan, a four-square effort in open-weave material, rough as carpet with finger-tip-sized spots that still appear before the eyes when I make them – mustard yellow, olive green, steel blue, albino-white on a red ground. The spots seemed to change shape when clouds passed outside and the cloth smelled of biscuit crumbs and mushrooms. Opposite the window recess, the divan jutted as far as the fireplace by day. From six at night, it opened to let me go to bed and became the room itself, a raised floor with a thin margin left for walking round and reaching the door. Hemmed in from six till she was tired or bored enough to get in too, my mother listened to the radio or read a book about a film star's life – Grace Kelly, Shelley Winters, Bette Davis. It would not have occurred to me she wanted things any other way. From where I lay, curled in a pink wool blanket and the fire on, something to watch till I fell asleep, this was bliss. Just the two of us: the only time in my life and hers that things worked out this way. We had no letters, no visitors, no surprises. What we did have was a lot of dependable monotony under layers of umber and bottle and burial-plot brown, this wonderful little rat-cage of a room. Silverfish, the odd roach, the occasional mouse. A ball and chain.

———

First was cleaning. First, last and always and for ever: the continual round against dirt, disease and decay. Mornings, when she went downstairs to freshen the close before the surgery opened, I spent on our rug in my train truck pyjamas listening to the clunk of brushes on lino, the shuddering grief of the carpet sweeper, the windows squealing when she vinegared them – sounds that always and ever after meant *mother*. The afternoon session of cleaning, her paid work, she let me join in on, because there was nothing else to be done with me at that time of day. It was not a secret. She said so plainly. *I wish I didny have you trailing my heels all the time.* But she did, she did, all the way down the head-crushing concrete steps in the wake of her skirt hem, the shushing noise it made on the stone.

You keep quiet in here, she said turning the big brown key to the surgery door. You don't want the man to come do you? Whoever the man was, he would hear nothing from me. Right then. You just keep mum and do what you're told.

I wasn't the kind that needed telling twice. The waiting room had posters of flies, lungs and gangrenous feet to jolly up its walls, warnings about coughs and sneezes, spreading diseases, chilblains and verrucas. Everything was the colour of drizzle in the twilight, even with the lights on because the shutters had to be closed to prevent people from looking in. Why people should not see the surgery being cleaned I have no idea. It was just the rules. There were lots of rules. The receptionist's cubicle was out of bounds, presumably to stop my mother stealing or making light reading of the medical histories of strangers, and papers on top of the counter were not to be moved. The receptionist, a woman with lips the colour of Ribena and wing-topped specs who pretended not to see us if we met her in the street, would call my mother to account for a shifted file, a missing pen lid, an imagined smudge insufficiently polished away. The calling to account was usually in front of me. During these dressing-downs, my mother would hang her head and say nothing, a lesson that taught me helplessness in the face of minor authority figures for years. After, she would call the receptionist a *sort*. That sort thinks it's special, she'd mutter, but only to me.

At least the doctors weren't sorts. Dr Deans, with a face like a fallen Yorkshire pudding, horse teeth, a pipe and a smile, made an occasional remark about the weather as he arrived in the morning, rattling car keys, and Dr Caroll would ask briskly how she was. It moved her almost to tears that these men, these clever men who had passed exams and healed the sick and delivered babies, took the trouble to get her name right and ask how she was managing. In return, she cleaned their desks as though the wood mattered, as though their paperweights and bottles and jars held the Secret of Life inside.

Don't you touch anything, she said, more than once. Not one thing. If you don't behave, the man will come and take you into a Home.

I didn't think to ask who *the man* was, just turned away from the forbidden as directed. *Swift and deadly!* the poster in the surgery said. It was about some illness or other but swift and deadly was how most things were, given half a chance. Just being there, among the tubes and glittery needles, the drawers full of the documented paperwork of illness, death and decrepitude, was enough to knock the wind out of the stoutest sails. Smelling of surgical spirit and bandage, these rooms weren't anybody's element. If the doctors had known a four-year-old was loose in there, traipsing over their hallowed floorboards in her Ladybird slippers, we'd both have been seeking employment elsewhere. But we were there all the same, the two of us in the half-light, imagining ourselves invisible. I didn't do much but rearrange dust and bump into chairs while my mother kept up the steady hiss of silencing noises – *shhhh* – and did everything else.

There was walnut, there was Bakelite, the odd patch of leather. Sinks and braces of books. Jars and bottles and metal bowls, racks of ruled syringes, snaky rubber tubes and surgical lint. She cleaned only the big stuff, left anything clearly medical, clearly the province of the professionals, untouched. The most thrilling things, the black cutlery boxes of doctor stuff (hooks and probes, syringes and clamps sunk up to their necks in velvet pile) were not only out of bounds but sacrosanct; a blazing pit might open at your feet if you went too near. On one terrible occasion, I lifted a kidney bowl from the lowest shelf and saw a horrible face ballooning back from the bottom. Ugly, pop-eyed and staring, a gargoyle embodiment of badness, it was also me.

Even then I didn't drop it. I unfocused my eyes, pretending I had seen nothing at all, and reached to replace the dish soundlessly on its baize cloth. Tiptoe was a mistake. As soon as I caught the edge of it on my sleeve, there was no going back. Three metal cups clattered and rolled on the lino, chasing in decreasing circles under Dr Hart's desk. Reaching to try and stop them tilted his chair, which fell forward against the desk lip with a crack, displacing the ink blotter and setting off his posh silver pen. After long seconds of ominous rolling, the pen fell off the table too. The moment it fell was the moment my mother poked her head round the door.

What did you do? she said, her voice accelerating as though it might chase off the damage. What did you do, what did you do?

The only answer – I dropped them – was no defense. It wasn't strictly true but there they were on the floor beside me, clearly dropped. There was no one else to blame. She took the cup in my hand and checked it over. There was a fine graze on the polished steel, nothing much, but distinctly there. She slumped, sighed and told me to pick up the rest, rubbing each on her apron as though her hands were heavy. Neither of us knew where they went, so she guessed, straightened the blotter and placed the pen just so.

If they complain, she said, I'll need to pay for it. She laced her fingers. If it's dear stuff, I could lose this job. We could lose the house.

She meant the attic. I stopped breathing for a moment, struck in the chest by her meaning. We could have nowhere to live just because I dropped things on the floor. I didn't know what to say.

She looked at me hard, wanting something I didn't have. Christ almighty, she said, her eyes filling suddenly, I wish. God forgive me I do. She slumped against the doctor's table. I wish I didn't have this. It's not fair. She dropped her eyes and big, fat tears fell on the leather inlay. I wish I'd never had you.

A wish like that wasn't expected, not then. A wish for presents or pots of gold I could grasp, but this was different. When she said no more, just took her duster and wiped the inlay clean, stainless, the sensation of stuckness rose in my chest till I thought I'd burst. Like swallowing a mountain. I slipped past her and along the gloss walls to the corridor, upstairs one step at a time, to the quiet of the attic. She did not follow. My lips seemed stuck together, a dry flat line, and I wanted to lie down, but the divan was folded. Outside, the street was more or less empty and still. The shops opposite when I stood at the window, my own face floating on the darkening sky. In future years, she'd say the same thing and say it a lot, and I got used to it, after a fashion. I could see her point of view. But that sensation of a stuffed gullet, of something huge that nonetheless had to be ingested, came back every time. She must have come upstairs eventually, but neither of us mentioned what happened. Not then, not ever. I didn't ask what it was that made her want to wish me away. Whatever it was, I was afraid of it, and when we went to bed, I imagine I was glad the day was finished. It would, I thought, seep away. It didn't, of course. Not for either of us. It seeped in.

———

The street, the cafe, the barber's with a blood-striped lance.

The rag man with a barrow and balloons.

The word VIRGINIA on a navy ground with golden leaves.

You and that window, my mother said, tickled by my indolence, my sober, Dutch-doll face. Godknows what you see out there.

I couldn't have told her even if it had been a real question. I had no idea what I was looking for, what it was I expected to come.

———

The drying green was a square with wallflower borders, beyond which was a weather-eaten wall. It was a place to put out crusts in the hope that birds would come and grew daisies with red tips that could be made into chains to wear on a wrist till they bust and got left behind like dead spiders strung up for crimes. Now and then, we had butter and sugar sandwiches, sitting on a towel while washing flapped over our heads, swatting at bees, fat fur-balls drawn by the smell of sweetness.

You shouldn't be scared of bees, my mother said. Bees are fine. It's wasps that sting you. You need to learn the difference.

By and large, though, picnics and the charm of bees was not a big feature of the green. It was a work-space and its work was drying.

The wash-house, on one side of the grass square, was exactly like the Cabinette store-room my father had burned down: dark, the pointing going crumbly, dissolving into slaters, beetles and nameless black things with wavy extremities. Touching anything in the wash-house brought forth legs. It had a window space that had never

embraced a window, that was open to the elements and anything
small and multi-limbed that fancied a night indoors. Sometimes a
bird sat on the sill, but came no further. Under this window gap
were the sinks and a round thing like a well in a story-book, that
sometimes sprouted leaves. The Brothers Grimm would not have
felt out of place. One door along was the toilet, gloss painted, redo-
lent of bleach, year-round freezing. In winter we put newspapers
on the concrete floor to warm it up, but they did nothing of the
sort. Out there at night you'd hear wood pigeons up late, leaves or
worse rustling too close while you shivered and tried not to picture
spiders, inching closer. Part of its cold came from damp. The little
room was scrubbed down every day and its corners flushed with
bleach so the place was never really dry. Sometimes there were
worms, attracted by the wetness, the cool place to hide. Worms
were OK, even if they died in the disinfectant. It was legs I didn't
like. And behind the whole lot, past the poky shrubs and the moat-
runnel of dirt, was the cemetery. Our garden wall was the cemetery
wall on the other side. Obelisks and angel wings poked over the top
of our wall and stretched out behind it as far as the Ardrossan bus
stop. This was the Old Cemetery, askew with age and sunken stones,
boiling with molehills and centuries old stiffs. There were people in
there who'd died in Burns' day, whole families fallen like pennies
down a well, solitary spinsters, teenage boys, infants. In summer
the grass was rich, studded like a Chesterfield with clover. If the bell
tolled, however, it was not a summons and it was not for you. It was
the Evangelical Union Congregational place next door being jolly on
a Sunday morning, cawing in junior Sunday School. The church that

attached to the graveyard was long closed, its gravestones hairy with
moss. Even if I'd been able to read better, the stones would have
told me little, they were so eroded, so thoroughly taken over by age.

That's where our weeds come from, my mother would say,
looking up at the wall through the washing. Dandelions and
wasps and Godknows creeping through. It's a bloody disgrace.

The last building, after the wash-house, the back-facing end of
the close with the wall made three sides, was Sophie's house.

Sophie was elderly but not like the Misses May. Not five feet tall
and with a pink hairnet welded to her head, Sophie aired her opinions with the authority of gospel. The border was for flowers, she
said, when my mother said she might plant potatoes; flowers *only*.
We planted lupins instead. Sophie disallowed washing on
Wednesdays and weekends, and pouring bath water down the
back-door drain made her threaten to call the police. Unlike any of
her neighbours, she owned a proper bath in a proper bathroom,
and an armchair that wasn't pink, it was *Damask Rose*. My mother
suspected she had come from money. Now she had only this share
of drying green, her cottage, down-at-heel neighbours and an
ancient Guinness-coloured cat called Lucky. Lucky spat at anyone
who wasn't Sophie, killed birds and peed backwards up the cemetery wall but I hoped he might be game for friendship. He wasn't.
Even in dreams he wouldn't let me touch him to save his life.
Sophie took to me as much as she took to anyone because I didn't
speak back. Charmed by my reticence, she suggested to my mother
I visit her on Sundays. Every Sunday for at least a year, then, she
placed four Custard Creams on a blue floral plate and tested me on

my Bible Knowledge while I sat on the damask rose easy chair, feet
not touching the floor. Jesus Loved Me even if her cat didn't, and
that, Sophie explained, was the most important thing in the world.
She told me repeatedly that God saw everything I did. I imagined
Him seeing the times I had stolen sugar with my fingertip from the
open packet on the kitchen sill, or worse, the time I dropped the
dishes in the surgery and almost made us homeless. But it was
worse that that, worse and more insidious.

He sees liars, she said. Drinkers and tellers of tall tales. There's
nothing He doesn't see. Nothing at all.

I didn't like these talks, they made me anxious and keen to get
away, but my mother worried that Sophie was lonely. She was
worried I was lonely. She shunted me down there claiming the
company would do me good.

On you go, she said. She's just old. She really likes you. She
gives you biscuits.

Opinion and fact hinged together, unarguable. Maybe it was
true. Maybe a barely-controlled bitterness tempered by biscuits
was love. Confused and reluctant, I kept going back. Over weeks
and months, along with the Vimto and assorted Tea Time
Favourites, I ingested that God knew everything about everybody. He watched me all the time. He did this to know what to do
with me when I died and came to judgment.

Judgment seemed to be the same kind of thing *the man* did
when he came to put you into a Home for being naughty. *The
man* and God were in it together, but God went one further. He
didn't lock you in, He locked you out.

If you've been bad, you don't get in to Heaven. There are no second chances. She nibbled a shortbread finger, dabbed her mouth with a proper cotton cloth. You know what that means, don't you?

I didn't.

It means you stay dead, she said. Forever.

Death. Forever. No second chances. Big ideas. Save for the terrible story of Tiger who had trailed off into the woods alone and comfortless, death had not much occurred, and never as something that would happen to me. Suddenly, it was an open pit. The shocking notion of *being dead forever* made me want sunshine. I wanted to get off the damask rose upholstery and touch the grass.

No second chances, she said, selecting another biscuit.

I thought about the Misses May, how one was very sick now. I thought about my mother saying *Godknows what'll happen when one of them goes* and understood her words, how she had put them, in a new light. God knew what would happen. Sophie's wrists were lavender, her eyes rimless, congealed as eggs. She chewed steadily, looked straight at me.

———

What's wrong with you, then?

My mother poked my rejected mince with a fork and asked again.

Are you not feeling well?

It was a bad stomach. I said I had a bad stomach.

What kind of *bad stomach*? I didn't know. Just bad. Sophie's expecting you, she said.

I tried to look fevered. She put her hand on my head, looked at my tongue and gave in. She must have known it was lies, lies and wickedness, but I didn't have to go and see Sophie, not that Sunday anyway.

You'll bloody go next week, she said. No nonsense.

I heard her out on the drying green as I sat on the cold concrete, halfway up the steps where the banister had fallen off, telling Sophie I wasn't well. She said it with her voice soft as though it was true after all.

Oh dear, Sophie said. Tell her to get better soon.

My mouth tasted like pennies, the foretaste of sulphur gurgling up from my insides. I was full of something rotten, something black and rotten as the gravestones behind the garden wall. What's more, I had dragged my mother into it. Like me, she'd have to stand before the Judging Panel one day, accused of aiding and abetting. And I had done it. I had filled her with my poison. With lies lies lies.

I began to watch her all the time. She went too fast down the stairs, sometimes when they were wet or still soapy from cleaning. She hung out of the front window to clean it, kneeling on a thin strip of rotten wood. She reached up standing on chairs to change the light bulb and burned her fingers on the cooker ring. I was a nuisance tugging at her apron strings, tagging at her heels.

Stop that, she said. Bloody clinging ivy. I've stuff to do. Away and play. On you go, shoo. .

I shooed. But I kept watching. I woke early to check for the rise and fall of her chest, counting between in and out breaths in case the gaps were getting longer. I thought about the bend in the steps where the concrete petered to nothing, pits and dips that could easily make the floor fall away underfoot in the dark stairwell. I thought about God watching all the time, taking stock, letting her make her mistakes. If she fell, He'd just let her. *No second chances.* There was no beard or flowing robe in this thinking, just dark; God sat in the gloaming and waited patiently, pencil poised to note all slips, mistakes and feet gone wrong. I thought about it too much and my mother had to buy a rubber sheet to protect the divan. Jesus, she said. I thought we were by this stage. So had I. But we were wrong. Even if she lifted me in the night, we both woke up damp. Part of the trouble was that I didn't want to go downstairs to pee. Not just downstairs, *outside.* Outside was the graveyard, not only visible over the low garden wall but watching back, cold and envious. I had done it once, forced myself down the freezing gloss stairwell, feeling with the tips of my toes for the chipped edges, opening the latch slowly so it didn't make a noise. I had walked into the orange glow filtering the sky a freakish navy-brown and fumbled as far as the wallflower border. But when the tallest of the memorial stones, a tumbledown angel, crept into view, my feet had refused to go further. I stopped at the privet hedge and stared out the big broken wings, in case, in case. But keeping my eyes on it hadn't been enough to keep the damn thing under control. It started moving anyway. Too slow to see, maybe, but I thought – no, I *knew for sure* – it was turning its head. And even if it wasn't the angel turning its awful gaze in my direction, its dead nostrils scenting blood, it was something all right; something hidden and huge and hostile. On guard and racked with sleeplessness, knowing everything in the world whether it wanted to or not, the thing was best given a wide berth. And it would get me, get me for sure, if I put one foot wrong. Slowly then, even more slowly than I had arrived in the haunted garden, I walked back the same way I had come. I did not run. I placed each foot carefully, feeling the ground beneath, worked the door like a thief, settled the latch back in place and climbed the stairs so quietly I couldn't even hear myself. The door was still open, light seeping under the curtains, shadows shifting on the wall. I got in beside her again, closed my eyes, tried to sleep, and wet the bed all over again. Next day there would be sheets to change, washing to hang, my mother with a peg in her mouth wise-cracking that the lucky ones were over there, nodding past the clothes poles to the tombstones. It was me, only me, who knew what they did at night and there was no telling a soul.

In desperation, I asked to go to Sunday School. Mr Moore, the minister that waved and laughed when he went by the surgery door, looked a better bet to be alone with than Sophie. Even though I was still on the young side, he might let me. I picked daisies and put them in the graveyard as a kind of peace offering. I asked if I could get a toothbrush. We didn't do teeth brushing in our family but I had seen other people doing it and it looked straightforward enough. My mother got me a brush and a tin of Gibb's SR the next time she went to get her dentures checked, pink paste, like scourer, that silted up the gaps between my baby teeth and tasted of sand and Vim. I had no clear idea what brushing my teeth was for but God's mysterious dental demands and His love of policing them were not for me to question. If He was watching – and He was – I wanted Him to know that in this at least, I was trying. If this was what it took to save us both from eternal darkness, midnight angels and no second chances, it didn't count as hardship at all.

So Sunday mornings became God's. Or at least Sunday School's. Mr Moore, the minister in his white collar and grey teeth, was boring but benign and seems to have left no impression on me at all. All I remember is fuzzy felt animals, a paper Jesus with a foot missing and songs. *Count your blessings. Jesus Loves Me. Running over, Running over, My cup's full and running over.* Not what they meant, mind, just the songs. I still went to Sophie's after church was over, but briefly and with no new consequences other than indigestion from the fizzy drinks. She went out shortly before two o'clock, so visits were more rushed. And that suited me fine. Where she was headed was none of my business and I never asked. I didn't care. The important thing about Sunday afternoons was that they were mine.

What I did with them wasn't much – there were the crayons, a cloth book, the fireside rug pushed into service as a passable mat on which to build towers out of wobbly plastic blocks – but none of it was frightening. There were the divan cushions, allowing the building of palaces, dungeons, dens, trampolines, burning buildings, mountains and stages to sing on. They could be hidden beneath or behind and dropped even from a great height with no more noise than snow off trees. They could also have been used for a pillow-fight but I was short of combatants. My mother was usually cleaning something elsewhere in the building, wringing mops, battering rugs with a wicker beater, scouring down the steps with bleach. Sometimes she'd sing up the stairwell and I'd sing back, hear her laughing when I did the words wrong. *Since the Lord saved me, I'm as happy as a bee.* Once or twice she sneaked away for half an hour, hoping she'd get away with it without bothering anybody else to mind me, but I always cottoned on. At such times, I made a point of thinning my breath down to silence in case, and since nothing sniffed me out and tore me limb from limb leaving only a mound of trembling viscera behind, the effort paid off. Looking composed was the hardest bit. I wondered if she really had left me this time, or called the Home; if maybe this was the first stage of an absence that would last for ever, but there was no option but to wait some more. If I was desperate, there was the hard Baby Doll and two bendy plastic efforts to play with, neither of which was much fun, but they were at least there. Never sure what it was other girls saw in dolls, I bent their limbs around, redressed them, then had to resort to other modes of play, such as hanging them by the feet outside the window, to keep them lively. I learned that biro eyebrows are forever and you can't hide accountability for your sins.

Who did this, she said when she came back, knowing fine. For goodness sake, you go out for five minutes and she's got pen over everything.

Relief must have shown all over my face.

What are you looking like that for? It's me. Mum. For goodness sake, your hands are covered in stuff as well. Get the bath.

And she'd pile up the coal, blow on building flames, rub her palms together before taking off her coat. From being full of nothing, the room was full of her, straightening, sorting, putting on a show. The fire on, two soup pots on the ring, boiling up water. This was home. This was where we lived. Sunday night, closed curtains, fresh towel under the kitchen sink, everything smelling of coal tar and dross. *My cup's full and running over.* When I was togged up for bed, my mother bathed in the same water, but behind a towel rigged up on a clothes horse with the radio on, a funny programme that I didn't get the funniness of because it was all in Southern English accents, but now and then, my mother laughed. She had a good laugh and used it often; getting in trim for Mondays, her work for the sick and the doctors at the foot of the stairs, the business of leading her life.

Christ it's freezing. God forgive me but it is. It's bloody freezing.

Mondays were always freezing. Traditional wash-day, picked to start the working week with that which was next to godliness, tedium and hard manual labour, a solid grounding for those who had not yet begun the delights of school and an improving exercise for those who had long left it behind. Winter brought snow on the sill moss and perishing cold at our backs while the wash-house was a fiasco of hot-to-hellish steam. It had no electricity, which meant no light, no takes-the-strain machinery, no heating. She started early when the grass was still crunchy, took down a handful of bread for the birds.

They die in this weather, she said, her fingers mauve at the tips. Drop like stones from the sky.

Lucky watched us from Sophie's kitchen window, knowing what the bread meant. It meant birds. Birds distracted by abundance, easy to catch. My mother saw him and didn't smile.

You can't win, can you? she said, dusting off her hands. Wee things have a hard life. No matter what you do, they die.

Washing was carried down the stairwell and through the back door, a brief fling with the sunlight before it surrendered to the wash-house: stone walls, stone sink, stone rinsing basin with a place to sit the scrubbing board and a big bar of Fairy. That was it: the technical equipment. The rest was brute force, hers. Her that brought the scalding water downstairs one pot at a time, her that lifted and poured it in the sink and her that sprinted back up for one she'd left on the ring before it boiled over while the wash-house got mistier. Something about the stone made the water hold heat: if the soap fell in, it was as likely to melt as submit to rescue by the big wooden tongs. Using an arm to find it quicker would have resulted in third degree burns and ham stock. The steam alone made her skin look marbled, flayed like an anatomy drawing. When the water was good and soapy, the things were tumbled in and stirred around by the tongs till they wilted. Then the serious cleaning kicked in, a rough skiffling of all garments, one at a time, on the Toblerone ridges of the scrubbing board.

We've still got a washing machine, she'd say, blowing a strand of hair out of her eyes. Me. I'm the washing machine round here.

The rest of her hair was under a turban to save the curl she'd taken all night to put in her hair from ravelling out. Arms raw to the elbow, buttons undone to the breastbone, she ground, slapped and bullied cloth into submission, then wrested it onto the line till the forenoon, her fingers creased like cold Christmas chipolatas. All I had to do was not fall in and hand things over: the plastic basin for the next load, more soap, an old towel for spills, the tongs, the pegs. Standing on a chair, I could stir the steeping washing now and then, but it cloyed at the stick and hauled me sideways like a sailor in a storm so she always took it back. I hadn't the nous. Once the scrubbing bit was finished, we pulled clothes sideways with the tongs into a cold rinse, then wrung them out by hand. They didn't like the cold. One freezing dunk and they lost all pliability, stuck, tangled and fought themselves out of twist. Cottons were bad enough but tweed was impossible. She had a go, but her fingers gave out and split at the knuckle, so heavy materials went up on the line sodden. I wrung the odd sock and bits of underwear and carried stuff in a basket when, if ever, it was dry. If there was a frost, skirts came off the line as ironing boards, the arms of jumpers were broken to make them fold. Then I stayed in nursing the nearly-dry stuff while she went down to the surgeries for her second shift. Anything that dripped

stayed outside, sometimes for days, but it was at the back of the
building and out of mind. Everything else got in with me, the
fire, the roof over our heads. Outside, through the misting front
window, I'd see the bookshop shutters coming down across the
street, hear the bang in the hallway beneath as the outer door was
closed, then the keys, jingling dark and heavy. No rest for the
wicked, she'd say, the word *wicked* bouncing off the walls, fading
as she descended. I was in on my own.

The attic was too quiet after the flurry, too full of shadows,
draped rigging on the clothes-horse, these damp human shapes.
The odd bumping noise was her, moving about beneath me in the
surgery. You'd hear her sighing, like a lost thing in a Greek under-
world. There were holes in the rug where live coals had fallen,
hard-edged craters in the nylon pile. It was the turn time of night,
ornaments on the mantelpiece barely visible: Queen Elizabeth I
with the face of a hear-no-evil monkey in a clumsy metal ruff, a
stag's head on a square, its eyes blind, and a brass bell that couldn't
ring. Two porcelain people *don't touch don't touch* turned apart cast
backward glances at each other, their glazed faces glinting like teeth.
She had a half-opened fan and a half-smile; he had knee-breeches
and a tricorn hat, his hands out-turned like a dancer. Their mouths
looked like roses. There was a story between them and I didn't
know what it was. They were all wrapped up in each other. The odd
car engine, weans shouting, the firework smell of powdered embers
in the grate. All it took was waiting long enough. Then, almost
before my ears knew for sure, I'd feel that lurch of heart, the sound
of her voice ebbing up from a distance – *if you were the only girl in*

the world – her slippers dragging like corpses on the stone coming
closer.

Maybe she knew what happened next and didn't say. Maybe it
was a surprise.

We'd been to see *Snow White* at the pictures and my head was
full of glass coffins, transformational potions, the shape-shifting
Queen who couldn't be trusted even with an apple. And when we
came home, with no warning and nothing otherwise out of kilter,
my sister turned up at the door. I didn't know who she was till my
mother said her name. Cora, it was Cora. She had a suitcase and
a packet of fags; no baby, no explanations, no return ticket. My
mother opened the attic out, the shipwreck of drying frames, the
sheets yet to be folded, and in she came. Her case, side-on,
blocked the door. She lit up a fag, shook the match to death and
scanned the place for an ashtray. There wasn't one. *Jesus,* she said.
Is this it?

Suddenly the place looked shabby, small, one too many. Her
perfume was creeping closer. All over again, ready or not, we
were three.

5

Within days of my sister's Great Return, we had a telly. It was black and white with a tiny screen and pushed out of sight with its face to the wall during the day to give us a bit more room. At night, pushed round to make the screen visible, it got in the way of the divan coming down and had to be dunted into the wall hard, smelling of hot wires and plaster. If the picture went wonky there was no room to thump it but it was fine. We'd have watched rain coming down in stair-rods if that's what had come on, and sometimes it looked as though it had. We had no washing machine, no bath and no kettle but we had the Test Card, *Muffin the Mule*, *The Woodentops* and *No Hiding Place*.

We huvny room for the telly, my mother said. It costs a lot of money. Cora didn't blink.

I don't put up with no telly, she said. I'm paying rent.

She had nowhere else to go and wasn't paying rent at all, just keep money, but she knew its power. She annexed the wardrobe and found a narrower than normal zed-bed that crammed into the corner, under the roof slant. At night, with the divan and the

zed-bed at full stretch, settled meant settled, no exceptions. Trying
to slide past her bed woke her every time and she hit. She had big
hands, the kind that made contact every time. She doesn't mean it,
my mother said. She's sleeping when she does that. She needs her
sleep.

Whether she meant it or not, it hurt. Even if she caught me on
the face, though, there was to be no whining. I don't put up with
whining, Cora said. She didn't have to because she could do
looks. Cora's special looks could wither trees. She had just got
shot of one baby and didn't want the disruption of somebody
else's, even if it was her little sister. That was my mother's look-
out. Her little sister, she said more than once, was not her
problem. If she missed her own look-out, her lost boy, she took
care not to let it show.

Bloody weans, she said, blowing a smoke veil that hid her face.
Who needs it?

And she went back to her paper. Cora was good at crosswords,
the harder the better.

My mother was middle-aged, tired and said nothing, just
watched as the attic turned into somewhere else. Cora bought
make-up, new shoes, a snazzy coat. She learned the names of our
neighbours. Sophie was *that moany old cow out the back door. If she
thinks I'm running messages for her she's mistaken*. The sisters May, in
their winter coats, were *Hamsters, bloody gerbils. Christ I hope I die
before I get like that*. And the cat, she said, was mangy. *Lucky, my
arse. If it touches my nylons, it's dead*. We got up to an alarm clock
now, and I had to stay in bed till Cora was dolled up for work and

my mother made her Nescafé – *just coffee, you know I don't eat stuff in the morning* – to keep out of the way.

Our day, the day I shared with my mother and no one else, a day that felt increasingly secondary to the infinitely more important day that Cora was having elsewhere, started when she was gone. It wasn't just the place that was changing, our routines. My mother was changing too. She was less likely to sing in the mornings or sleep with me in the afternoons. She crashed my dolls and building blocks into a box so the three of us had enough space to move. Up on the mantelpiece, the Bakelite radio we were listening to less and less was shifted aside to make way for a mirror; bigger, higher up than the pocket affair my mother had made do with. The size of a tray, it was still too low for an adult to see in properly without genuflecting but Cora didn't complain. She dipped at the knee as though making a curtsey, waved her mascara brush like a magic wand. About the business of transformation, nothing put her off. At bedtime she'd reverse the process, return to her human shape, swabbing off the layers of pan-stick and thick eyebrow pencil. Behind her back, I watched her melt and change. Now and then, I'd catch a fleeting reflection of a skinny girl in a tin bath in front of a coal fire, the water getting hotter with every passing moment. Flat-chested, faceless, being boiled for a feast. *Me.*

———

Cora's job was in a café. It was in West Kilbride, up the coast road, and her boss, my mother said more than once, was a real

Tally. Exotic, sun-kissed, capable in more than one language, a left-behind POW blessed with a family ice-cream recipe, who chose to make a go of life by the storm-tossed Scottish seaside. Italian cafés were the only cafés. Nothing else came close. You got proper coffee with froth and decent sweeties, the freshest of fresh fish and chips. My mother liked Italians despite what they'd done to her brother during the war.

They weren't the ones that hurt Willy, she said. The ones we've got here are the ones that came to get away, and we locked them up anyway.

She had no time for Mussolini, whom she suspected was *not all there*, but not all Italians were Mussolini. She did not feel the same about Hitler and the Germans, but what happened to the Italians, she opined, was a damned disgrace.

They've had to work for everything they've got, she said. And another thing: they're good to their mothers.

Not only that, but the men dressed nice. Cora liked Italians too. She liked Spaniards and Americans and men of any stripe she had a notion could dance and wore aftershave.

That stuff counts, she said. Some men don't try.

Like him you just left, my mother said. You and your big ideas. He's your husband. You canny just *leave*. Are you even going to tell him where you are?

Cora ignored her. She ignored most things my mother said. Dolled up for work, her nails slick and her stilettos sharp, Cora had her mind on other things, most of them in the mirror.

How's that for *gorgeous*? she'd say, a deliberate interruption so my mother gave up. Pouting, flicking her hair, she got into character, you had to hand it to her. For gorgeous, she was good. *Pretty* was not an adjective to which she aspired and she was constitutionally incapable of *winsome*. If Cora laughed, it was out loud with all her fillings on show, a big, guttural, dirty laugh like she meant it. Her other laugh, a smirk, had nothing to do with humour. Delight to spite took seconds: there was no middle ground. How she dealt with being a waitress and dealing with the general public was anybody's guess.

She'll be found dead up a close with her stockings round her neck one of these days, my mother said. Too bloody cheeky by half.

Cora barely registered that anyone had spoken. Voices she chose not to hear did not exist. She could do the same trick with people, stepping firmly in front of anyone else at the mirror or the kitchen sink as though they had no substance at all. Cora, on the other hand, was a *presence*. Every morning, she painted on eyebrows like gull wings, curled her thick, black hair and set it rigid with whole cans of hairspray. She put on a dress with a sticky-out skirt, a clasp belt as wide as a man's forearm, seamed nylons and a too-wee cardi with buttons open at the neck to show the dress material and low-cut neck beneath. Her lipstick was red or coral and patted down with powder. Cora's lipstick did not wander to her teeth or come off. It wouldn't have dared. Ladders in her stockings was neither here nor there: people noticed my sister in the street and some of them smiled. Whether they did or not was of no consequence to Cora. She was, apparently, self-contained.

I like a good time, me, she said. I do what I bloody well like.

Twenty-one, just clawed herself free from motherhood and sprung like a steel trap for what she imagined might be *Life*, she never sat still. She read four books a week, knitted like a wild thing and watched anything that moved on TV, sometimes all three together with added fags. Stillness was not in her nature. Even wedged into a chair, Cora charged the air with electricity. Something around her crackled fit to kill flies and drop them at her feet in crispy little packets. I couldn't take my eyes off her.

My mother told me, in hushed sentences and over weeks, that Cora had left her husband because he'd smoked the last cigarette one morning and left her with none. That was the story, she said. Cora was full of stories. But the baby was the *real* reason.

She doesn't want to look after anything, my mother said. She wants all the looking after for herself. That's why she's here. My mother sighed. That's exactly why she's here.

My head buzzed even thinking about it. People left babies because of cigarettes. I pictured an infant left in the rain, squalling in a basket next to riverside reeds, his mother walking away. I imagined a door banging and a man waking up in a room of spilled-out drawers, realising the mess was all his now. I imagined my sister's long, slim fingers, turning a cellophane packet over and over while she sat on a train. Now here she was, the whole uncontainable package, doing what she bloody well liked under the same too-small roof as me. It occurred to me then that whatever she was running from, she wasn't going back. I would have to live with her for ever. I was mousy, withdrawn and nearly five: in bed at night, I barely breathed.

Creeping bloody Jesus, Cora said. You wouldny know if she upped and died.

And we were sisters. Imagine. I tried to and failed again, again. This was blood tie, whatever that signified, wherever it led. *Sisters*.

———

Over the weeks, Cora being there became normal. She went out early and came back from the café late. She did not talk about work or offer anecdotes. What she did bring home were gifts – chocolate pennies, Five Boys Bars, Cadbury's Creme Eggs and Refreshers – all sweet and immediately functional. On the odd occasion, there were surprises.

Spell cent, she said. *Cent* like American money.

I spelled it fine and she fished something out of her pocket, leaning forward so close I could see the freckles round her eyes, the crumbs of mascara between her lashes, and held out a fist. One by one, she peeled her fingers back to show the open palm. Inside it was a circle: small, dull, not chocolate.

One dime, she said. We both looked at it. Real American Money. You hear me? That's *Real American Money*.

She spoke the words singly, like she was enunciating the names of gemstones, then flipped the coin in the air to let me catch it. Go on, she said, take it. She shook her coat off, casual as you like. It's yours.

It had a man's face on one side and some bits of trees on the other with the words written clearly. ONE DIME. This wasn't money. It was a token from a magic place, a country rife with washing machines and fridges like wardrobes and flashy cars, the country of Snow White, Elvis and Lassie. It might have been kissed with pixie dust, had lines radiating from its surface marked *splendour*. It wasn't the size of a halfpenny and not shiny at all, but it would buff up nice. And she had given it to me.

Her gifts were magic tricks: no explanations, no need for occasion. I let myself think she gave things for the sheer pleasure of giving and didn't ask questions. It was Cora who bought me the Mickey Mouse toy that made me so excited I was sick, the purple make-up bag I kept long after it bust from being stuffed with sweeties, tissues and pocket-money pennies, who painted my nails crimson and taught me to shuffle cards three different ways. I could play a mean game of Blackjack by the time I was six and my card houses never fell down: two cards on one side of each trestle and first-class lung control were all it took.

Don't breathe, she'd whisper, down on her hunkers as the towers grew taller. Just don't you bloody dare.

Cora liked to win. She beat me at tongue-twisters and games of tig and cushion-fights: no concessions. She's got to learn, she'd roar, belting me in the face with a pillow and howling with laughter: do her good in the long run. And maybe it did: it never pays to be too sure about what you can't prove. Sometimes, more rarely, Cora would take me out. She'd flick the crayons or Plasticine out of my hands and whisper with intent: *I canny stick any more of this, cmon we'll go up the café*. It was not an invitation, it was an order. We were going up the Melbourne.

The Melbourne, at the top end of Hamilton Street, was a Saltcoats institution. Sold ice-cream and sundaes, sweeties in quarter-pound bags, assorted chip suppers and café coffee in café coffee cups. It had been around since my mother and father were courting and had thrown hot peas down the bell of the owner's gramophone while they ate a late-night romantic repast for two. By the time Cora was a regular, the Melbourne had a jukebox. Cora jabbed the buttons for Pat Boone or Lonnie Donegan, jiving her shoulders to the tunes. Sometimes the wrong disc fell down and she'd dunt the machine hard to make another tumble into place. Once the music was sorted, she'd order coffee with a thin layer of foam on top and watch the talent, crimping lipstick rings on the unfiltered tips of her fags. Sometimes she talked to men, sometimes not. Either way, all I had to do was eat my ice-cream and keep my head low.

Cmon, she'd say eventually, stubbing out a dout and gathering up her lighter, her beaded purse, her frothy spoon, laying it just so on the saucer rim; let's scram. And whether I was finished or not, we'd scram, Cora's bangles jingling as she walked. She could blow smoke-rings and hand-jive and nobody in their right mind would have challenged her to an arm-wrestling competition. She had a laugh like a sewer when the notion took her and no time to lose. This second bite at the cherry, she insisted, would be nothing but sweet. Whatever she had or hadn't done, I bet the baby deserved it. High on adrenalin and ice-cream sauce, I drank her in. My mother's dutifulness, her pride and tenacity were nothing to this. Cora was glamorous, glamorous, glamorous and I loved her to death. I had permission then. *Carte blanche*.

The attic was now undeniably tiny. Two at a time was the ideal. My mother chose to go to see her own mother more often, take herself to frosty, doleful Aunty Kitty if the notion took her. Cora didn't have any truck with my Granny McBride or Kitty. The only one she had time for was Kitty's daughter, Marie. They'd been clippies together before Cora got married. Marie had a touch of sunshine about her, a generous smile. She let us on the bus free if there was no inspector and called people *doll*.

You'd wonder how that came out of Kitty, eh? she'd say. Wonders never cease.

And my mother, normally so reticent, would snap. You don't know the half, she'd say, her voice cracking. That's my sister. My *sister*. You know damn all about it.

It was startling and not that easy to grasp. But one thing was clear. My mother loved her sister even if I had no idea why. The same thing happened when she talked about her brothers: Saul, the eldest, like a face on Mount Rushmore; Jack, who was pompous and had a pencil moustache; skinny-to-death POW Willy with eyes hollow as drill-holes; Allan with his mind never able to settle and Tommy, the baby of the family with his baby-smile intact. *My brothers* she called them, missing them, alluding easily to growing up with all those boys in the house, an alien notion not able to be grasped at all, *my brothers*. Auntie Kitty, who possessed pieces of my mother's face only older, scared me. But she knew what *sister* meant. At those times, I was ashamed for not liking Kitty, but it didn't change the fact. At least now I didn't need to go and see her any more, get put out on the back step with a Penguin biscuit and be told to play with boring Alma while the adults talked inside. I didn't need to go and do these things because Cora was there to look after me. Cora, my mother explained, could babysit. Foolishly, I was excited. I should have dwelled on the words *looking after, baby*. I should have not have taken for granted that Cora grasped them at all.

On a good day, babysitting meant a game of Hide and Seek or Tig or building houses of cards. They did not last long. The possibilities for hiding and running in the attic were not rich, and the cards eventually fell. Sometimes she tickled me till it hurt, then she lost interest. Fairy tales bored her, but she liked rhymes – big spiders, falling down the hill, choppers intent on the chopping off of heads, and poems about children coming to terrible ends. *Matilda Who Told Lies and Was Burned to Death*. Eventually, fed-up to the teeth, she'd begin another tickling game, which brought us full circle, me weeping and Cora having played her last card, casting me off like a finished sleeve.

Soon, Cora hit on a solution. And the solution was company. Not long after my mother left, Cora might change into a dress, put on lipstick and swear a lot looking out decent stockings. Then

they'd arrive. *Is your big sister in?* Men I'd never seen in my life, by
and large, smiling like crocodiles. *Is this Cora's house?* Strangers
knew where we lived. The company that came for Cora were
never women. Not one. But I said nothing. This was a secret, she
said, having her friends come to see us. Most times, there didn't
seem like much *us* to it at all, but two of the men turned up more
than others and I got to like them. More surprisingly, they got to
like me.

There was Sandy with his Teddy-boy quiff and Brylcreem and
golf-type jumpers, calling me his girlfriend and laughing. Sandy
wasn't like Mr Dixon, the Woodbine man, whose girlfriend I was
no longer: Sandy was young for a start, a boy-man, rubbing his
hands and jiving and talking with a movie drawl, a transatlantic
Scots that made him sound concussed. *How's my wee girlfriend eh?
Still love Sandy? Sure ye do. Everybody loves Sandy.* The other one
was Big Davie Stuart, who looked like a Highlander taking time
off between shot-put events. Eventually, they were *bona fide*
enough to come round like proper people and meet my mother.
My mother liked Sandy but Davie Stuart became *That Nice Boy.*
He had blond eyebrows, a Rock Hudson chin and shoulders
broad enough for a brickie's hod on each side. He called me
Princess and Sweetheart and told me I was better fun than Cora,
and even though it was lies, I liked him for saying it. My mother,
charmed, forgot Cora was already married and put in a good
word for Big Davie with Cora.

He's a nice boy, that. You should give it a go.

Cora, drying a bra at the fire, took it badly. Christ almighty, mother, she said, pushing the cups inside out, back again. Give us a break.

You need to settle down, she said. You canny stay here for ever. If you're never going back to Glasgow, you need to get settled with somebody.

With Davie Stewart? Ha bloody ha.

How not? she said, pinking up. Davie Stewart's a nice boy.

Cora stretched the black elastic straps till they made a snap noise and looked my mother in the eye.

Because I'm no wanting just the one, am I? Did you a lot of good, *settling down with somebody*. And I don't think.

My mother, wounded, had no answer. Of course not. She looked at the consequences of her actions. I didn't look up but I felt her doing it. She looked at me.

———

Church had a Harvest Festival. Mr Moore talked about goodness and things being ripe, then people came forward to put offerings in a pile: apples, potatoes in brown paper bags, a lot of tinned stuff, the odd plant and bag of sweeties. This was for the poor and the elderly, he said, for those less fortunate. I hoped somebody nice got our cling peaches. Mr Moore's hair shone with pomade and he lifted up his hands like a crooner during the blessing. Giving thanks and being grateful was very pleasing. At the door on the way out, Mr Moore gave Sophie two tins of cat food.

Lucky does us the odd shift, he smiled. There's no mice left in the vestry. It's the least we can do.

He was the kind of man who always looked thrilled to death to see you. He turned away from Sophie and did it now, a great big smile: full beam, a lighthouse, right at me.

Tell your mother I'm asking for her, he said. He slipped a bag of red lentils into my pocket. And see if you can get her to come with you next week. I don't know why she doesn't come.

The lentils dragged at one side of my coat, unearned, unearnable. She didn't come because church was boring. It was a social club like Rosebuds, and I had forgotten why I wanted to be there in the first place. Now I wanted my mornings back. I didn't say anything to Mr Moore, not even *thank you*. Guilt was choking me. Mr Moore kept smiling, giving gifts to the perfidious while God gazed down, seeing everything.

It could have been any day when the Big American Sailor came round, but it felt like Sunday. The door knocked like an accident and it wasn't Big Davie. It wasn't anyone, just a wall of blue uniform. It wasn't till I looked up, up a long way, I saw the face. Bowed like a beanstalk just to duck under the doorframe, he was taller than anybody I'd ever seen. Mr Dixon in the Cabinette and Uncle Angus who had stood on a step to look nearly the height of Aunty Rose at his own wedding, were five foot four on a good day and probably shorter in winter. Sandy and Big Davie were handsome, light on their feet and five foot eight. The vision at the door was six foot seven at the shortest estimate, and now I'd spotted him, remarkable in other ways too. Davie and Sandy were confections of bequiffed Celtic creaminess with pink apple cheeks and decent biceps; this bloke was a rickle of bones with bad skin, a hardly-any haircut and ears like colander handles. He took off his tiny white hat and crushed it into one hand.

Is your sister home? he said softly. I did nothing. Can you tell her it's Jack?

Jack. His voice on a slant like Elvis, only shy. Cora swept past me and took his arm.

That's my wee sister, she said quickly. She's a bit simple. Don't bother with her. Just you come away in.

So he did. His ear touched the ceiling even when he ducked, but he managed and sat down almost immediately on the settee where my sister was already patting a place next to her in welcome. Sitting, he could at least raise his head but he sunk deep into the springs and they groaned. His nails were chewed-to-the-wire. Cora spoke slower than usual, sounding her Ts and Gs like bells and the man smiled a lot at random intervals. It's possible he had no idea what she was saying. A beer emerged from somewhere, smelling sour. Cora swished about in her good frock, showing off. She gave me one of my own dolls, a hard plastic baby with a pink dress and painted brown hair coiling on the nape of its neck. I didn't like the doll and she knew fine. When I put it down, she picked it up and gave me it back, firmly. The hand she placed on my shoulder dug in like a peg.

Now you play nice with your dolly, she said. Here you go.

Dolly was not a word she used. I looked at her, bemused.

What's your dolly's name? the big lad said.

I said nothing, and Cora didn't know. Of course not. My dolls didn't have names. They were all called *doll*.

She doesn't have a name? he asked, and he made the noise you make to a horse. Whoa. A doll with no name!

He laughed briefly, nodding his head. For a moment, nobody knew what to say.

Me and Jack are just going to sit here and talk, Cora said with a cough. Jack's away home to the States tomorrow so this is a *special visit*. He's not wanting to see the silly dolly. She was enunciating as though I was deaf. So off you pop and play.

Cora never said *silly*. She said *stupid*. If not, *bloody stupid*. I looked at her, desperate for clues.

Do what you're told, she said. And take dolly. Her mouth tightened and the words more bitten. On. You. Go.

She glared till I went all the way over to the window. Then Jack got up while they giggled about something, shoving the divan about so it tilted away from my line of vision. I focused on the doll a lot when the whispering started, the muffled laughter and the tilting. When Cora's skirt flared like an open flower showing all her black net petticoats, the metal and rubber buttons of her suspenders, I looked out of the window instead. I heard their kissing more than saw it, the gullying and swallowing like drinking lemonade too fast, and Jack making a snorting noise like a pig. She didn't make any noise at all, but she kept at it. I took the doll's bootees off and put them back on, then rolled her on her face and just waited. There wasn't a lot else to do. I didn't play with dolls. I drew eyeliner on their faces, but I was too old for dressing and undressing games. I was bored and embarrassed. Something wasn't right, but what it was escaped me. Sitting here while whatever it was carried on felt like waiting while a puppy drowned. Things quieted down after a while, so I craned round to see. Jack, neck tilted to fit under our ceiling, was adjusting the band of his navy trews. Cora snatched something like a dishrag off the edge of the rug and tugged at her dress, and I realised with a shock the thing in her hand was knickers. Jack had seen Cora's knickers. Furious without knowing why, my neck burning, I turned away sharply and glared out of the window at Rankin's sign across the road. I imagined being over there instead of here, looking at the ordered rows of pens and writing paper, the comics and Observer's Books in clean, white covers. Next to Rankin's was a striped barber's pole, a man emerging from the close with freshly shorn hair.

She never saw nothing, Cora was saying, almost quietly. For godsake, Jack, it's fine. Come on and we'll go out for a coffee. It's all right.

But it wasn't. My face was stiff and refusing to ease out. Jack held out a half-crown at the door. You like ice-cream? he said. I didn't look up. Your sister here will buy you something tomorrow. OK?

I felt the half-crown being pushed into my hand, how warm it was from his fingers.

You say thank you when you're given something, she said, an edge in her voice. It's manners. Say it.

She made me say it three times before it was loud enough, then they left. I heard them going downstairs, Cora apologising and saying the word *ignorant*, quite clearly. She meant me. I ran to the window and watched, but after the bolts sounded, only Jack came out. I pressed my face into the glass to see down but there was no Cora, just the big man, holding a lighter inside a cupped hand. Then the door burst open. Cora wasn't downstairs because she was here. All the time I'd been looking out, she'd been striding up the stairs behind me. There was no time to say anything before Cora was hauling me from the window to the zed-bed with her fist tangled in my hair. I remember tripping over my own feet and dropping on to my knees, like a bird landing badly, then there was a crack, a camera-flash, and something sharp stinging into the bridge of my nose. I opened my mouth to yell and a hand went over it, hard.

This is what clever gets, she said. The voice was distant, an echo through the metallic bloom where my nose had been, but I could hear her clearly enough. I could taste nicotine on my lips from her fingers.

You just mind your manners in future. My life's not going down the drain for *you*.

On the last word, she hit me again. Then something – it had to be her – shook my neck sharply from side to side, tugging the hair to snapping point. When she opened her hand, my head seemed to surface from deep water, ringing with pain. Opening my eyes made it sure: the only person here was Cora, my sister, filling all available directions, looking hard into my face as though she'd lost something on it. She looked puzzled, not angry. Confusion made my eyes fill up.

Did you bump yourself? she said. Her voice was gentle, almost sad. She took her hand off my mouth. Are you all right?

I was sore but my breathing had almost stopped with trying not to cry. I may have nodded.

For goodness' sake, she said, making a face. Butterfingers, eh? Look! Your nose is bleeding.

She fished a hanky out of her sleeve, pressed it against my face and it hurt. It hurt a lot.

You're all right, she said. Look. It's only a wee bit.

Red spots growing on a crumpled tissue, seeping.

You must have banged your nose on the bed, silly thing.

I looked at her, the hanky white and crimson like a fairy-story mushroom.

You tilt your head back and use that hanky. Don't you dare let that on your clothes till I get back, you hear? She stood and inched towards the door. You're all right, OK? If mum comes back tell her you bumped yourself and she'll fix it. You tell her the truth, now. You fell down. She chewed the inside of her cheek briefly, considering options. I'll take the money OK? I'll look after the pennies Jack gave you. Just in case.

I had forgotten the half-crown. It was hurting my fingers, making ridges on my palm.

Right, she said, prizing the coin out and tucking it down her

brassiere. That's you. Jack's waiting downstairs. She sounded
bright, expectant. Ta ta then. She lifted a glove as though it had
been what she came back for, smiled. No be long.

I heard the sound of her heels, the big door cracking open,
thudding shut again, the faintest echo of laughter as though it
came up from a tunnel. Jack's voice saying *Cora Doreen*. He called
her by her full name. Then they left. A gull sat on the sill, side-on
to the glass. When it flew off, there was nothing but sky, the pain
in my face ebbing back, ebbing back. My legs were stiff when I
moved, unbuckling them from beneath the rest of me to sit
upright again and check my nose with my fingers. It was OK,
still in the one place. I checked there was no blood on my top or
anywhere else, but wasn't able to work out how the blood had
happened in the first place, except vaguely. Perhaps I had fallen
after all.

I sniffed a lot and chucked the hanky in the rubbish bag under
the sink and waited on at the window with the doll that had no
name while the street lights came on and made pools on the pavement beneath. My eyes felt swollen but the soreness was perfectly
bearable. I was fine. Every so often I went back to the zed-bed,
looked at it and tried to believe I had fallen. There was no other
explanation, but it didn't feel right. I did it often enough, crossing
back and forth across the rug, but it kept making no sense.
Eventually, my eyes got leaky with confusion, then with something else. It wasn't fair. She'd let a stranger into the house and
gone off quite the thing, chirpy. What was wrong was suddenly
clear. She should have been with me. It was cold and it was

frightening in here in the dark. I could reach the light switch but that wasn't the point. She had left me here alone and it wasn't a mistake. She knew she was supposed to be with me and had gone anyway. I was ignorant. I didn't know when to say thank you. I was to say I fell. None of this was *right*. It felt entirely familiar, entirely new. I banged the doll's head against the window frame till the hard line of her eyelashes broke off and lay on the rug like a nail clipping. No one came to stop the noise. And my face still hurt. My chest hurt. It was stuffed with lies. I wept till my nose ran pink, melting the dried blood inside. It ran over my wrists, my fingers, the edge of the red divan, where it sunk with only a snail-trail trace. She should have been with *me*.

6

You're a moody bugger, you, my mother said.

Stop looking out that window all the time. Make yourself scarce. I'm away to Kitty's and I need to get ready. Away and make a tent with the sheets on the line. On you go, away from the window. Shoo.

There must have been times she thought I was deaf, the number of tellings it took, but I liked the window. Seeing the world through glass was tranquil, and with Cora not even up, unproblematic. But things were moving around me, preparations in the offing. Knowing the day was coming to a rolling boil, I succumbed to another cardi and shooed the best I could.

Hamilton Street was a better bet than the back green. It had the shops, the dump at the side of La Scala picture house, the sideroad to the cemetery and drains to drop pebbles down. Out the back there was only Lucky hiding under a bush, birds down for scattered bread and things to avoid under stones. The street was good for watching seagulls, running sweetie wrapper races in puddles and classifying the shoes of passers-by varying degrees of shine. Going up to the war memorial reeled in the chemist with its displays of Liver Salts and Buttercup Cough Mixture and the Melbourne with its music, coffee smells spilling outside. The War Memorial was a soldier with names, sometimes a wreath. After that, there was the walk back down. Very rarely, there was the rag and bone man's donkey, a dog keen to sniff my socks in case anything for eating was hidden in the folds. There were no children. The apartments of Hamilton Street, every one of them over a shop or warehouse, had only older people. Mine were the shortest legs on the street. I didn't mind. Since Rosebuds, I preferred to avoid people my own age. Children were noisy and unpredictable or whiny. Some were the whole lot at once, like cousin Alma. Being a child meant being thrown together with other short people and expected to play, no matter how little you had in common. I wasn't much good at play. Other children made me feel disappointing. I belonged with adults; older adults, singing *Silver Threads Among the Gold* at the Bowling Club, my uncles' fingers crab-dancing over accordion keys, being chucked under the chin and given pennies by grey-haired strangers. I belonged with the shop customers, my father's sisters, aunties Anna, Rose and Moira when I saw them; the matching sets of uncles, all of them quiet men who grew tomatoes and collected stamps and fed ducks in public parks, men who were not Galloways or McBrides at all. Now, since we'd come here, I hardly saw them. Except for the odd visit to Granny McBride and her eye in a matchbox, we were pretty much alone, me and mum. She was going out this afternoon, though, which meant a shift in the pairing. This afternoon, it was me and Cora.

Even if she stayed in, being with Cora was not an unalloyed pleasure. You had to be braced. Want something nice? she'd say and hold out her hand. It could be chocolate, a wrestling match, a feather, a belt to the side of the head, no clues which. I didn't even have to choose a hand. That's what *want* got, she'd say, whether the surprise was nasty or nice. That's what you get *just because*. What she was trying to teach me I have no idea: what I learned was a lifelong suspicion of treats, promises, the expectation of pleasure. Curiosity was a known cat-killer and cheek was simply *asking for it*. Other times, she might haul a chair over to the window and insist I stand on it to sing, opening the latch to let the sound carry to the street. *What do you wanna make those eyes at me for, when they don't mean what they say?* I crooned as she waved at Mr Rankin and the shop girls across the road, apparently thrilled. *That's my wee sister!* she'd shout, smiling big red smiles at strangers, while I belted out the refrain again, again, sure a policeman would come any minute and I'd be arrested for the racket. *Some kid, eh?* she grinned, tossing her hair before she banged the window shut, the smile too, announced they were nosey bastards. *Some bloody kid*.

Other times, I'd turn round from playing with dolls because the air in the room seemed suddenly heavy, and see her staring, eyes rimmed with flaking liner, mind off the hook. Her eyes without company had something frightening and sad about them, like the eyes of a drunk leaning back against the shut station door at night, the way home forgotten beyond recall. She looked without blinking at the carpet for minutes together, as though she could see something there. As though the person inside Cora had just disappeared. I didn't speak at these times, but I felt I wanted to. I wanted to make her snap out of it, smile as though it was all a mistake – she had just been distracted for a split second and was really fighting fit and raring to go. I wanted her to put on the radio and jive round the settee in her best stilettos, know for sure there was nobody she'd like to do it better with than me. *Dance with me, hen! Cmon, Let's show them!* She never sang, Cora, but she could dance to beat the band. And while I couldn't jive to save my life, I sometimes took her hand and tried to make it happen. Sometimes, she let me. This dancing, I knew even then, was a kind of medicine. She was my sister, after all, my sister. For both our sakes, not knowing it at any conscious level at all, I wanted us to try.

A red and yellow scooter turned up in the wash-house. Maybe it had been Alma's or maybe it was a cast-off from an unknown admirer. Whatever its origins, it had been used. The bumps on its footrest were rubbed black and the rubber on the handlebars was crumbly, but it was fine for scooting, and its worn condition meant I had no fear of letting it fall. The scooter took me down to the shorefront with a plastic bucket hooked over one handlebar for shells, crab claws, dried bladderwrack and doll limbs. Collections to throw away. Stick-drawings in the sand and slicing my fingers on dune rushes. Falling on the rocks left bruises, huge

purple and yellow continents on the blue-white sea of my thighs.
It was possible to walk about alone in those days at five years old
and mostly that's what I did, along the prom wall or poking the
dunes with a stick. I fell off the prom wall and straight into the
Galloway Burn once, wearing my Best Thing, a purple tartan
padded jacket Aunt Doreen had sent me at Christmas, all the
way from America. The Burn was just a freshwater runnel
through the sand, really, the fall over the side no more than five
feet. But my ankles were sore from the landing and my jaw
throbbed where I had bitten down. There wasn't a soul on the
beach, only a dog, snuffing up seaweed and miles off down the
dunes. I fished a sodden tissue out of my purple pocket and
moved up to the council bench, trying to look as though I was not
shocked, embarrassed or soaked to the bone. Even though there
was no one to impress, no one to laugh or shout at me, I tried to
look as though falling off a wall and sitting sopping on a bench
happened to everyone, every day. After five minutes, there was
still no one in sight. The bench was all mine. Bored and shivering,
I sat on wondering how long it would take to dry off in the whipping wind. There were towels at home but so was Cora, and Cora
didn't believe in accidents. The best thing was to stay put. I closed
my eyes, prepared for a long wait. Next time I opened them, there
was Colin.

Colin had taped-up specs and a haircut like a hedgehog. He
was staying with his aunty in a flat in Windmill Street, he said.
His ma lived in Paisley. He looked at me through the circle of one
lens. Colin, he said. It's Colin. Then sat down without being

asked. He was pale as a mushroom and smelled faintly of mould, but he had a nice voice. It was soft.

You six? he said.

I said nothing.

Five? You look wee. Any brothers or sisters or that?

Nothing. We listened to gulls in the silence, watched the dog bolting from side to side on the sand, demented with a find of something dead. A tiny head was flopping on either side of its jaws.

You scared? he said.

I thought he meant was I scared of dogs, which struck me as a pointless question. There was no reason to fear an animal. But it wasn't that.

You scared to go hame? I looked at him. His nose needed blowing. Know what it's like, he said. That's how I'm staying here. With my aunty in Saltcoats.

I fell in the burn, I said. I'm just sitting.

Cagy of his intentions, I kept my eyes on his knees. He was wearing grey school shorts. School shorts on a weekend. We saying nothing for some time.

Have you anything for eating? he said eventually.

No, I said. I had a threepenny bit, though, and handed it over. Maybe he wanted money. He didn't.

That's yours, he said. You keep it.

After a while of the pair of us staring out at the water, he changed his mind. I gave him the coin and he ran away. I thought I'd solved the mystery of what Colin wanted, but he came running back and stopped in front of me, looking keen, fished a half-bag of chips out of his V-neck. Good chips from the Melbourne. They were, he said, *ours*. I tried not to touch his fingers, his nails bitten down to the blood, but sharing the food was fine by me. Rubbing my warm hands over the jacket to get rid of the salty grease afterwards revealed the purple cloth was drier now, almost bearable. I told him what I knew. I had to go home.

Too bad, he said, crumpling the paper, chucking it under the bench. Ah hate my da as well. Know what it's like.

He said he'd watch out for me. He went down the beach sometimes and his name was Colin. Colin. He was very keen I remember his name. I nodded, but this was a seaside town. People came and went all the time. I had no doubt I'd never clap eyes on him again. All the way back home on my own, I could feel damp tugging at the thighs of my trews. At least it wasn't leaving puddles. Damp was OK, easy to conceal. Given the bedwetting was back, I did it all the time. If I was lucky, I wouldn't have to say a word.

The scooter must have opened up my sense of adventure. It could even have been Colin, the fact of meeting someone new and nothing bad happening during the whole encounter. But I felt ready for the wider world. My mother had the surgery, Cora had the café. I wanted my place in the scheme of things. I wanted *work*. I'd already had a crack at tidying up the cemetery, poking crumbly, olive-coloured moss out of the headstones with a stick, hacking off the decay to let the words rise clear. I knew an H and an L after only one shift, my hollowed-out letters drawing the eye to the HERE LIES parts and making the people beneath seem that bit more visible. But there were too many stones and I knew I was walking on dead people. The location of my new work was in a stretch of broken-slabbed concrete behind the Countess Cinema, filling the cracks with gravel. The gravel had been dumped there by builders, and since I found it, I was keeper. The idea was to make the abandoned ground safer to cross for people going to the pictures. Cora had broken a heel there once and called it a *death trap*, which meant I was, potentially, saving lives. Part Public Art, part Public Service. I might get a medal. Work required a plastic bucket and spade, a KitKat and a firm jaw-set. The cemetery stuff had had its heart in the right place, but this was *real work*, dull, strenuous and necessary. My uncles who had gone down pits for coal would not have scoffed. I dressed in old clothes and planned to turn up at the same time every day for as long as it took. I imagined a year. Finally, after some false starts, I had found something useful to do with myself. The method was simple enough:

1. scooter to work with head held high, park scooter sideways near gravel;
2. scoop up said gravel in spade to half-fill bucket, balance half-bucket load on the scooter handle carefully for journey to the broken slabs;
3. slabs attained, tip out bucket contents, spread over the cracks with spade in a thick layer for maximum coverage, then
4. scooter back to gravel pit and start again from step one.

I had the impression I did this for hours. When the first round of boredom hit, I ate the KitKat and made the exhausted cloth-cap worker faces I'd seen on TV and sat on my hunkers on the kerb. Sometimes people asked what I was doing or stopped to offer sweeties. I could take to this, I thought. This was fine.

It might have been the third day, even the second, that Colin came. I knew him right away: he was in exactly the same clothes with the same pattern of tape on his glasses. He wanted to help but gravel went in his gym shoes and he had to empty them out too often. The soles were peeling off and his socks were missing heels. Braving it out, he shared bucket-ferrying, scattering and shovelling. In our break, while Colin sat next to me, I imagined we might put a garden here one day, a bench. People could sit out on their way home from the shops, enjoy the view and wonder out loud: who made this lovely place? And I'd step modestly forward and confess. I told Colin but he thought the whole idea was daft. It's just messing about, he said, shrugging. This place is a dump. I gave him half the KitKat because he'd earned it, but ignored him for the rest of the afternoon. He went home first.

Next day, when I came back alone, the slabs were clear. A council sweeper or maybe just a dog had undone the lot. I spent time trying to put it back and Colin came back for another go, but it was dispiriting. Third time killed it. Third time the gravel was cleared and the place looked worse than before we had started and I admitted the truth. This was never going to be a pretty place and what we were doing wasn't real work; it was wasting time.

Colin was right: it was a dump, and nothing I did would make any difference. I pictured innocent women catching their heels in the cracks, toppling headlong, split skulls and rivers of blood, but it was all beyond me now. It felt terrible, like how I imagined my mother had felt when Tiger died. The whole thing had slipped away. I told Colin it was finished and he might as well go home. He got agitated and his specs steamed up, but I didn't care. It was finished, I explained. He should just go away and leave me alone. When he kicked me and ran, I was pleased. I deserved it.

He came round a couple of times after that. My mother gave him a biscuit and he said, Thanks Missis. Can I eat it the now? When she showed an interest in finding him a better pair of socks, I'd had enough and walked us both to the end of the street where we stopped and surveyed the former work-space. There was no sign we had ever worked there and it seemed daft to think there would have been. He looked at it for a bit, then at his shoes. I didn't want to go for a walk and neither of us had any money. He turned to go away then looked back.

Are we still pals? he said. Sheen on his specs made it hard to see what he was looking at. Can lassies be pals with boys?

The question threw me. I didn't know. I'd never been pals with anyone so far as I knew, not anyone the same age as me. I knew I liked Colin. He had never called me a name or hurt my feelings or tricked me, not once. I liked him very much, but that wasn't what he had asked. I had no answer. He took my silence as some kind of answer, and turned away. I understood, with a pang of terrible guilt and pity, than he was disappointed.

OK, he said, before I had the chance to mend it, to work out exactly who he was. Fair enough. He crossed the road abruptly, almost huffy, then thought of one more thing. I remember him looking back across the road to ask it.

Did your da batter you? That time down the shore when you got your stuff wet – did he give you a doing?

For a moment, I couldn't think who my da was. All that popped into my head was Cora. No, I said. No, he didn't. I asked him nothing in return.

He looked at me hard, biting his lip as though he thought I was telling lies or simple and he wasn't sure which. OK, he said. I'm away back hame to Paisley next week then. Cheerio.

He stood another moment, deciding. Then he cleared his throat and ran down to the corner of Windmill Street towards the sea.

———

Near Christmas Eve, we foraged out the tree from the back of the wash-house. An assemblage of green bottle brushes about eighteen inches high, the tree was more than it looked. We brought hardly anything from Wellpark Road – there wasn't the space apart from other things – but we brought this. The tip of every branch sported a chipped red wooden berry and the prickles drew blood, but it was a tree beyond reproach. This is *my* tree, she said, hauling it out of the box. *I* bought it, she said, her face smooth with pleasure as she unfolded the branches, laid them straight. I was buggered if I was leaving *this* behind.

She had brought the ornaments too, layered inside leaves of tissue so old they had turned the colour of kippers. There was a string of lanterns on a frayed cable, glass teardrops and four metal balls with hearts and clubs, diamonds and spades indented in red and black on the sides. Mostly, there was tinsel, ropy old strands of silver on balding string, shedding more every time they were touched. Past the wear and tear, the scratchy bristles and awkwardnesses of cables, though, they came together and the effect was beautiful. Gilded, ethereal and still a tree, it sat in the middle of the bay window-sill, a wild thing content to be caught. The fairy had only one arm and the paint on her mouth had come off, but angled the right way, you couldn't tell. The whole lot tilted when anyone tried to pull the curtains at night, but it was worth the effort, the extra care. It'll be down sharpish in a couple of days, Cora said. She wouldn't put the fairy-lights off at night, though. They stayed on.

She did my Santa list when the time came, writing out a short roster of items in her tiny, curlicued script. My mother chose what went on the list, approved it, then folded it once. If he has these, he ticks them, she said. She looked behind the telly. In pencil. You'll have to wait and see.

The sheets were rough with toast crumbs when I fell asleep, watching the little lanterns glow on their green wire. It's the first Christmas I remember, the last I believed fairies were a reasonable, if rare, proposition.

The shift started with Cora's voice, repeating single words. It took a moment to work out that *what* she was reading was my letter. In the crackling and shuffling that followed, I heard them take things out of the wardrobe, checking them over against the list: Beetle Drive, a nightie, a deck of cards, a plastic swan full of bathcubes. It clicked right away. There was no magic, only your own family hiding things in wardrobes and taking them out when they thought you didn't know. Aunty Rose, Aunty Doreen, Tommy and Allan, one after another in Cora's voice, out of the bag like cats. It was shocking, their not knowing I could listen like this, when their voices were low and easy; shocking and touching at the same time. We were all pretending together now, even me. Lying with my eyes shut, listening, I drifted back to sleep. When I woke again and there was only their breathing, the tree, the shapes they had arranged just so in the paper the givers had chosen, cut, bound with tape and raffia ribbon. I watched little drawings of penguins and holly, bells, stick snowmen with hats and smiles glowing red at the edges from the grate embers. The short-circuit buzzing of the lights had stopped and it was quiet, just Cora, wheezing in her sleep. There was no real dilemma here, no excuse for the terrible feeling of hollow space that was filling my chest. I should have known. It was stupid not to and I should have known. In the morning, I would pretend the presents were a fine surprise. I had no desire to be a disappointment. But I had a sneaking feeling they'd see a difference in my face and *know*. This had something to do with growing up, the lying and the knowing at the same time. It changed the look of you, the way your eyes met someone else's. It made you feel torn in two.

Get back to sleep, my mother said. It's not time.

And neither it was. I had a dim grasp of that much. Stuffed with secrets and trying to forget, I slipped back off to sleep. In the morning, the thing that surprised me most was a school tie.

Haha, Cora said. That knocked you off your perch.

You wait, my mother said. You're going to love it. I bet you're going to be really good at the school.

Santa's passing was the least of my worries.

On Tuesday 10 January 1961, I rolled up for school for the first time and almost fell at the first hurdle. The entire half-mile walk had frozen overnight, turned treacherous beneath the soles of my brand-new flat, lace-up shoes. Jack's Road Primary, normally within easy walking distance, was awash with mothers and kids with scarves and gloves that would be long lost by the afternoon. Everyone preparing to shunt inside, clueless, was five. I wore a black blazer with a Saltcoats crest on a wavy line, a grey skirt, a vest, a shirt and long socks, none of it cheap. We had been to Corner Duncan's and bought the lot in one go. Be good, she said, waiting at the gates, and I dithered off, after the other children, inside. A tall woman with white hair rang a hand-bell. Anything else relating to that first proud day is a blank.

This noble start fell apart by the morning break. I know from telling, she had been sent for because I was howling. This was followed by a solid week of crying and hyperventilating during the course of which my mother was called a further twice to calm me

down. She was, she said, mortified. For years, she did not tire of
telling me that she was mortified. My second week was more or
less the same. The janitor found me in the junior toilets after milk
break, flattened against a wall, and they called her in again. I
don't know what's wrong with her, she told them: she's usually
so *good*. I know all this from telling because I don't remember
any of it. They, by which I mean the headmistress, told her I was
clingy, anxious and withdrawn. The words *separation anxiety* had
been bandied. My mother rolled out the phrase now and then,
hoping it was a diagnosed condition and therefore not her fault.
Separation anxiety. It meant the plan of me shining like a star in
Infants 1b had all gone to cock.

They know what they're talking about, teachers, she'd say, at
the end of her tether. It's like bloody Rosebuds back to haunt me.
I'll never get rid of you.

It got worse. I wouldn't hold hands readily, was reticent when
spoken to and, during a chorus of Old MacDonald, had offered
only the words *I want to go home* when called upon to suggest
what the duck said here, there and everywhere. My mother knew
that teachers were people to whom apologies, explanations and
obeisance were due, but she didn't know what apologies, explanations or types of obeisance were appropriate for this kind of
thing. It had never happened before.

My other daughter wasn't like this, she said. Cora loved the
school. She was desperate to get there. This one – she looked at me
and sighed – this one's different.

They commiserated and she chewed her lip, trying not to look weak. Sympathy made her uncomfortable. Somehow, the whole thing passed. It must have, because they put me in charge of the class scissors by February. But it was a rocky start and she took it hard.

Are you going to stop this *mummy mummy mummy* nonsense? You that's supposed to be clever? Are you going to try and be a big girl like Alma?

She posted a sweetie into my mouth and took one for herself. By the time we had walked back over the railway brae, sucking had made us calm.

Kitty's right enough, she said, as we struck out down Argyle Road. Weans will take you over if you don't watch. You'll just have to sink or swim.

I didn't argue. I'd drain her dry if she didn't get me sorted out. Kitty said that too.

Alma's good with hair, she said, clacking the sweetie from one side of her mouth to the other. She'll get on.

It was true. Alma was blonde. She was good with hair, had the top bunk in a real bedroom and still thought Santa was right enough. Alma would get on just fine.

I wish I knew what the hell you were good at, she said. Godknows where you're headed.

Only one thing was certain: sooner or later I'd get what I got. What happened to you in this life was random. It was sudden, often frightening and always judged. What was true for everybody was true for me: nobody got to pick and choose. That which was not terrifying deserved our gratitude and the rest was a puzzling jumble. Even the terrifying had its own excitements, like walking along the shore wall in the wrong shoes over seaweed. The miracle was that you stayed on at all. That you kept going. Yes indeed, that was the measure of the thing. It was all about hanging on.

Stick in at the school she said, and you learn things. Writing your letters and spelling, sums. Important things. You'll be good yet if it kills me. And it might.

She drew me a sideways look. I smiled, hoping it was a joke. She bit down on her Polo Mint and just kept walking.

Count your blessings, name them one by one
Count your blessings see what God has done
Count your many blessings, name them one by one
And it will surprise you what the Lord has done.

Aunty Doreen came from America. She had escaped to upstate New York and sent clothes every Christmas, the party dresses in which I was pictured, to-the-nines stuff from another world altogether. My mother's pleasure in Doreen's gifts was real and unstinting. She didn't resent: it was a law of nature that Americans had money. She'll like you, my mother said as I left to meet her at Rose's house. She's got no kids. If she gives you anything don't say no.

Rose and Angus fetched me to their house in Angus's car, and Doreen was waiting at the door, all ready in a red shortie jacket and a hat with a pin. All the bones in her hand showed, but she had a generous mouth, good, straight teeth. She liked Sunday School songs and insisted we do *Count Your Blessings* before I got in the door. Her singing voice was every bit as terrible as Rose's. It was so bad, I blushed.

Who does this look like? Rose asked, thrilled to bits, pointing at Doreen's face. Doreen kept smiling, rolling her eyes like a model. I didn't know. Eddie! Rose shrieked. Like daddy! This is daddy's big sister! Him and Doreen, they're two peas in a pod. She didn't know how I could miss it.

Doreen, there was no two ways about it, looked odd. She looked odd the way all my dad's side looked, swollen-ankled, bony and badly jointed, but she had a lovely smile. Also, Doreen was talkative. She had a husband called Cliff, who wasn't with her because they couldn't afford two, but she had brought me an outfit instead, a yellow dress and Easter bonnet with white cuff-length gloves. She showed me a picture of Uncle Cliff – *Cliffy* – then held me by both shoulders at arm's length, checking me out.

Don't you look cute? she said. Something special brought me all this way, she said. Did I know what it was? I didn't. She shook her head, still checking, smiling. You, she said. I came to see *you*.

Angus took us out to the beach in his car, my only outing with my father's big sister. Somebody took three photos. I still have them, dark as the day they were taken, no fading.

The first is Doreen, up to her ankles in sea with a cinched skirt billowing in the wind, middle-aged and laughing with her knickers on show. The second is me and Doreen and Aunty Rose, sisters and their shared niece digging a hole in the sand. I'm the only one with missing teeth: theirs are flush and false. Like gates in their mouths. I wear a shirred Ladybird swimsuit tied halter-style at the nape, its neckline at the front barely high enough to cover my nipples. Rose has a big bag hiding her entire skirt and Doreen is putting on lipstick. There is a sandwich off left, a Thermos tilting like the tower of Pisa, two discarded spades and a spoon. We are peering and grimacing into the sun.

Doreen didn't want to be in the third snap. She was, but before the deal was settled there was some old-times conversation between adults who have forgotten a child is there, so I went toward the shallows and left them to it. Two other kids strolled up, blond and chicken-skinned, and we made a game of jumping over incoming waves for a while. Some time during the jumping, I fleetingly felt a tug on my ankles, seaweed maybe.

There was no sensation of falling, just the sky zipping up over my head, then a roaring sound, everything reduced to muffle and fog. A ribbon of bottle green with tentacles drifted near my hand. Weed. Looking towards it, I could see my arms were splayed, making me bob on my hunkers without falling, and overhead there was a light, distant echo of laughter. The sun was up there, but through wavy lines, electric streaks and dashes moving through the blue. Not far away I could see a misty red costume, pallid limbs stretching out of it towards where a face might be, arms melting like wax. Children's voices were audible, but distant as foreign radio waves. They were looking at the place where I had been, a little ripple of disappearance. I am – I thought it clearly – drowning. The water was calm, unflurried, no colour at

all. I felt mist in my eyes, but no panic, no appropriate survival
instinct. Till something tipped my ankle with its fingers, a dogfish,
a strap of weed, and the washing machine thrum coming closer
became my own heartbeat, a craven need for air. My legs pushed
down and my head split water with a sound like silk shearing. And
I was teetering upright, head roaring, ears pouring out the whole
Firth of Clyde. The kids I had been with laughing out loud. They
thought I was playing, trying to amuse them. I could barely see
or stand upright, so sat for a few minutes on the rocks, coughing,
waiting till my eyes stopped blurring, my heart slowed, getting
over the feeling that something huge and unreasonable had taken
things in hand. When the pain in my chest had died back, I inched
up the beach to where I had left them. To Doreen and Rose and
Angus, waving the camera like a flag.

Hurry up, he was shouting. Cmon, quick, while there's still
something to eat!

I was still here, after all. And starving. They had bananas up
there, biscuits, bread. I ran, even aware of the shells and the dune-
rushes underfoot, the fear of falling. I ran.

Despite everything, then, this last picture is the full line-up:
Doreen in her dirndl, Rose with her gargantuan bag spilling flasks
and paper-covered food, Angus's thumb in the far-left corner. We
look the same as in the last photo only this time my costume is
wet. And there's a fifth member of the party. He must have been
with us all day, in on the paddling and the sandy meat-paste
sandwiches, but appears only once and only here, a man with
deep lines on his forehead and false teeth too big for his face.

Dad, trousers and shirt-sleeves rolled up, open-necked, bare-footed. No one is touching him, but his hand is grazing my shoulder, hardly there at all. My eyes stare past the camera, astounded. He is looking down calmly into the sand pit. He is, almost, at peace.

The day before she went home, Doreen gave me a brooch and an invitation to come and see her one day. I said yes because I forgot it was America. She also gave me an envelope with the pictures, freshly developed and shiny as plastic. They showed Rose and Doreen, glowing for the camera, me, fresh from drowning, and my father. We're ghosts, the two of us, on borrowed time, with only the faintest idea how lucky we are. I didn't know at the time but I know now. That's why Doreen came all that way. Not for me, for him. His peeled-back sleeves, a pale score where his wedding ring had been, his eyes fixed on the sand.

I saw him three more times after Doreen had gone. Angus collected me. Rose and my mother were still not speaking, so I had to go outside and not let Angus in, and we drove all of six streets. My father was in a brown armchair in the corner of their front room, the one they never used, with a rug over his knees. He had a Disney book, *101 Dalmatians* with spotty cartoon dogs on the cover, and I read bits off the pages out loud, making it up when the words got hard.

You're getting to be the clever girl, he said. He sat in shadow, flicking pages to find more. I bet you're good at the school. Clever like your daddy.

The second time, Rose made jam sandwiches and I hid the pieces down my sock rather than say I didn't like them. He ate nothing and didn't give me away. On neither occasion did he ask after Cora or my mother. I thought he had forgotten who they were.

The last time was a longer journey to a place I didn't know full of corridors. I recall a high bed in a tiny white room, his head on a pillow like a buoy on the sea. A cable came out of his arm and attached to what looked like a coat-hanger. He was the colour of boiled chicken and wearing pyjamas. Striped. It was the pyjamas that threw me. I'd never seen him in pyjamas. It still occurs to me to wonder where he got them. Whatever we spoke about next, whatever else happened, it ended with singing. I was doing *Wooden Heart* in my best radio voice, though there was no table to go under. Just me, up front and no pretending.

There's no strings upon this love of mine
It was always you from the start.

My voice sounded thin without the table for an echo chamber, not like Elvis at all.

Treat me nice, treat me good,
Treat me like you really should,
Cos I'm not made of wood
And I don't have a wooden heart.

I was about to say it was no good when he started crying. It looked like extra lines on his cheeks to begin with, but they were sliding. The rims of his eyes turned suddenly red. I stopped singing. An ambulance could have driven into the room, lights flashing, siren wailing, and I wouldn't have broken my gaze. He was turning into something else. Rose put a hand on my shoulder as he moved, tugging the wires, flailing his arm. And I realised he was reaching. That what he was reaching for was me. And Rose was hauling me backwards, away from the weeping man who was trying to touch me, my own arms not long enough to help. The distance between us widened, Rose repeating it was all right while she dragged me closer to the door. My hands open like starfish, fingers at full stretch. It's all right, she said as she closed the white door, shutting him out of sight. But it wasn't. Any fool could see it wasn't. I shivered on Rose's knee all the way back in the car, seeing him reaching, knowing everything she said was lies.

When the time came, my mother told me straight.

We'd been up the scheme on the bus, stayed so late Alma was being bathed in the sink when we left. We got off the bus and I was running, wild with being past bedtime, the unaccustomed freedom in the dark. They were building something on the corner of the street near the war memorial, meshing the street with barriers and cordons so it seemed festive, strung with colour, and the lights were on in the Melbourne. You could hear the sea crashing if you listened. But I didn't. I ran not bothering with her telling me to stop till I had a stitch and turned and she said, Your daddy's died. I looked up when she said it, staring as though the words might materialise in the sky over Hamilton Street, the words *Your daddy's died* drifting up into the sodium-filtered blackness like smoke-rings from a cigarette mouth.

You hear me? D'you hear what I'm saying? Your daddy's died. You've no daddy any more.

There was nothing, not even a gull, nothing to account for the whistling filling my ears. I looked at her, amazed she couldn't hear it too.

Your daddy's died. Look at me. He's dead.

There was only the noise of waves from the shore wall, keeping going, crumbling the rocks and shells first to powder, then to nothing. It struck me I'd have to go to school tomorrow, knowing this, that Cora would be home when we went in. Eventually my mother had to shake me to make me see her again. She said *shhh* repeatedly. *Shhh*. It was comforting, this evidence of breathing, but it made me start to cry, the kind of crying that could only get worse. There was a stone angel in the graveyard, and I didn't know what happened now. Where did they take dead people? Nobody told you. I felt a sudden flash of anger and heard the crying turn to howling, baying, wailing at the moon. Nobody told you anything. *I have school tomorrow*, I yelled. *I have school*. Cora's face appeared at the attic window. She pointed a finger, made a zipping gesture across her mouth. I turned away from being able to see her, covered my face with my hands, but the anger was gone. *I have school*, I said to nobody in particular as though it made any sense. *I have school*. It was a whine, a dreary, childish complaint. Nothing to say at all.

I wasn't at the funeral and neither was Cora. Cora went to work and since it was a Saturday, I went to Aunty Marie's. I recall sitting in her kitchen, roaring. Big drops fell off my face and on to the Formica table-top, the black Sputnik shapes of its design pock-marked with craters of salt water. Alma was out. It had not been seen as healthy for Alma to talk or be near me because I was tainted with death. Marie made comforting noises but it was her neighbour, a black-haired woman with arms like salami and a fierce warmth in her chest, who took me up on her lap and stroked my hair and let Marie get on with Alma's tea. For an awful moment I thought I might have to live here from now on, call Aunty Kitty *granny* and have Alma for my sister. But it was all right. My mother arrived in black with her powder thick and we went back to the attic, one end of Saltcoats to the other, walking the whole way.

We'll not be staying at Hamilton Street any more, she said. We'll be moving. Do you remember the old house?

I said nothing.

Well, we're going back there. Soon.

She crushed a paper hanky over and over, snowing her good black gloves with white fibres. Soon, she said. Soon.

———

It was. We went back to Wellpark Road, the garden, two bed-rooms, indoor toilet: all change. Shortly before the flit, I did something I should have done before. Nobody else is doing it, my

mother said; it's your responsibility. I shouldered it and told
Sophie I wasn't going to Sunday School any more. I had to say it
twice. There was no mention of my father, of moving, just my
desertion of Christ. The desertion earned me a flaccid slap on the
ear. It didn't hurt and it didn't soothe her.

Well, my mother said, shrugging, They just do what they like
these days, don't they? They don't know they're born.

Sophie stumped off, not speaking and my mother turned back
to the washing line. We had signed off, ticked the last box on the
list. We were free to go.

———

We did not call on doors or make formal goodbyes. It would not
have occurred. My mother left a basket of shopping on the Misses
May's doormat, tins and things, eggs and two ounces of mince, a
leaving gift with no leave-taking. She did knock on the door but
there was no answer, even though we knew someone was home.
Leaving the Misses May was the only thing my mother seemed to
regret. Cora was at work the day we moved stuff. It was only me
and my mother doing the lifting to Angus's car. We took no
photos, had no last looks round. None of the room, the garden, the
wash-house or the outside toilet with its surround of tombstone
teeth and its peeping-tom angel or the EU; none of Sophie or the
Misses May or Big Davie Stuart or the view all the way up
Hamilton Street to the Melbourne, or anything else. Nobody had
taken a picture the whole time we had lived there and nobody

saw the need now. We left the red divan, the tin bath and the potty behind as though they had never been ours. This, my mother said, holding her restored set of council keys, was a second chance.

We already knew he had left us nothing but debts and a set of expensive lawn bowls with his name on the hubs, *Eddie Galloway* in fancy gold letters. No insurance, no savings, and, given he'd spent his last weeks before hospital at Rose's, no clothes.

He was a neat man, my mother said when she found the shelves of nothing, not even dust.

Thank god the second chance was there. It was all we were getting.

7

The block had been built by an *architect*.

She had said it already, but it was worth repeating. Swedish or Danish, she said; the *architect* who designed our council block was a Foreigner with Big Ideas. That was who had Big Ideas: Foreigners. Wellpark Road was a return to great things, not least cupboards. She said *cupboards* like it meant golden floorboards. She lost the cleaning job at the surgery, but you didn't get everything in this life. Given the choice, it was easy. This place was *ours*.

I knew I had lived there before, but had forgotten what it looked like. Taking in the unaccustomed space – two bedrooms and a living room, a bath indoors with cold *and* hot – I understood what tempted people to chuck their money away on Vernon's Pools. If he hadn't died, she said, godknew where we'd have ended up. But here we were. Everything was luck, in the end: luck and accidents.

We went in and out of the doors – front and back – for sheer novelty, thrilled with acquisition. There were even two gardens: a vegetable plot and washing green complete with washing poles out the back; floral borders and grass for its own sake, just because it was grass, out front. The people in the apartments above, to the right, and above the right, each had their own double plots, paved round to show where one ended and another began. There would be no more arguments about what days you could do the washing, who could hog the line, whether we could grow potatoes. Grass was permission. Everyone had their own.

Thank god, my mother said, poking her nose round the kitchen door. He didn't sell the washing machine. We don't need to use that bloody wash-house ever again.

We had an oven, hooks for kitchen knives, a counter, a drainer, a cupboard for cups. It struck me more than once and in every room, that my former life here must have been enchanted. I had forgotten almost the lot.

———

The first thing Cora did was set up a mirror in the hall. She checked the height and got my mother to hammer in nails.

Some of us prefer to look smart, she said, stretching her neck at her own reflection. She tapped her front teeth, watching the mirror tap back. That'll do nice.

After that, we didn't see her much. She had her bed to make, make-up to sort, the telly to find. Cora had a lot to do. We did the rest, at least that's what I remember. The business of transformation was all ours.

My father had left his mark most outside, mostly in the narrow little shed. It was really a coal-house, laced with dirt, cobwebs and leftover dross, full of filth-covered bits and pieces that had belonged to my mother before she had made a run for it, but since it held garden utensils as well, the name notched up to something grander. In this shed, then, beside a leftover hummock of coal, we reclaimed a hoe and a spade, two sets of heavy trowels. We found a dibber, a big plastic bottle slathered with brown stuff that claimed to kill dandelions and a blunt-to-buggery scythe with which to slice their carroty roots till they wept out milk. We dug up a rake with prongs rusty as mole-claws; a watering can with a clogged-up rose, a medium-weight fork flaking ancient dirt like dandruff and a set of hedge clippers, gone green and seized shut. He must never have used them, she muttered, shaking her head as though it was a surprise. He didny touch them once.

Opposite the coal, there was a display cabinet full of almost-finished tins of enamel, gloss and varnish, a couple of dried-hard brushes and stirring sticks with gone-solid drips in royal and bottle green. Boxes of nails gone orange with rust nestled in what was left of the space. This, she said, tripping on a stack of giant screws, was what he left us: all the rubbish he didn't want. Anything that could be used again – garden tools, a set of cobbler's lasts in cast iron, hammers and screwdrivers, saws, sieves and assorted other stuff – we kept: the rest went along the side of the pavement for the bin lorries. She dusted the lasts of mouse-droppings and put them on top of the cabinet in a box, sets of skinny little robot feet waiting to run away to a bright new future.

They didn't fit Cora's stilettos, my mother's courts, my T-bar sandals, but we kept them anyway. You never know, she said.

Indoors came together at less of a tilt. Over weeks, the house found a place for everything, and we put everything in it. My mother did the kitchen. It was her kingdom, her crockery, cutlery and cooking things. My forte was the quiet stuff. I came into my own with a J-cloth, dust and things to fold and stack. Most of my sorting applied to bedrooms.

It was obvious from the start that Cora would have one to herself. The front bedroom, the nice yellow one, the only one with any sun and the view of the front grass, was all hers. She had a single bed, a dressing table with doileys on it, a bedside cabinet and a walk-in cupboard with a rail that took all her fancy frocks and pencil skirts, all her nifty wee cardigans and their perfume smells and kept them safe. The back bedroom, the one that fell in the shadow of the house but showcased the potato drills, the washing lines and the sound of Mr Gregg's pigeon loft every morning, was my mother's. My mother's and mine, that is: two people, one double bed. We shared it till I was sixteen: ten years, starting now.

Bloody pigeons, she said, peering out of the window. They'll shit on the washing. Still. She looked round at the buff walls that smelled of ash, the mahogany-coloured headboard, the bedside table bullet-holed with fag-burns. You got nothing without effort, she said. But we'll get there. This will do us fine.

It was a man's room, she said, but that was about to change. She opened one of the wardrobe doors, a statement of intent.

She'd stored her clothes at Kitty's, not taking any risks. Now – she opened the double doors wider, wider still – they could come home.

My mother didn't smoke, didn't drink, didn't gamble. She wasn't man-crazy. She didn't gossip, do coffee mornings, overeat or fill the house with knick-knacks. She had given up singing and hadn't held a party for years. Bar lipstick, she didn't even wear make-up. Her secret pleasure was clothes. They weren't that new, and they weren't that many, but they were bought as carefully considered outfits, paired and accessorised, and she kept them for *years*. Careful darning, button-replacement, hook and eye realigning and threading of ropes of stray broken beads were one of the very few things we did as a mother-and-daughter pair. She had antique bags, polish-rich shoes, jackets with belts, brooches that had formerly been diamanté-effect but were now empty-eye-socket skeletons, contrast-trim suits, and at least three coats, detachable collars, scarves, head-squares, wild-coloured gloves. She had church-going cloche-hats and turbans, berets and snoods and wide-brim straws, woolly button-through balaclavas and printed rain-mates (pink and lime to go with navy, scarlet to offset black, orange or turquoise with beige), and all were cherished. Not only that, but she knew how to wear them, how to mix and contrast colours so the outfits looked like something. She was, and she knew it, stylish. I was not stylish. I had sherbet dab on my pullover, graphite up the sides of one hand from my pencil sharpener and dirty marks on both socks. You're as much like me as an alien from outer space, she said. If somebody came from

Barnardo's and asked for me back, she wouldn't argue. You're not a McBride, she said, looking almost pleased; that's for sure.

Of course not. I was Galloway down to the bone. The most cursory glance at photographs proved it. I had the Galloway chin, their offset teeth, their glassy, flat blue eyes. My failure in the elegance stakes was not in dispute. What puzzled me was my mother's pinning her dress sense to her name. To Granny McBride.

My granny wore the same thing every day: a patterned floral pinny over a round-necked black sleeping-bag effort made of something not far off wool. She wore her hair the same way, in a loose Edwardian-style bun by day and down over one shoulder at night for bed. Twice I saw her in a Fair Isle cardigan, but that was for Hogmanay and then only till she'd finished the required stick of shortbread and one schooner of Harvey's Bristol Cream. She was four foot ten and not beautiful, but she was, when I forced myself to see it, trim. The only electrical gadgetry she possessed was a telly she couldn't much see, a fan heater with a faulty cable and an iron, and the iron mattered most. Near-blind, she knew the U-bends of her clothes by feel. She burned nothing, scorched nothing. This was discipline, not patience: a choice about what mattered. She had raised six miners, one big lad after another, and every one of them washed and dressed in a clean shirt before sitting at the table at night. No wash, no eat: clear and simple. Dirty nails were not trivial: they were going to hell on a handcart. Whitewashing the front steps, returning library books on time, not running up debt and turning out nice were the mark of the man, the sum of the woman. She called it *making an effort*. If my mother believed that gut-crushing rubber corsets were essential daywear and that curlers were worth the pain – and she did – she was not crazy. She was *making an effort*. Cut-price chic and caring for it showed a right attitude to the world and one's duty. You did the best you could.

The attic must have driven her mad with dowdiness. Now, back at Wellpark Road with her clothes restored, she could be her own woman again. Or something like. She filled the huge double-coffin of a wardrobe, the chest of drawers, the hanging cupboard near the bed with emerald greens, royals, stripes and tartans. Her good things were not many, but they seemed more because they were vivid. She adored vivid and generously sprinkled it round the rest of the house. She changed the dingy candlewick to a Co-op quilt in tangerine nylon, put up floral fibreglass curtains to let in light. She got a lampshade with fringing Marie didn't want any more and a purple bedside rug. The smells of talcum powder, ladies' shoes and MUM deodorant took over from varnish and ash. I had my own chest of drawers full of home-knitted jumpers, stirrup trousers, socks and school things, the new-fangled anorak Doreen sent from New York. We could hardly move between the items of storage furniture, but that was immaterial. We were truly settled in.

We were so settled, that by the time the Coat came back, there was nowhere for it to go.

I had nearly forgotten I had the damn thing, my mother said, shocked by her own laxness. Kitty hadn't. She needed to be rid of it, she said, and I could see why.

Thick, reddish, fox-like and falling to mid-calf, the Coat might
have been swish once. Now, it looked raddled. Even when she put
lipstick on and peeped over her shoulder like Betty Boop, trying
a smile for good measure, the Coat did not revive.

Nobody in their right mind would wear that out any more,
Cora said. It makes you look like King Kong.

My mother's face was so sad I toyed with suggesting I use it
as a Viking Cloak, but didn't. I didn't want it either. The lining
was cold, and beneath the chilly mock satin was coarse hide,
rough and suggestive of violence. That the Coat had been something living once, something butchered out of its skin, was all
too obvious. Not only that, but the thing smelled. It was animal,
wild.

What a shame, my mother said, peeling it off to show the lining
torn and stained at the armpits. But you can't just throw it away.
It's *fur*. You never get a fur coat again. Your granny would have a
fit if I threw it away.

My granny's opinion counted, so we all paused to think. You
didn't throw out fur: it was unarguable. Even if no one ever wore
it again, the Coat was staying. It was hung in Cora's yellow bedroom, hidden in her clothes cupboard next to too-tight jumpers
and patent plastic buckle belts. It looked like a bear in a suitcase
and smelled like it too, but there was no argument. I've no room
left, my mother said: Cora would have to give up the space. I
could always move Janice's stuff in instead, she said, arch. She'd
need to dress in with you, mind. You'd not get peace.

The Coat or me. Cora, as she was meant to, chose wisely.

My mother never grew to like the pigeons, but I loved the sounds, the soft crooning there before I woke up for school every morning, Mr Gregg cawing in his homers last thing. I dressed, read and did homework in that room, lying spread-eagled on the nylon quilt. My mother didn't mind. She seemed to seek no privacy of her own, but must have found it somehow. It did not occur to anyone that Cora might share with me. The idea was outlandish. Cora was sure of her place in the world. It did not resemble my mother's. With dad gone, Cora saw a vacancy and filled it. She was the man of the house, no contenders. Or not often. For all that, Cora believed she looked like my mother. I couldn't see it myself, but what did I know? You're not entitled to opinions, Cora said; you're entitled to bloody shut up. Anyway, you know who *you* look like.

I knew. I was *him* all right, nobody could deny it. But at least I hadn't inherited the hair. I wasn't, thank god, ginger.

Godknows what colour you are, my mother said. Mousy or something. You can always dye it when you're big. It's not what you look like that counts.

I turned my face from the possibility of beauty and counted my blessings. I had my very own hair colour, unclassifiable. I was scissor monitor at school. I could make my mother's face light with pride when I whipped out a duster and offered to polish the brasses. We had an indoor bathroom, two gardens, the station at the end of the road that led to the outside world. This was living. This was *life*.

French roll, Cora said, tucking stray tendrils away with the end of a comb. Hair in your eyes gets you nowhere. French roll, now – she stuck out her tongue, concentrating – that's smart.

She was on a typing course, gaining qualifications. My mother was all approval. A lot depended on this typing course and it better come right. It was her big chance. All she had to do was make the bloody effort.

Cora didn't wear eyeliner to college, just a dab of lipstick paler than her usual. She must have wanted the typing diploma very much. She caught the seven forty to Glasgow – *late gets you nowhere* – and always left the house running. Uneaten toast lay around on sideboards and the top of the telly, not so much as a bite missing. Cora had places to go, people to meet; she had to catch the A-train. Cora's was a fag on a front-facing seat, heading inland. Whether she thought about the husband and son she had left behind as she travelled, whether they even crossed her mind as she shunted through the Ayrshire countryside, its mottled milk herds and rain-begrutten sheep, is anybody's guess. Nobody mentioned it even behind her back. Cora's old life, like ours, was unspeakable, unmissed.

She'll not be travel-sick anyway, my mother said. Eats bloody nothing.

Then she turned to me. We all had places to go now: new routines, new lives. Cora was training to be a *typist*; I was no longer a wee girl in silly floral prints, but a schoolgirl in a new-build primary with *all mod cons*. My mother did up my tie, checked my face for smears, my shoes for scuffs. It mattered to look well to the world. Only my mother stayed home, no longer a skivvy in a wash-house, but a modern housewife surrounded by a modern apartment with time-saving amenities. We had an electric mangle, a flip-top coal scuttle, an egg-timer that buzzed. None of us liked eggs but it didn't matter: what mattered was what science could do. It was 1961. We had not merely shifted home, not merely shifted decades: we had shifted centuries.

With the newly found rush, mornings were short and far too sweet. Nobody ate cereal. Only people in adverts ate cereal, and they did it because they were paid. Toast meant butter and only my mother liked that. Jam was stuff you put on semolina and semolina, as any fool knew, was not worth the waste of milk. Milk was for tea. Pancakes and sausages were tea-time foods and bacon went with mash and cabbage on Sundays. Eggs stank, rusk went mushy and porridge didn't bear thinking about. The ideal breakfast was an item of food ready-made, wrapped and sturdy enough to bounce off the head and wake the sleeper whilst presenting itself as the first meal of the day. The ideal breakfast was a biscuit, preferably coated with chocolate to protect it from shattering when it landed. KitKats, Blue Riband and any flavour of Club were good ones, though the edges could give you a black eye if they weren't well aimed. I was injured only once: chocolate

biscuits were worth the risk. Thus reinforced, I was ready for anything. What I had was school.

This was mine. I thought it every day when I walked down the
pale blue corridors, the bright, beautiful drawings of children
older than me. I'd be here for ever. At least longer than I'd been
alive already, till my age was so big it needed two numbers to
write it down. There was no point in having an opinion about
school. Its requirements were not open to opinion. School just
was. It was not *education*, the fancy thing Cora did at college. It
was reading and writing and sums, art and drill. I was expected to
be good here, for all those years and with all of them.

Reading was *Janet and John and the Dog with the Big Red Ball*.
Janet and John had a daddy in a suit and a thin mummy in a
frock. How she kept it clean with no pinny was a mystery. They
were polite sorts with a tree in their garden, and the collie had a
lead. Miss McKillop forgave me for being able to recognise letters
when I first arrived (*It's not their fault is it? It's the mothers*), but she
read out very slowly. This made reading more boring than it
might have been, but at least there was a story. Sums, after the fun
of simply making the numbers out of circles, sticks and bendy
lines, were a disappointment too. The jotter having squared pages
could not live up to expectation. No sooner did you master
adding the numbers together than they wanted you to take them
away. It was learning the same thing inside out and I knew it
would get worse. Sums were just tricks: the same old numbers
forced through different obstacle courses. After the initial excitement, sums were just the same games, over and over.

Writing happened in a small jotter with wide-spaced blue lines: two thick bordered by two thin. Making writing happen was largely a matter of hitting the jotter guide-lines in the right places and had something of a fairground game about it, only touching the wire with the wand instead of not. It was oddly thrilling. Sometimes an **O** turned out as a tomato (correct) or an ear (incorrect) or a bean (nearly correct) and each was a surprise. Balancing the bar on a **t** took the skill of a tightrope walker, dotting an **i** or the bar on a capital **J** was marksmanship, bridging the legs of an **m** the right distance apart was engineering. Writing let you imagine your way into all sorts of people. Some of my classmates were less impressed – the letter **s** reduced Lena Mills to tears – but I practised them all the time. Putting the letters together was a whole new territory. It was spelling, which heightened the whole thing: **c**, **a** and **t** were just letters, individual, awkward, strokes – **cat** was a *word*. If you let your mind float looking at the word, a picture appeared too – the animal in question! Letters made ideas. Joined with spelling, you could make your own words up and say the thing you wanted to say. Spelling wrote down what you were *thinking*. It was astounding. The day we wrote whole sentences on cardboard strips and put them up on the wall for everyone to see, I thought I would burst. *I see kitty. The ball is red. The dog runs.* A story all round the walls and into the corridor, going on till it reached the world outside. *Look at kitty.* Look. A story made of words made of letters: ideas made of marks. It was the cleverest idea ever invented.

Art, where a picture was a picture, was wonderful too. Art

allowed standing up and walking about sharpening pencils, picking paint and filling jars at the tap. You got thick, bleachy paper that left dust on the fingers and pencils soft enough to chew. I was good with scissors (*Janice is very neat*) and unfailingly quiet, so I prospered. Whether with pencils or wet paint, I became an asset by obeying orders and being no trouble. I could do this, I thought. I could, given the lists of red ticks, the gold and silver stars next to my work, the letters stacked like jumpers on flat blue lines, *shine*. Then they rolled out drill.

It might have been the running about in navy blue underpants and a shirt that did it (drill was undignified and knickery); it might have been the noise (the thunderous rockfall of gym shoes pounding); it might have been the incitement to move at all (I took a pride in my ability to sit still). It might even have been the smell of the place, all rubber and unwashed human skin. It was certainly Miss McKillop, an otherwise staid lady with a melon-seed necklace, who started it by showing another side to herself, a side I'd rather have known nothing about.

Just let go and enjoy yourselves, she roared, let me see you smiling when you run! Make a big *whoosh* sound like the wind!

I all but swooned. Orders to comply with dull things, repetitive things or even sore things I could follow, but not this. Enacting smiling enjoyment whilst whooshing was something I'd get wrong every time, something at which I would only disappoint; something I'd do if I thought for a moment I could, but I couldn't, I couldn't, I couldn't. I adopted *rigor mortis* and one thought: *this was cheating*.

I thought I had this place taped. I was studious. I excelled at being quiet, was great at being good. I exceeded expectation at anything that let me keep my head down, safe. I got gold stars and my mother was showing me off to Kitty, putting her sniffy nose completely out of joint. School was something I could do and I was doing it, finally, *right*. Now, there was more; a whole set of sly new demands that flew in the face of all the others. Don't be quiet, *make a noise*; don't sit at peace, *run*; don't fret about the rules, the possibility of failure, getting it horribly, hideously wrong – *abandon all caution. Just let go*. Let go. They might as well have insisted I lay an egg. It wasn't fair and it wasn't in me. Like a horse at a gate, I refused. I was as surprised as anyone else, but while the others gathered speed around me, I did not move. I could barely breathe. Miss McKillop blew her whistle to ask if I was all right, her old eyes a picture of concern, but there was no way to make sense of it, no defence. Silence was obstinacy. It was rudeness and refusal to cooperate. It was wrong, wrong, wrong – but I did it anyway. I hung my head and said *nothing*.

There was some jeering from shirtless boys, Miss McKillop shaking her head and telling me I was a nuisance, some reining in of tears, but nothing shifted, least of all my ability to join in. She gave me one last chance but it was no good. Furious, with a whole class waiting to let go and whoosh, Miss McKillop blew her whistle and threw me out. I'm surprised at you, she said as I gathered up my skirt, my shoes. You usually make the effort. You've let me down.

Dishonour apart, being sent back to class was no hardship. I knew where I was in a classroom, among the ordered ranks of desks and pencils, the injunctions to behave. The sound of rubber squeaking on the polished drill hall floor kept me company while I bided my time, still in my knickers, and practised the cone cups of my **ws**, the bridges of an **h**. I didn't mind the others having fun, not at all. What was terrible was the shift in Miss McKillop's eyes, the words she had spoken. *You've let me down.* Guilt curled in me like smoke, replayed the phrase again, again. *You've let me down.* It wasn't *her* I'd let down at all. Not really. It was mum.

I pictured my mother, crestfallen, having to lose face to Kitty and admit she was wrong about me being clever, I was just a drain after all. I imagined word leaking out from school and covering the whole of North Ayrshire, people pointing at me as I walked home, head down, scarlet with shame – *There goes the girl that let her mother down.* I imagined Cora, smug as a monkey with a bag of peanuts, saying, *I told you she'd come a cropper sooner or later.* I imagined all this and knew one thing: whatever happened I'd have to keep this dark. Cora's job was to be out in the world getting qualifications; my mother's was housework and cooking and everything else. My only job was to be good. It was my part in the family story, the role I'd been given. I had to make it come right. It was my big chance. All I had to do was make the bloody effort.

We had hot and cold taps. We had neighbours who knew our names. We had nice clothes with which we might present a brave face to the world, and an architect-designed council house. Our heads were above water and full of things we did not say. This was just one more. To keep the whole show on the road, I'd have to *lie*.

8

Cora bought everybody ice-cream. She came home from the station with it, roaring *I passed my exams* in at the window, holding the cones up like the Statue of Liberty, her wrists slashed with raspberry sauce. We had no fridge and it wasn't winter, so we ate the celebration right away, reckless of the mess. My mother was thrilled. Cora had a *distinction*. You'll get more money for that, she said. *Distinction*. You can get a decent job and a fat pay-packet with distinction, then maybe give me more keep. And another thing, she said, crumpling up the tissue wrapper, I've found a job.

Only widows could be dinner ladies, and there was a long queue of hopefuls. She thought she'd need to wait at least a year, then she'd bumped into an old neighbour in the butcher's who was already dinner-ladying locally, and this neighbour had put in a good word. It started next week.

Cora looked cool, but my mother's mood was too good to break. Dinner lady, she said. I'm going to be a *dinner lady*. She'd been a servant in a big house in Yorkshire once, and the best that could be said for it was that they didn't hit her. By contrast, being a dinner lady was all perks. It's walking distance, she said. Kyleshill Primary, just up the road, and part-time so I'm back for everybody coming home. You'll never know I've been away.

I'd never seen her so chipper.

The cook's easy to talk to, *and* I'll get to talk to the wee ones. I like children, she said. You always know where you are with children.

That's right, Cora said. Steal my thunder. Bloody weans.

It was hard to tell if she was hurt or annoyed. Keeping the peace, I pretended to be pleased, but I wasn't. I was appalled. As long as I'd known my mother, she had worked with me. In the shop, the surgery, *with me*. Now there was a hidden side-road, a world of pay-packets and other people, the news she *liked children*. Every day she'd go to a school that wasn't mine to serve up dinners to children who weren't me. Children who didn't tell her lies; who, in all probability, would not be clingy, anxious or withdrawn. *Of course* she liked them. They only wanted her for caramel cake. Jealous, I imagined her dressing up in a white coverall with her hair in a net, radiantly blessing smiling infants with huge spoonfuls of stew and mash, beaming as she drizzled their currant cake with custard from a blue-striped jug. *Our* dinner hall smelled of mince all the time, even when mince wasn't on. There was a lot of noise and bits being stolen off your pudding, tiny people staggering under the weight of eight sets of crockery and a water jug on a tray, but not much smiling. *Our* dinner ladies looked run off their feet. Her school, however, would be lovely. It would be lovely partly because she was in it. Suddenly lonely, I wished she'd come to my school, then I'd see her in the middle of the day and she'd smile at me. Then I remembered she couldn't. Even if she wanted to, it would be terrible because she'd find out my secret. Just because I was monumentally lousy at drill, my mother would need to serve up the dinners of rivals after all.

I learned as the weeks went on and the work became routine, that what she did had no glamour. She stacked trays and served at hatches, cleared, washed and dried dishes. She lifted racks of plates, glasses, cutlery and tumblers exactly the way they did at my school. I knew from her stories that she wore nothing beneath the regulation white shift because of the heat and the constant steam, and her face gave away the high blood pressure coursing under the net turban. But I never let my imagining go: Our Lady of the Dinner Hall, suffering little children while I was out of sight, out of mind. I tortured myself with it for fun. Knowing nothing of this, my mother brought home rewards. The wholly unexpected side of school dinner-ladying: free food. Remaindered trays of mince and onion slice, uneaten cheese and macaroni crumbles, big white bowls of jaundice-green blancmange that the Kyleshill children hadn't got round to. The blancmange came home so often you wondered they kept making it. But they did, and we were the beneficiaries.

I liked it even if the Kyleshill children didn't, scooped it straight out of the six-person bowl with a serving spoon. I made appreciative noises, hoping my mother would see me afresh as more deserving of her approval than the ingrates at Kyleshill who hadn't wanted it at all.

Greedy pig, Cora would say, a fag slant-wise on her lip and fiddling with her stitch counter. You needny think *I'm* touching that.

A proper secretary now, *pool* and everything, Cora turned up her nose at all sorts of things. She called what my mother brought home *leftovers*. The canteen that had served her during her time at college was now *poky* and anyway, she didn't eat *bloody sandwiches*. At work, she drank coffee brought round on a trolley and wouldn't touch the biscuits. *Custard Creams, for christsake. You think they could afford chocolate*. It was home cooking or nothing, no half measures. For the office do she'd put up with a restaurant, but what Cora liked, *loved*, was chips. Most nights she asked for chips and most nights she got them, fresh from the pan of slimy white lard we kept in the kitchen for that express purpose. It meant peeling, washing, slicing and double-frying for one, but my mother never said no. She has to eat *something*, she'd say, up to her elbows in fat, as though without her, Cora would fade away to thistledown. Tumbled to the truth that my mother's need was to serve, serve up and do both well, Cora was sitting pretty. She didn't cook, didn't wash dishes, didn't tidy up, hoover or dust. She didn't buy groceries, wash her own clothes or iron. The only thing Cora did was knit. My Granny McBride thought Cora should be thrown out on her ear, but if Cora heard, she never let it show. Cora didn't go to Guthrie Brae and my granny never came to our house. Never. The chances of their meeting were slim.

If they did, my mother said, she wouldn't be surprised if they didn't recognise each other. Granny McBride and Cora, she said tersely, did not get on.

Kyleshill and my mother, however, did. Everyone, even my Granny McBride, agreed; her face took on a bloom now she was *out and about*. She had more to say, enjoyed the company of the other women, felt *useful again*. Kitty said it was the best thing she had done in years and my mother didn't disagree. She brought home a photograph of the kitchens, all steel table-tops and women with their hair tied back in makeshift turbans, arms bare to the elbow. Two of them wore lipstick and their cheeks *glowed*. It looked jollier than I'd have guessed, and made me jealous all over again. It seemed likely she had a better time there than at home. She had friends now, people I'd never get to know, people who took snaps of her in clothes I'd never seen because they stayed in her locker in the kitchens. Looking at the photo made me uneasy, suddenly adrift. I didn't know the half any more. What Cora did in her typing pool never crossed my mind. But here, in a little four by four curl of photographic paper, was evidence of something more unsettling: my mother was out there being someone else. My mother was crossing roads in front of grinding bus tyres, lifting weights of scalding, slopping water, braving stacks of dishes that at any moment might fall, shatter and slice through to the bone. I dared not think she was happy. Apart from me and heedless, safe, content. That, like Cora's baby, I could melt away and not be missed. That would have frightened me to death.

My Granny McBride had no truck with fear. She was seventy-odds and four foot ten, but not infirm. She walked every day for fresh air, refusing the white stick in preference to kicking dogs out of the way if the need arose. Her glass eye was legend. She did all her own cooking and cleaning and ironed clothes in the evening by the light of the TV.

She can't hear you right, my mother would say, though her hearing seemed fine. My granny's ear trouble seemed more to do with wanting peace. Her eyesight, however, was worse than she pretended. The glass eye only came out for practical jokes and impressions of cyclops and triffids, but the other eye wasn't much better. She had glasses, but didn't like them. They were heavy and lacked style. The white stick stayed largely in the umbrella stand in the hall. I don't want that, she'd say. It's just a badge for burglars.

It was easy to forget how poor her vision was till something gave her away. I remember being told to go outside and pick up a dishcloth that had appeared on the front step. I must have asked why, because she told me she was afraid of it. Every time she went near the damn thing, she said, it *moved*. She'd paid a wee boy threepence to take it away, and so he had, but it had been right back on the step next day when she opened the door. It was haunted, she said, looking genuinely wary. She wasn't touching it. My imagination boiled: a haunted dishcloth. What could it want? What, come to think of it, could it do? What I found when I stepped gingerly outside was a tortoise. An escaped pet, maybe, but that's all. It moved when I tried to pick it up as well, but it wasn't hard to catch. I put it over the wire fencing into next-door's garden, under a hedge for shade and told her the story. If it came back all over again, she never said.

Are you sure she wasn't kidding you on? my mother said after. She's a great kidder, your granny. She kidded us all the time when we were your age. She can tell terrible stories with a straight face.

No, I said, scandalised. She was frightened. She said so.

Oh well, my mother said. She laughed out loud. If she said so. Your granny was a Catholic. Maybe she worries about unusual things.

I tried to imagine a religion that taught people to be afraid of moving washing cloths in case they were haunted, but it wasn't that. It was the idea of things coming to get her.

She was a dynamite worker, and she had a big accident and married your granddad. But she married *outside the church*, and priests don't like when you do that kind of thing. So they tried to make her feel bad.

I still didn't get it. She gave up beating around the bush and went for the nub.

Some bloody priest told her she'd go to hell for marrying a Protestant. For goodness sake; she was only sixteen.

And even though she had gone ahead and married who she liked, the priest and his god shenanigans made her *how she was*. It could have meant anything. I knew no more about Catholics than I did about the Scout Movement, no more about any kind of

church-going beyond the Harvest Festival and being bored stiff. I
had seen a priest though, a solitary sighting. He'd been bouncing
around outside my granny's window when my mother and I
came down Guthrie Brae, a young man in a black dress looking
agitated. He moved to the door as we watched and roared
HELLO at the letter-box, in no mood to go without a fight. I
KNOW YOU'RE IN, MRS McBRIDE, he yelled. And since we
knew it too, we walked past, right round the block and back again
by a complicated route to make sure we didn't give her away.
Even then, we had to say more than once he was gone before
she'd open up.

Bastard, she said, rattling the inside chain. They know when
you're in. They turn up at tea-time and hope you feed them.
Bloody creeping Jesuit bastards.

Shh, mother, my mother said, embarrassed. Don't swear,
mother. He's just doing his job.

Don't you dare get one of them round here when I'm going,
either, she said. I'll die in my own time without somebody trying
to frighten me when I'm not fit.

When I die was a favourite topic. Whole evenings could be
devoted to allocating ornaments, funeral invitations and catering
arrangements – *no sandwiches, Beth, if they didn't want to come and
see me when I was alive, they can whistle* – till my mother's eyes
were moist. I know she's difficult, she'd say on the way home, but
she's had a terrible hard life.

If I said nothing and the night was dark enough, she sometimes went on.

I love my mother, she'd say. It's important to love your mother.

I couldn't have spoken if I'd wanted to. We walked on under the sodium lights, listening to our own feet.

After a while, she said, I miss my dad. It was a sorry thing to hear, this fond name for a dead man I'd never seen. *I miss my dad*. It made me wonder if I missed mine, but I had no idea. She wasn't looking for my insights or any kind of shared feeling in any case. The night, not me, brought these things to the surface: she was saying them aloud only because I happened to be there too. This was not an exchange, just thinking out loud. He was a good man, her father: his name was Sam. He had worked down a mine then had to watch all the boys, one after the other, getting ready to do the same. It must have broken his heart, she said. Maybe it did. Because he died and my granny got the seven of them to deal with on her own. Seven, she said. That's why she's the way she is. In the end, the boys got out. He didn't live to see it, but they did: every one of them, she said, *escaped*. Uncle Willy had been put in a POW camp by Italians, but I knew what she meant. She said it as though that was their great achievement. They *escaped*. She did not say that about her and Aunty Kitty. Not the girls. Some nights, she went further still.

I picked the wrong one, she said. Her voice went cold. I should have had a good man too, but I made a mistake. I wish I'd stayed in England.

Footfalls, while I pictured rolling pasture, milk and honey, sugar and spice and things much nicer than they'd any right to be. The next pause would be so long, the picture had time to fade away while I counted my steps, became distracted by snatches of half-recognised theme tunes floating from tellies behind the single-pane windows along Gladstone Road. Into the home stretch, it would come, though. Just when you thought she had finished.

Don't you get married.

Gulls and buses. Me trying not to feel the sensation of vanishing, seeing my mother young and carefree in a deck-chair, a snap from the bag of photos. More gulls.

Don't have weans. It ties you. It ruins your life.

I said what I always said. Nothing. *Nothing nothing nothing.*

Even on the warmest nights, these confessionals, when they came, made me shiver down to the roots of my hair. I liked the stories about her brothers washing after work, the family singing with accordions, my granny chasing women away from the house if they came to speak to her wage-earners. I knew which boys had run away from her to get married, which had come back with the deed done and a hopeful smile only to have their new wives chased down the street with the words *dirty whooer* ringing in their newly-wed ears. I liked the stories about England, full of wild-flower fields and playground games and girlish hopes, even if they suggested that Scotland was the place where such things fell to grief. But I did not like the feeling they left me with. I did not like the undercurrent of discontent; the cold sensation under the skin that everything good was in another time, another place and this life she led, the *here and now* was waste, ashes, ruins. It made me, the street, the night itself with its howling full moon, unreal. The only way to keep my head above water at these times was to remember *she wasn't talking to me*. Not at all. Even at six, I was under no illusions. She'd rather have been walking with a reliable husband, a good friend, a warm-hearted sister, someone who knew what to say. But she didn't have these things. She had a walk every day in the half-dark to get home from her widowed mother's, ten bob a week widow's pension of her own, a job as a dinner lady and two daughters. None of it was a patch on what was no longer there.

Cora disappeared. It wasn't that unusual. She disappeared at weekends regularly, dancing or just out. Where are you away to now, for crying out loud? *Out*. Door-slam, heels clacking into the distance, shouts of *You'll catch your death* etc., was a frequent enough weekend exchange. But this one was longer. I recall waking in a room with a yellow spread, yellow walls. It was Cora's room with no Cora in it. Why I was there I don't recall: what's remembered is being there. It meant Cora was not. I didn't mind. When Cora disappeared, things went quiet and quiet was just how I liked it. I could play Red Indians out the back in among the washing hanging on the line, with nobody to tell me I looked a fool with lipstick stripes on my face, and that I'd be on the other side of next week if she found out I'd used hers. I could poke about in the wild flowers on the waste-ground without being told they were full of ear-wigs and they'd crawl into my brain and eat it all up at night. I could watch Mr Gregg's pigeons without being told they were rats with wings and encouraging them was a sure-fire way to catch a fatal disease. I found a stray tabby on the waste-ground wall and could tempt it nearer without her saying she would kill it if the bloody thing came in the house. I liked the lack of drama, the peace, my mother rushing less. It was dawning on me, however, that perhaps my mother didn't like it as much as I did.

This dawning was my Aunty Marie's fault. She came to the door and my mother went outside to speak to her. As covert operations went, it was hopelessly amateur. All it did was draw attention to something secret happening. Hidden under the window, counting out pennies from a bowl of loose change, to sound busy, I heard Marie asking softly how she was doing. *She* was Cora. My mother said *She's fine* so much the repetitions merged – *Shesfineshesfineshesfine*. A foreign language. They said just about nothing else: I logged the word *salvation* then there was just a lot of breathing and sniffing. I turned back to the coins, thinking there was nothing to learn here at all. Then there was. The words *I miss her terrible* filtered in at the window crack, almost shocking. It was my mother's voice all right: there was no mistake. *I do*, she said. A stack of coppers tumbled over. My mother missed Cora.

It took some time, this idea; some thinking through. I tried to imagine them in the living room at night together after I had gone to bed, talking. I tried to imagine what on earth such talk might be. Maybe it was food. Maybe it was Old Times. Maybe jokes and stories about what happened at work. Maybe – and this was a big one – maybe she *really liked* Cora. The more I thought, the more possible it seemed. Lots of people liked my sister.

Cora went out in party frocks. She was a regular at the dancing. Even if we never knew them, she had friends. Strangers shouted in the street, the café, the train station: *Tell your big sister I'm asking for her*. Big Davie Stewart had vanished for ever, but Sandy still showed up now and then, crying and with his quiff gone flat when they'd had a row, desperate to see her again. Sandy, as my mother never tired of pointing out, had a soft spot. She got *distinction* at the typing college and had certificates to prove it. She worked in a *pool* with other girls, and had a boss like typists in romantic books, dark-haired and curt, but who nonetheless had time for Cora. She got a Christmas card with his name on. Even Kitty liked her and Marie thought she looked like a film star. Then there was my mother.

My mother brought Cora's food to the chair, cleared her empty plates away. Cora didn't clean the bath, mow the lawn, flex a duster, answer the door or handle neighbours. *I don't do domestic* was a mark of pride, a chalk score in the air. If she snapped her fingers for coffee, it appeared, and with a biscuit on the side. It appeared because *someone made it for her*. My mother called it laziness, but she fed it nonetheless. Cora was not a Good Girl, an Angel or a Help around the House, but my mother fetched and carried for her nonetheless. Even in her absence, no one sat in Cora's chair. No one called her names or told her to tidy her own room or fetch her own bloody meals for a change. Maybe what you got from life had nothing to do with how you behaved: maybe it was who you were that did it. Cora called shots *by nature*: nobody said boo *because she was Cora*. She attracted care. My mother, on the other hand, gave it. She was never going to snap her fingers for coffee right here, right now; she would always be the kind who turned on the telly on her way out to make Nescafé for someone else. Where I fitted into this terrible split was already more apparent than I wanted to know. I'd never have boys lining up at the door to take me dancing. I couldn't dance. Like my mother, I sang. I did requests, didn't let myself go as the mood and the music took me. The word DOMESTIC was probably surfacing in red ink on my forehead even as I thought about it, horrified, ready, quite pointlessly, to run.

Cora came back, of course. Wherever she had been, she returned to find her chair untouched and her knitting exactly where she'd left it. The chip pan came out of retirement and the telly started warming again not long after the arrival of the five-thirty train.

What are you looking at? she said. Away and get me a cushion. And she sat back, sure it would come. It always did.

I remembered Marie at the door, asking after her, my mother's voice, owning up to abject loss. At my granny's house, though, Cora still did not exist. The split was stark and puzzling. I mentioned Cora only once at Guthrie Brae and my granny froze, momentarily, barely at all. *Whooer*, she muttered, and it passed on by. My mother turned up the volume knob on the telly and didn't even blink. I logged the word, the word my granny had thrown at her son's wives, and carried on with my plasticine as though butter wouldn't melt. Whatever it meant, like so much else, I was not meant to know.

Cora got a new job starting in Glasgow where stockbrokers and solicitors and people to do with money filled up the narrow-windowed buildings.

Stockbrokers, my mother said, impressed. They get *manicures*.

Thanks to Cora, we were going up in the world. We knew somebody who knew somebody with pretty hands. Cora's eye-liner got softer, her lipstick less thick. She bought satin gloves and a scarf with roses on it, perfume. She fetched home shoes, beautiful kitten-heel slingbacks in shiny black with a bright green trim, and kept them in tissue paper in the box rather than slot them in with the ordinary shoes. She grew protective of her room. Once, it had been all right to sit at the window in there and look out at the lupins in the garden, to lie full out on the yellow spread. I was allowed to teeter about in her shoes and put lipstick in circles on my cheeks. Not now. Now she took to shutting the door, banging around with boxes and rails, rearranging.

Out, she said. And don't touch my stuff. I'm warning you. If you touch my stuff I'll thump you senseless. And stop the bloody snivelling. Stop it *now*.

She's needing peace, my mother said. Just keep out of her road. This new job is a lot of strain.

Don't you be so soft with her, she yelled through the door. I'm telling you and I'm telling you straight: if she comes in here, I'll bloody murder her.

That's you warned, my mother said. Keep clear.

Warnings and death threats: I had no excuse. But I did it anyway. Cora came home earlier than usual off the train and found me in her bedroom, wearing the black kitten-heels, the box with its green tissue empty beside the bed. Her best shoes were cobbled sideways on my too-small feet, her best silver belt draped over my non-existent hips like a deflated swimming ring. I'd have put on her gloves if I'd known were they were, but I didn't, and I hadn't touched the make-up. The make-up was exactly as she'd left it, but not something I could bargain with. I knew as soon as I heard the door rattle, the iron cleats on the tips of her heels scraping in the porch, I had no defence. My mother was still at the shops. It was just us two. She didn't even have to open her door to see me.

She looked once, put down her keys and started, slowly, to unbutton her jacket.

Are you worried? she said. She flicked a nail. You should be.

The jacket slid down her arms. She folded it, lining side up, over the arm of the wicker chair in the corner. Then she strolled closer and stood next to me, bending to let her eyes settle at my height.

I told you not to come in here, didn't I?

She smelled of trains and ash and distant cologne. I could see a piece of myself in the dressing-table mirror, a panel of pigtail and

Cora's cardigan, tilting closer. When her arm reached up, I ducked and shut my eyes tight, but nothing hit. No smack, no dazzle, no pain. All she did was push. The heels stayed put, and I tipped sideways, lost for balance. I felt one hand near my collar, dragging, saw the other reaching for the cupboard door. All it took was one more push, and I was on the other side of it, the cupboard door pressing in, reducing the place I stumbled inside to shade and cloth. She was shutting me in the cupboard. I could see a tiny slice of Cora, shoes off for better traction, in what was left of the opening, red toenails like burglars under a mask of American Tan. Then it went dark.

I pressed the door and it pushed back. She was leaning against it, fiddling with the catch. Shoving hard, I saw the crack of light wink once before it thudded back. I heard the scrape of the key in the lock, and yowled like a cat. Once only. Then we fell quiet. I could hear her breathing. I could hear me breathing. After a while, she spoke.

Think about it. Her voice slithered down to a whisper. Some people die in the dark. They die of fright.

I said nothing.

There's no good shouting so don't try it. I don't care what happens to you in there and your mammy's not here.

Panicked, I thumped hard against the door and felt her thump straight back, her voice rising as she rattled at the handle.

Just don't bloody try it. If I have to take my hands to you, you're dead. You're bloody finished. You hear me?

I could hear her behind the door, waiting to catch me out. So I made my breath shallow down into nothing, like I did when I was sleeping. I made myself as not-there as I could manage.

She'll be away for ages, she said. She's at court seeing if the judge will send you to a Home. They send the police and that's what they do. They put you in a Home.

My heart was deafening. I said nothing and closed my eyes.

Nobody likes you. Nobody liked him and nobody likes you. If we tell them what you've done they'll take you away, no bother.

She moved back now, floorboards creaking gently under her stocking soles.

We don't need *you*.

She sighed, a pleasure sigh like she'd just solved a problem.

Right then. I think I'll go for a walk. Her voice was like cigarette smoke, molten in the blackness. You better behave in there in case there's something nasty in the dark. Bye bye, she said, her voice almost a child's. *Bye bye*.

I listened till there was just dark and me, breathing in gusts through my nose like a sick fish. Sometimes I thought I could hear her listening back, but it never came to anything. I could feel the hard edges of shoes beneath my toes and hoped the low drumming noise was only my own blood, dunting in my ears. Shutting and opening my eyes was exactly the same: black. I imagined spiders and was afraid they'd hide in my hair. Shouting for help was not an option. It was better, it was always better, not to know for sure that no one would come. Shouting for no one was the worst thing in the world. I chose to go for the handle, try it softly, gently, and see what happened. So I reached, put out my other arm for balance. And touched hair. For a split second I was slipping under bath water, all texture and heat and wavering unreality. Then I knew what it was. The Coat. My fingertips nudged fur, found the hide, like a guilty secret underneath. There was the thick lip of pocket lined with satin, the hard cotton-coated clasp hook. It was only the Coat. The same instant I knew it, the door made a clicking sound and there was Cora, looking down with the key dangling from one finger.

Well? she said.

I gripped the nearest sleeve to hide behind, aware my face was running. The fur reeked of moth balls, making my eyes worse.

I said – she leaned closer, opening her eyes wide – are you ready to say you're sorry?

There was an awful moment of nothing. I couldn't say *no*. But then again, I couldn't say *yes* and not tell a raging, roaring, wholly defeated lie. I was still trembling from the terribleness of the choice when the outside door opened and I didn't need to make it after all. Fresh, cold air curled into the stuffy cupboard and I heard the wet-feather ruffle of an umbrella. My mother was home and bringing the cavalry. I almost bolted. Alert to that exact possibility, Cora grabbed my arm hard and told me to shut up and stay put.

Don't you dare go out. She doesn't want to see you right now, she said. She doesn't want to see *you*.

And astonishingly, as though she'd pulled a power cable, I did what I was told. I let her close me in the bedroom while she went out and did her perky voice. I could hear only bits of what my mother said back, something not being finished yet, the words *unfit mother* over and over. Cora was still way too near. But mum was there and I could hear her. My face was red and puffy and embarrassing, but I wanted to see her and I wanted it now. Edging out of the cupboard, avoiding the Coat, I heard something that stopped me dead. Three words: *She's staying put.* They were very clear. *No change. She's staying put.*

It came back that Cora had said something through the door, something about the police coming and putting me in a Home. I had no doubt they really could do that but was too busy being scared to think it through. Maybe she really had been there asking and they'd said no. I could still hear her voice, carrying all the way down the hall.

And how would Mrs Campbell know what's fit when she has no children? That shut her up.

Mrs Campbell was Aunty Rose. What had she been doing there? Maybe she'd gone to put in a good word, said I would behave. Maybe the Homes were full up, or I hadn't been bad enough yet. But they'd have my name. I was sure they'd have taken my name. Maybe – I was grasping at straws now – maybe my mother had changed her mind. Then again maybe not. Only one thing was clear: I was staying put. She said it again, making sure. *No change of custody order. She stays.*

Whatever had been said or not said, the judge wasn't sending me away. Not yet. It was good and terrible at once, the hugeness of what might have happened making my nerves tingle. None of it felt right, allowable, even real. Things were wrong in our house. Things were not the way things should be.

My mother came down the hallway sniffing behind a hanky and saw me standing at the crack of Cora's door.

What are you doing in there? she said, blowing her nose. Come and get juice. We're in the kitchen.

Her face wasn't right, but then neither was mine. When Cora saw me trailing in after her to the kitchen, she looked unhappy too. Seasick. We all looked seasick.

Aunty Rose is asking after you, my mother said, tight-lipped. She poured water into a tumbler. She's saying she'd like to see you more often.

Cora snorted.

She's wondering if you'd maybe like to see her on Sundays.

I thought you were out playing, Cora snapped. On you go back out. Nobody wants to talk to you just now.

Stop that, my mother said. Leave her alone. She turned to me. They'll take you up the road to see them on Sundays. I said it was all right.

I knew she was looking at me because the words tilted more into focus in my ears, but I didn't want to look back. I wasn't ready to meet her gaze, meet anybody's gaze. Not yet. There was a silence and Cora lit a match. She threw it into the sink and lit another one. My mother foraged in the cupboard and handed me a biscuit.

On you go and enjoy yourself, then, she said. We've things to talk about. I'll shout you when it's tea-time. Off you pop.

I hung back a bit, desperate to tell about the Coat and the cupboard, what Cora had done. I wanted to know if Rose had gone to the police too, how she came into anything. But both moments had gone. Something else was in the offing now, something big by the feel of things, and whatever I had to say was beside the point. I went out and sat on the back step, watched Mr Gregg's pigeons. They circled out over the whole expanse of the grass and came back, their wings whipping. The odd grey feather fell from the loft and cradle-rocked to the dirt. Pairs sat together, bills touching. They were graceful things, pigeons. Not rats at all. The way they wheeled and came back, knowing where home was. If you held one, I thought, you'd feel its heart beating, the warm roots of the feathers. A cage of crushable bones.

9

This is me and Alma. We're six or seven, standing dazzled by sun outside the solid concrete scheme-end shops. In knee-length skirts and socks with ties and short-sleeve shirts, schoolbags flopped at the toes of our scuffed school shoes, we are unremarkable children against an unremarkable backdrop. Except for our teeth. Not one white chopper between us, we present terrifying black stumps straight to camera. The reason is in our hands. We are holding toffees. My mother is off right holding a bottle of pop, a packet of biscuits and a paper bag of something nice for later. You can bet your boots it's made of sugar. Alma and me have no blazers, but we have bulges in our cheeks to keep us warm. The bulges, packed hard against whatever enamel is left, are melting.

Q: How much sugar can one child take?
A: How much have you got?

What's here is a picture of the West Coast of Scotland's addiction to crystalline carbohydrate, the mainline to award-winning levels of dental caries. Sweeties swilled around our pearlies every day.

Plentiful and cheap, they were rewards, promises and tokens, affordable pieces of demonstrable Good Life. Every night I was sent to the corner shop for a shilling's worth of things from the penny tray to bring back and share while we watched the telly. White mice, lucky horseshoes made of lardy white chocolate, MB Bars, Blackjacks and Fruit Salad, Refreshers, Sherbet Fizzers and liquorice watches and pipes and straps. Halfpenny caramels covered in suckable brown wax, Rhubarb Rock and Coltsfoot Rock and Lucky Potatoes. Cough Candy and jawbreakers and aniseed-middled gobstoppers, pineapple cubes and Big Soor Plooms. And that's before we admire the forms and textures of the plethora of mints. That I retained any teeth at all seems a small miracle. Cora, at twenty-three, had dentures already and my mother had them too. Every so often she needed a refit to keep in line with gum erosion, and they sat in her mouth like the teeth of a completely different mammal till her face adapted. A grinning glass by the bed was a future none might avoid, unless they opted for gaps and not much smiling. Sweeties, pop, penny caramels, chocolate biscuits, any old biscuits, scones, jam, shortbread and Dundee cake, jam doughnuts, ice-cream and candy floss were the only sops for grief. A cough could be soothed by a little ball of butter rolled in grains of demerara till it crunched, sore throats needed Victory Vs, and headaches were rendered bearable by the liberal sucking of Parma Violets. Rosehip syrup was doled out by the government as health-giving, slipping toddlers some vitamin C in thick glucose syrup. The school dentist, a grim-faced woman with sideburns and a blond moustache, had her work cut out and knew it. Whole classes queued on her days in school, and they queued from the age of five. You had to be a stretcher-case to qualify for gas, but we bore up well under the drill, holding on to the arms of the chair against the spray of splintering white enamel, kicking only when the pain was beyond reasonable control. My second time in the chair, her drill slipped and dug into my gum spraying blood and little flakes of tissue in several directions, mostly hers. You ate the sweeties, she said; this is what happens. Night follows day. And she wiped her eye and carried right on. I don't care how much the lady was paid, I wouldn't have had her job for a two-pound presentation box of Dairy Milk.

Mornings began with it, playtimes ran with it, after-school freedom was full of it. Sugar, not religion, was our opiate of choice. We chewed at the scheme-road shops and were merry. And tomorrow, just as our sisters and mothers and our porcelain-enhanced elders before us, we decayed.

Yet all this time, despite the reassurances of biscuits and Irn Bru, I had been developing what the teacher called *distracted tendencies*. I hesitated before answering questions, single words dammed behind my teeth, or forgot what the question had been as soon as I was called on to address it. Sometimes I'd look up and Miss Murchie would be standing over me and asking whether I was listening. If she had to ask, the answer was probably *not enough*. I seemed not to be able to account for the missing moments of focus, to explain my lapses of attention; even to notice how long they lasted. If I'd been a noisy child, prone to chatting in class and dropping pencils, it could have made me *naughty*.

Because I was quiet, thank god, it made me *special*. Along with three others in the same year group (one with round-framed glasses, one with lank blonde hair, one who smelled more than faintly of pee, and all girls) I was selected – *selected* – for tests with a tall woman called Miss Shand.

A special teacher for special pupils, Miss Shand knew her worth. Like a woman waiting for Sunday, she wore a hat made from a whole chicken's-worth of feathers and huge horn-rim glasses that gave her the distracted look of an owl out at the wrong time of day. She also had a heavy lisp. We chosen children watched her intently, avoiding each other's eyes. Aware we were all suspect in some way, we were not sure whether to feel rival-rous or united but were there so brief a time, all we managed was compliant. The tests were short, easy and unexplained. We listened to bells being rung on corners and bits of music that Miss Shand played herself on a xylophone and a maraca out of the Infants Music cupboard. After that, there were matching squares and triangles and a pairing game, putting words with their oppo-sites. The blonde girl looked as if she might cry during the shapes part, and she didn't bother with the opposites at all. Miss Shand kept me behind to read something out of a book using only one eye at a time. The whole thing took ages and I missed drill. It was a good swap. All in all, I felt things had gone well. If this was as hard as tests ever got, I was in the clear.

Next day, Miss Shand appeared at Miss Murchie's door as we were waiting in twos to leave. She gave me a letter to take home. I knew these only as invitations to trouble but it was official, not optional and I had no choice but to deliver. My mother waited till Cora was in too and they both looked worried at the sealed envelope, but didn't open it. It would wait, Cora said. If it was something terrible, it would be better to know after we'd eaten.

We had lentil soup on our knees at the fire, thick with orange goose-bumps and molten leek. Cora took the spoon out of hers when my mother was in the kitchen fetching salt and burned my neck with it. *Behave, you two*, my mother shouted from the kitchen when I yelled. *Behave*, as if we were both small. Bloody letter, Cora whispered. It better not be trouble.

I hoped so too. If being rotten at drill had caught up with me, or any other hint of *not sticking in*, I might have to leave home. In the end, the letter turned out to be more mysterious than a direct complaint. It was a summons for my mother to go to school and meet Miss Aitken, the Infant Mistress. It was some kind of big deal if the Infant Mistress was involved but nobody knew what. Mum turned the letter over looking for explanations and hints, but there was nothing; just a time, the name of the teacher, the tight little request.

Search me, Cora said. She's your wean. At least she's not set fire to nothing.

A disclaimer and a cause for hope. But communications from schoolteachers were not taken lightly. Teachers, as my mother saw them, were keepers of gates to better worlds and nothing was shutting this soon if she could help it. Cora, despite herself, was nervous too. She helped my mother plan a suitable outfit for the meeting, the two of them crashing about with hangers in the

wardrobe for ages, and poured them both a sherry. It was the
Christmas sherry and a million years old, but we had the real
glasses. That night, we did not watch TV. They stayed up talking
and I went to bed. The sherry was still there, untouched on the
mantelpiece next morning, and I had a blister on my neck the
size of Denmark. I had to wear my collar high all day, even next to
the radiator. Miss Shand waved at me from the outbuilding in
which she worked as I left school, and I felt marked. Being *selected*
was scarier than it sounded.

The meeting, when it happened, was brief. Miss Shand, hale in
her feather hat, opened the door and Miss Aitken sat behind a
folded piece of black plastic that said INFANT MISTRESS in
white. It looked like chalk on a board, only the lettering was too
uniform and too narrow. She had no drawings on the walls. There
was a chair and gestures to take it, the word *please* several times.
My mother preferred to stand. Nobody spoke to me.

Well, Miss Shand said, beaming. The first thing to say is that
Janice is very fluent with tests. She knows how to pass them!

My mother looked keen but wary.

She's a bright girl. No worries in that direction. But that's not
the whole story.

No, said Miss Aitken.

No, said Miss Shand. Despite her written results, it must be
said that Janice makes a poor showing with regard to some basic
communication skills.

My mother, who had walked in keen to make amends for whatever I'd done, straightened sharply.

That is to say her verbal skills are good *on paper*, but she is reluctant to be very forthcoming *one-to-one*.

My mother's brow furrowed and Miss Aitken had a go.

Your daughter seems unsure of people. Withdrawn.

They looked at her as though she knew what to say next. She didn't. Miss Shand rose to the occasion.

For example, she never says *That's a pretty hat, Miss Shand*, or *What pretty perfume, Miss Shand* – conversational remarks don't seem to pass her lips. She didn't say, *May I have a sweet, too, Miss Shand?* even when they were offered.

It was true. Miss Shand had had a bag of iced caramels on the table and asked us if we wanted one. I was the only one who didn't take. I thought it was a test to see if I was greedy. Now I realised it was a test after all, but of a completely different kind.

I see, my mother said, but she saw nothing of the sort. She was confused and so was I. Questions nobody was asking out loud hung on the air, refusing to be drawn. I could see from her eyes that my mother was weighing Miss Shand in a balance, wondering what was so special about her hats, her perfume, her bloody caramels. Miss Shand didn't notice. She simply waited for a response. What response was there to make? I had got the tests right, for goodness sake; I'd sung little phrases and pointed which side the bell had been rung and matched stuff like a trouper. But they didn't matter. What mattered was to chat to Miss Shand. The tests were tricks. School wasn't meant to do that. They were only allowed to make you sit tests and if you passed them they had to leave you alone. I thought that was the *whole point* of passing:

you did your bit and they had to *leave you alone*. Now it was much more complicated. I'd been swizzed, duped and double-crossed. I was uncharacteristically furious. Miss Shand must have noticed something too: even in silence, she and mum were not hitting it off.

And this, she said, nodding at me. This *dumb insolent* look. I've seen *this* more than once for no reason.

They all turned to see. I tried to clear my face but I knew it was still registering unhelpfully. Miss Aitken looked uneasy and coughed.

Mrs Galloway, your daughter has a stammer. It might be helped by speech therapy.

Miss Shand brightened up. And the ear problem. Her hearing is far from perfect, so I've arranged for her to sit at the front in all classes.

We wanted to arrange reseating, Miss Aitken interrupted, to ensure your daughter is hearing as well as she should.

My mother nodded.

And, Miss Aitken continued, this time more slowly, some sessions, this time with your permission, to see the School Psychologist.

She spoke the last two words with capitals. My mother heard. Her eyes flitted from Miss Aitken to Miss Shand, back again.

Psychologist, Miss Shand said. She clearly thought my mother was deaf. The *School Psy-cho-lo-gist*.

My mother sighed, allowed her silence to deepen. This was all wrong. They were saying I had things wrong with me and needed to see a doctor. It wasn't fair. Eventually my mother stopped chewing something at the back of her throat, and found her voice.

Right, she said. Tell me something. Is she doing what she's told?

Yes, I was very quiet.

Well, is she slow on the uptake?

No, no. Miss Aitken was getting flustered. She's not slow by any means. She's ahead with her reading and –

Is she being a nuisance? Is she giving up cheek and keeping other people back?

Not at all. In fact, she's rather too –

Well, my mother said, putting one glove back on, she's not in trouble. If everything's fine, I've got things to do.

There was a bit of shilly-shallying as she made for the door, a brief flurry of apologetic protests, then the brokering of a last-minute deal on speech therapy. Miss Shand said I shouldn't go through life with a stammer if I didn't have to. She'd had a lisp once and look at her now.

Whatever you think, my mother said. Both gloves were on now. She wanted off. You're the teacher. If she's not in trouble, just you do what's best.

I trotted after her, thinking I'd missed Art for this, and all I'd had to do was stand and control my face. It was a crêpe paper underwater scene today, and I'd missed the chance to make sea anemones. I could have cried. There was nobody in the infants' corridor as we left, and only a dog in the playground. Outside and safe, my mother started fizzing like a bomb.

Bloody psychiatrist, she said. There's nothing wrong with your brain. That's half the trouble. It's the Birdwoman of Alcatraz in there needs the psychiatrist, not you. Bloody cheek.

She crunched a cinnamon ball to rubble and didn't speak again till we were halfway down Argyle Road near the billboards. A man was up a ladder, changing a row of faces into a big red box of washing powder in strips, covering up a collection of smiles. *Pretty perfume*, for goodness sake. Who does she think she is? And you huvny got a stammer either. Behave.

It was the only time she ever referred to my speech defect. Maybe she never noticed, but it was there. My **b**s and **p**s, my sibilants jammed at the jumps till I was into my thirties, but I was quick-thinking and could reroute a word at the last kick so it started with something else if I had to. The interview with the Infants Mistress was over and done. She shook her shoulders at the turn of Springvale Street, like shucking off rain, and I ran ahead, pulling the leaves off the private house privets and throwing them in the air like confetti. I was *fluent with tests*. My ears didn't catch every word that was said to me, but I knew how to pass things, tilt my head to make the most. I was *a bright girl* and my cutting-out was lovely. The whole thing had gone better, in some ways, than anyone could have foreseen. Flushed with success, I made a clean breast. I ran up and grabbed her coat-buckle to keep her still, closed my eyes and spat out what had to be said. I was terrible at drill. I couldn't do forward rolls or run in circles to save my life. There was a long pause filled with sucking.

Och well, she said. I loved it. Highland dancing, races, all that kind of thing. But you'll be clever. She reached into her pocket and popped a humbug in my mouth. Right, let go my coat. I've Cora's tea to get ready. She was captain of the hockey team at Ardrossan, Cora. Come on, shift.

I imagined my mother, light on her feet, running through English greensward peppered with buttercups, laughing head of the pack; Cora in padded leggings, her black hair tumbling as she fronted the opposition. I couldn't have imagined anything more wonderful, more unexpected, more perfect if I tried.

My seat was changed first thing on Monday and I started speech therapy. No rest for the wicked. Thereafter, speech therapy was Monday afternoons for four weeks or so, always during music, which drove me crazy. I made diphthongs and consonant clusters and moo-ing noises with the speech therapist while my class-mates got to bang wood blocks and sing. To make matters worse, the speech therapist was Miss Shand. I don't know why I hadn't seen it coming. *What nice shoes, Miss Shand*, she said at the end of one session, *What a lovely hat. Honestly, it's like training a monkey.* We both coped with our frustrations as best we could. After the month, it was finished. The stammer was exactly the same but I now understood clearly that I had no social graces and would not be getting lunch invitations or Christmas cards from the Shand household, not now, not ever. I was not her type. The day it finished, Miss Shand informed me she did not expect me to buy her a gift: the speech therapy was provided free. I said, *Thank you Miss Shand*, so something rubbed off. I'd paid my debt to society and was free to go.

———

Two things happened before Infants washed its hands of the whole intake and sent us on to be Big Boys and Girls. Both happened in the same week. I got back to music sessions just in time for sets of jungle bells to emerge from the store cupboard, brand-new temple blocks and tambourines. These were percussion, lovely on their own, Miss Murchie said, but better with a melody. Maybe we could sing. There was some giggling and practice trilling, but nobody starting out for real. I was astounded. People who'd thought nothing of rushing about in their knickers pretending to be vegetables during gym periods were hiding behind their hands turning pink. I almost laughed. Singing was easy. Come on, Miss Murchie said. Who wants to sing? Singing didn't need thinking about. It wasn't making a show of yourself or even *trying*. It wasn't starting an argument or asking for trouble. You opened your mouth and there it was. Me, I said, standing up. It was no effort at all.

I saw Mummy kissing Santa Claus
Underneath the mistletoe last night.
She didn't see me creep

Down the stairs to have a peep
She thought that I was tucked up in my bedroom fast asleep
Then I saw Mummy kissing Santa Claus
Underneath his beard so snowy whi-i-ite
Oh, what a laugh it would have been
If Daddy had only seen
Mummy kissing Santa Claus last night.

It wasn't my favourite, but it fit in with the jingles and I tried not to feel funny singing the word *daddy*. The room was quiet when I stopped. I was beginning to be uncomfortable when Miss Murchie clapped and thrilled me to bits. It was like being under the table over again. I'd pulled it off.

Who taught you that? she said. What a lovely song!

I remember her smiling. I didn't know who had taught me it, so I told her it was the radio and she laughed. She went to fetch Miss Aitken and I sang *I saw Mummy kissing Santa Claus* again. Miss Aitken clapped this time and took me round the older years' corridors so I could sing it some more. We went past the dinner hall with its thick, near-food smells, and I wished my mother worked there and not in mile-away Kyleshill, so she could see me being a spectacle. The Primary Fours couldn't have cared less about the singing – they were putting cotton wool and glitter on the windows – but the Sevens clapped and cheered and made cooing noises, so I did *Love Me Tender* as an encore. My first tour. We went back down to the Infants' corridors again, past the crates of milk in half-bottles ranged near radiators and pegs at baby

height strung with duffels and Burberry school coats, and Miss
Aitken held my shoulder just before I went back inside. The class
were doing sums with blocks, rectangles and cubes in blue and
red, just visible through the glass grille on the door. I liked counting blocks and moved to open the door, but she held her hand
in place till I looked up. You have a lovely voice, she said. There
was a hiatus. The hiatus expanded. I was waiting for a rider, a
proviso, a *but*. What came was repetition.

I said, you have a lovely voice. Do you know that?

I almost said *yes*, then caught myself. What did she want me
to say? My head was racing while I looked at her face, sniffing in
the dusty scent of her cologne. If I agreed, she might think I was
too sure of myself. Aunty Kitty said I thought I was *It*. She said
it regretfully, as though duty compelled her to report me to the
It police for everyone's good, but she did it every time I sang. On
the other hand, Miss Aitken was asking me a real question, she'd
think I was being cheeky and ungrateful for saying nothing.
Maybe I could just say her necklace was nice and hope for the
best. Treading a line that seemed thinner in all directions, I fell
back on what I knew best and said nothing at all. If it went on
long enough, she might just get fed up with me and let the
whole thing go. She gave me a run for my money all right, but
finally Miss Aitken shook her head and opened the classroom
door.

At least you're coming out of your shell, she said, more to herself
than to me. But she squeezed my shoulder. I ambled back through
the tables of blue and red, the rubbers and pencil shavings, the rich

atmosphere of children learning, arms crossed on my chest, hugging the words so they wouldn't fly off too soon. *You have a lovely voice*. I knew I was smiling.

———

Next day, Cora set fire to my hair.

I have no memory of what kicked it off, where we were standing when the drama caught light. I may have said something that was past bearing, or at least past bearing for Cora. Then again, sometimes, things just happened with no warning. This one surprised her as much as me. It was an accident, Cora said afterwards. She was lighting a cigarette and I got in the way. She said *christ* a lot and cut off the frazzled ends to make it look better, but it was obvious something had happened. So she owned up when my mother came home.

It was an accident she said. An *accident*. It was her own bloody fault.

My mother narrowed her eyes and told Cora to watch her step and Cora hit her. Then she hit me.

It was her fault, she yelled. We were fine before. You and me before *she* turned up. Bloody Smart Alec thinking she's *It*.

When the screaming was finished, I went into the back bedroom and sat on the tangerine spread. There were two bottles on top of the chest of drawers, nice bottles, with silk tassels and rubber bulbs to squeeze for the faint whiff of vinegary perfume that was inside. One had a crocheted net over the bulb, a white filigree.

Their prettiness was encouraging. Outside, washing was waving
its arms, the sky turning lilac. The garden was nothing but sticks.
This time of year, everything had rotted down or died. But it came
back in spring, bursting with rain and sunlight into leaves. Gardens
made food. That was the bit that you forgot every year, then it
happened anyway. A patch of clay-logged earth turned into
potatoes and leeks and cabbages. Then, of course, it turned back.
I stayed in the bedroom thinking till it started to get dark. And
what I thought was that the singing and the hair thing were linked
in some way. Good things were followed by bad, as though something did it on purpose, something that didn't want you ever to
feel sure, too safe. It had to remind you the ground you stood on
was not, would never be, stable. The problem was you didn't know
what kind of something it was, why it was like this. It didn't seem
right. Mum shouted through the door eventually. Tea was ready.
Marie would come and give me a trim, she said, muffled through
the chipboard. She'd do it nice again and everything would be fine.
Now come and get your tea.

I thought of Alma's hair, the job Marie had made of that.
Outside, the washing had turned to random black shapes looping
and jerking like monsters lowering over a hill. There was nothing
for it but trust.

10

We were no longer Infants.

We were Primary Three, the newest kids on middle-school block behind the toilets and sheltered playground. In twos, we trouped by the dinner hall to our new rooms on the first floor, passing the Secondary Modern block on the way. The Secondary Modern smelled of Cookers and Chemistry Labs. It was where tough-nuts played cards for money and did experiments with Rizla papers during breaks. They were nearly old enough to get married, the pupils here; they had sideburns and earrings and brothel-creeper shoes. Even so, we'd share a playground with them, a tarmac area wide as a field. No more free milk for us, but we could borrow lighters any time. Some people cried when Miss Aitken said *Good Luck!* but not for long. Danny McFairlie blew a raspberry and broke the mood.

A fresh squad of teachers was shown off at first assembly in a giant hall we'd only glimpsed before through open doors. From the inside, it was bigger and had a stage. The new teachers stood on it and looked down, every one of them grey-haired and every one of them female. Except for Mr Waverley who did all the talking. Did we know who he was? His voice zinged around the polished wood veneer and bounced off a sports trophy. He was The Head of this Great Big School. When he came into a room, we were to stand and say *Good morning, Mr Waverley* in chorus. He was, he said with a tight little smile at the ladies who were his *front-line troops,* a Very Important Person.

Except for the janitor, Mr Waverley was the most powerful man at Jack's Road and wore a tawse round his neck to prove it. He looked like General de Gaulle, my mother said: all hooter and self-regard. It was true. His hair, a pepper-and-salt sea of carefully pomaded Marcel waves, made sober little boys laugh out loud. They didn't laugh long. Mr Waverley did not much approve of jollity. Robert Patterson, who sat next to me, thought the Head had been in the army. The teachers were *troops,* the bell was *signal to fall in,* and home time was *retreat* if he felt light-hearted. He patrolled the corridors with his eyes swivelling, looking for *slackers,* and his yell made even the Junior Secondaries freeze. Robert Patterson took to calling him *Sergeant Major.* My mother called him something else.

Look at him, she said after a school concert, watching him tweak his hair back into place. He thinks he's God's Gift.

She was still annoyed about the whole speech therapy thing, but I didn't argue. Now and then, I'd seen him belt someone who'd been stranded in the corridor announcing his reason as *wiping off that silly smile.* Tiny children, eyes trained on their *Startrite* shoe-tips, were frightened stiff when he hove into view: older ones made signs behind his back. The Infant Rooms, with their smells of baby-sick and bandage, seemed far away at the end of only a day. By the end of a week, how things had been slipped clean off the edge of the world.

———————

I walked to school, along Argyle Road and over the railway bridge down the length of Jack's Road, alone. I'd been doing it since halfway through Primary One without mishap. There weren't many cars then, and children wearing satchels on their backs seemed set apart, safe from all but other schoolchildren. A wee boy called Ian chummed up with me for the first few days and we made the walk together. He had filthy knees and his tie squint even first thing in the morning, and the ability to talk to strangers marked him off as *not local*. Ian's utterances were short – Nice day the day, eh? Want a sweetie? – but longer than mine. He reminded me of Colin but with proper shoes. Maybe he was from Paisley. After a couple of days, though, my chances of finding out more about Ian were over. His parents had told him not to talk to me any more. You're not a Catholic, he said. That other school you go to, it's for Protestants. So I'm not to walk with you. I was dumbfounded. He had a vague idea it was because Protestants didn't believe in Jesus, but he didn't really know why. His parents said so. He was just doing what he was told. OK, I said and we separated, meek as collies. Even the day it happened, he crossed the road. Step for step in the same direction, a street apart. I saw him from time to time and we said hello, but always across tarmac with cars between. Weeks later, he was chucking stones at me over our school wall and calling me a Proddy Bastard but I tried not to take it personally. Outside home and school was the wild world. Trying to make sense of it was a waste of time.

Random ambush from next-door's Catholic establishment apart, school became more formal by the day. Words refined. *Drill* re-tricked itself as *Gym* which meant star jumps and wall bars and games of rounders. *Sums* fattened into polysyllabic *Arithmetic*, and *Grammar* reared its ugly personal pronouns. Counting sticks and tangrams gave way to project jotters and graph paper, finger paints to brushes. There was a lot less help with coat buttons. I suspected I would never be asked to stand up and sing out of music periods again and I was right. Different things – things like *doing exactly as you've been shown* and *doing only what you've been asked* – became the centre of the picture by stealth. More sitting down was required, less drawing and more numbers; fewer stars, more spiky little ticks. We were expected to buckle under and, as best we could, did. Soon, we could all sit – or at least sit through – a class test, read simple words in more or less the right order, write our names and a short paragraph about MY BEST FRIEND even if we didn't have one. Some of us could make up MY PET and MY DADDY to a band playing with coloured pencil drawings as decoys. *I can do this*, I thought, every time another star glittered up from the blue-lined page. *I can get the answers right.* Red ticks were addictive, tens out of ten, an adrenal rush. To acquire a *good*, a single word penned in the teacher's neat and joined-up script, made me tingle with pleasure. These things were proof: this trick, whatever it was, of *knowing how* was not arbitrary. *Good*. The more she wrote it, the truer it became. I could get right answers. I could do this, repeatedly and provably. I was *good*.

Drawn by numbers, Cora took an interest in my homework.

Sums, she said, poking a knitting needle into my Arithmetic jotter from the height of her chair while I lay on the rug, struggling with subtraction. You should have said you were doing sums. Sums was my best thing, she said. I was a wiz with numbers. Well, till we got Algebra. Christ I hated Algebra. It wasny even real numbers.

She drew faces in Geometry, my mother said. She put eyes and noses in the circles and got the belt. *Cora takes nothing seriously.* That's what they put in her report card. Left the school with damn all.

Algebra and *Geometry* meant nothing but getting belted did. The belt was serious. People were taken out in front of the whole class, told to put their hands together palms up, then raise them like Oliver Twist for *more*. What they got was struck with a long leather tawse anything up to six times. It was horrible even watching, and refusing to watch could make you next. I looked at Cora and imagined her with her hands on fire, Mr Waverley urging her to *understand what this is for*, and wondered how she had survived the shame.

I got belted lots, she said, smiling. I was a naughty girl, me.

She could have been clever if she'd behaved, my mother said, poking the fire so suddenly sparks spilled. You couldn't behave. Bloody *boys* came into the picture and that was it. You were never done chasing boys, and I got hauled up to the school. You took nothing seriously all right and it was boys that did it.

Cora took a long drag of her fag and laughed. Nae chance of that with you, is there, hen? Goody-Two-Shoes.

I bloody hope not, mother said, still annoyed. She's got a head on her shoulders. She's not going to throw her chances away *like some*.

Cora rolled her eyes.

You wait and see. She'll be a teacher or something, something decent, not a bloody secretary.

Cora stared at my mother and slowly stubbed out the fag. After a long, pregnant moment, she lit another one.

That's rich, she said. Great job you've got, eh? Fetching and carrying for kids. She picked up her knitting, settling the needles into place and casually glancing at the slim little watch round her wrist. Is it not time you fetched my tea?

My mother lunged forward in her chair, but Cora stared her down, chewing smoke in her mouth while she did it, then blew. My mother, with no talent for violence, had no counter-bluff. She looked furious but threatless, a born push-over.

You're a cheeky bitch, you, my mother said. You'll get your comeuppance once day. God forgive me, you'll be bloody murdered up a close one day and deserve all you get.

Cora had heard it before. My mother got up and turned the telly off – it was the worst thing she could think to do that wasn't active violence – then went out banging the door behind her. I knew, and Cora knew, she'd gone to fetch Cora's tea. One nil.

Put the telly on, you, Cora said, going back to her Aran needle, twisting a rope into a collar. Make yourself useful. Dimly aware she was feeling bad and it was my fault, I kept my face blank and turned back to the pale aqua squares of the discarded jotter, trying to hide the teacher's red pen endorsements. Right now, the word *good* might tip things entirely the wrong way. It might, I judged, be an idea to do the homework *slowly* and look puzzled in case she thought I was showing off. The numbers were looking at me, expectant. Fours were dead ends. Nines were apples on a long thin branch. Twos were swans making for the edge of the page. Equals signs were merely emphatic. The whole page was dashed with minus signs. I filled in the answers laboriously while *Double Your Money* quizzed contestants from the box in the corner. If they got the questions right, they won. It was that simple. You only had to know the right answer and some oily bloke with fist-fuls of it gave you money. Everyone on it looked thrilled to bits. That was all pie in the sky, though. My mother said the folk on these programmes were actors who had to hand the cash back at the end of the show. Nobody got anything free. You only got things by *sticking in*. Cora was still ignoring me. Even in the huff and without her make-up on, she looked gorgeous. She was ter-rific at cheek and dancing and boys and had a *distinction* for typing, but she had thrown her chances away. I had to *be some-thing* to make up for it. It didn't make sense. I looked at the door my mother had slammed behind her and didn't know who to blame for how rotten I was feeling. Cora was angry and mum was angry because I was good at sums. It wasn't fair. Good things never stayed good, not really. It was all cons and pie in the sky. It wasn't, any of it, *fair*.

I started doing my homework in the bedroom. Home and School, like rival pit bulls, were best kept in separate cages: if they had to meet, the bedroom was at least contained. Not only that, but belly-down on the lino tiles gave a better writing surface than living-room carpet and I could write the required paragraph on *My Hopes and Dreams* with nobody looking over my shoulder and telling me I was a dope. In the bedroom, I could dispense with schoolwork altogether when I was finished and turn, quite naturally, to books.

We had around a dozen permanent books in the house, all well-thumbed: *Alice through the Looking Glass*, six book-club efforts with the titles in gold on the front and the authors, ignored, on the spines, four paperbacks on top of the wardrobe about someone called Angelique whose clothes were falling off, and the door-stops – a fat *Works of George Bernard Shaw* with a little picture of a beardy man inside, a *Complete Shakespeare* with a different beardy man inside, and a hymnal someone had strolled out of church with by mistake. *Alice* had doubled as a plasticine table in her time, and all of Humpty Dumpty had been torn off the cover of *Alice* by plasticine animals, carelessly left there overnight. The hymnal had red-dyed edging with a faint blush of gold leaf that showed other people had touched it over the years: the music inside was a foreign language made of holes. I could stare at staves for hours knowing the notes were trying to tell me *something* and stay none the wiser what. My favourite was the Shaw, largely because it was enormous, but also because of its excitingly lengthy contents list. *Mrs Warren's Profession. Sister Barbara. Saint Joan.* One day, I thought, I'd read a big fat book like that all the way through and understand every word. You could learn everything you ever needed to know from a book like that if you read it all, no skipping. *Androcles and the Lion.* You could learn how to *save your life.* The idea made me dizzy. Schoolbooks didn't have stories. They were spelling primers and books of sums, but since Janet and John, nothing joined-up and nothing about people. The place for those was the library.

We were all members, but only I fetched the books. I fetched them under strict instruction. Cora took six a fortnight: no non-fiction, nothing with pictures, nothing historical and nothing by women. Women canny write, she said. Bring some bloody romance by some bloody woman back here and you'll get your head in your hands to play with. She liked war stories, thrillers and almost anything American. My mother's tipple was biographies of film stars and philanthropists. I was a Folk Tales and Mythology buff. Beside the *Famous Five* and *Chalet School* (which seemed to be about a bunch of girls who slept in a castle with their teachers) stories about magic beans and women being turned into olive trees came out with dignity. My other love was Fairy Tales, but I was too afraid of the librarian to take them out – she tutted and snorted at adults' choices never mind mine. These delights could be had for only threepence each from Woolworths, my secret vice between being sent to bed and my mother coming through in her curlers for Laurence Olivier, Aneurin Bevan and Bette Davis. All these books, school stuff included, lived under the bed. It made me feel better if I woke at night to reach under and touch them, feel the coarse grain of cheap paper nuzzling back like a pet. We kept no books in the living room and would not have read there even if we had. Books were *anti-social*, my mother said and I knew what she meant. To read them properly, you had to ignore other people. Books made you unselfconscious – it was their chief delight. In bed at night, open to talking trees and never-ending ice-creams and all sorts of daft tosh, you could believe what you liked. The words had shape and order and did not change their tune according to the weather. Books made solitude into intimate company and they did it best in private. I'd no more have read in the living room than bent over and touched my toes naked. The living room was no place to be off-guard.

Fetching and carrying to the library apart, I had few fixed chores. I did the family food-shop most Saturday mornings. I cleaned the bath, ran to fetch the local paper every Thursday and helped haul in the washing if it rained. I worked the washing-machine mangle. I wasn't allowed to iron in case I burned myself. Anything involving ladders, though they attracted me, was out. I bruised like a banana. I caught on door handles, fell off steps and shredded my knuckles off grating cheese. I had bruises and bumps and grazes and scuffs and could make up stories about how they had got there without even realising I was doing it.

This ability came in handy, since some of them were gifts from Cora, some from a big Primary Seven called Dora Rose who had taken a dislike to me and thumped me under the railway bridge when I walked home at night. I don't know what happened to my ribbon, I'd say round-eyed: I must have fallen/stumbled/got caught on the brambles at the corner of Springvale Street. Keeping home from school, school from home, plausibilities slid over my tongue easy as sherbet. The less one knew about the other, the better. I showed good marks only to my mother if she promised not to tell and hid any crosses against my work as though they were obscenities. I pretended my sister was keen to take me out to gather rosehips for the rosehip appeal when I hadn't even asked her. Asked for a baby-photo for the school wall-chart, I simply pinched one I thought no one would miss and kept my mouth tight shut. Everything was *fine*.

The only real crossover was when I wrote my mother's letters. Something instinctual made her ask me to do it only when Cora was out or sleeping and I knew to keep it to myself. It was, almost, a secret. *You do it*, she'd say, waving sheets of paper in my direction. *I'd do it myself but I'm not good at this kind of thing. It's easy for you. Come on, pet – write to Tommy/our Jack/Willie so it looks nicer*. Her handwriting was copperplate so this wasn't true. What was true was that the words got stuck in her head when she as much as thought about writing them down. *Put Dear Tommy*, she'd say, then falter. *Dear Tommy*. She'd look at me. *Put Dear Tommy. Have you put it?* I nodded, sucked my cheeks in, waiting. She'd recover, run through a few trial sentences, retract them and look at me again. *What will I put? I never do nothing to put in a letter. What will I say?* And I'd just look back at her, bouncing the end of the pen. I wanted her to look up and see it was me, that I could do this thing for her if she only asked. Almost ashamed, but with feeling she'd level her eyes on mine eventually and say *You do it, hen. You tell them something.* And I would. Running the sentences by her first, then writing them if she approved. I'd hand it over after and she'd read it like a novel, moving her mouth to the words, questioning spelling. Mistakes meant rewrites, the whole lot from the top. She didn't want *crossings out* going in her letters as though our family didn't know any better. And when it was done, I'd hand it over, pen and all, for her signature. *Beth.* Not *love*, just *Beth*, her name at the end a validation. Sometimes when she signed it her eyes would fill up. I thought she was disappointed by my handwriting, that seeing the account written was never as fine as she hoped, but in retrospect that wasn't it. Maybe it felt like getting Cora back, the time during the war when Cora was wee and still willing. But it moved her, this simple thing. Her daughter, the one who hadn't wanted to go to school at all, could write a letter. Lined Airmail paper and a blue Bic pen, running to the Post Office for the stamp. Alone, I would practise my cursive, hoping to make it better, whatever it took. It was as close as I got to making clothes from wool like Cora could. Writing letters gave me a use. It hurt no one. It was one bridge between home and school I could cross no trouble, arrive without harm or fear of it on either side. I could do this. I was fine.

This is my school photo. It's the whole class, buckled under, socialised, emerged from infancy with shining success. We are an assemblage of future citizens, hair combed nice and ties done up right showing the effects of a year's *sticking in*. Babies no more, our efforts have reaped their own rewards. We have, every one of us, grown. We're a team, a class and in it together: a credit, a tribute and a tonic. Resplendent in our Jack's Road uniforms, we know we know the ropes.

There's me in the back row with my plait over my shoulder, the end still sporting its ribbon. The bundle of nerves beside me is Moira-Elaine Murray and the fat lassie with the hair-band next to that is Jennifer Brown. We hung about together in the playground, watching other girls being good at things. We were natural enders, the girls who turned the rope for the skipping of others; not the in-crowd, the photogenic stars of basketball or Step-Up-Tig. Mr Waverley used the word *misfits* when he passed us walking in as a trio from morning break, and I assumed it was us he meant. Probably, it was. We were not good at rough and tumble, trouble or sudden change. It's there in the braced set of our shoulders, those sober little chins. Look deeper, however, look harder and there's something of defence even in the faces of the children I thought were popular, the sporty ones, the kids with bikes, the collected-at-the-gate set with proud big sisters and brothers the size of men. Every last one of us carries the wary interdependence of strangers thrown together, working around our differences, hoping to find our place. In tiny Irene Waters who peaked her school jumper into points and knew the word *tits* too soon; in Jeannie Chapman with the yellow Edwardian ringlets and fat, ready tears; George Crawford with the neck like a coal-man's horse and scarlet sausage fingers. In Alan Paxton who was slow, Brian Coultard with the twitch, Robert Patterson with the lisp and a mole like an exclamation mark; in high-strung Alison Bean and earnest Bobby Cameron and English-spoken Marion Sheerwood with the blonde moustache. In moody Lynn Floors and huffy Margaret Hastie and timid Tom Pye. And Esther Baillie and Iain Collie and May Anderson. Stewart Turner and Suzanne Davis and Margery Thom and Donald McKie. And sallow June Woods and pasty Lorna Carol. And red-headed William Shannon, and tiny wee Lena, and Jean and Pat and Tina and Cheryl and Mina and Danny McDanny McDanny McFairlie who was strange and speccy and the biggest queen in Ayrshire by the time he was eighteen. There we are, the whole class, merely children and unsteady on our feet about something. But we stand up, shiny and new for the bored photographer, the prospective gaze of our loved ones, this fading, captured moment, its lifelong show. I'm right at the back, on the left-hand side in a knitted suit, wearing elastic-sided boys' sale-price winkle-picker boots. You can't miss me. I am, almost, smiling.

11

2 oz beef ham, /4 lb cut tongue, /2 lb mince, ham bone
4 apples, Ayrshires (/2 stone), 2 nice peaches (not soft)
a leek   four carrots   greentails
2 fruit scones, 1 iced bun (currant), 1 plain bun
beans   milk   Oxo
aspirin

Not a letter. Not even a poem. A shopping list. Saturdays started
with shopping lists, items whispered aloud in the kitchen while
Cora had a lie-in. I was too shy to ask for items outright, so my
mother peered into the larder and intoned what she'd need while
I wrote it out on the back of last week's receipt. The list was
wrapped around money, my mother's ready-reckon of the cost,
and the resultant hard little parcel tucked inside a glove so I
wouldn't lose it. My job was to hand the whole thing over and
hope the recipient thought I was mute rather than just ineffectual:
their job was to select the items their shop could provide and put
them in a bag for me. Any change went into a purse the size of a
bible kept in my coat pocket. There were no supermarkets in

Saltcoats: shop-keepers stood with the goods behind them, out of harm's way, then passed them hand to hand for inspection and payment. This system meant children could fetch and carry for whole households and often did. My Saturday routine included Mr Gray and his son Charlie for milk and tins and dry goods; MacIntosh's for fruit and veg; Braine's the butcher, The Kandy Bar bakery and McPherson's The Chemist for my mother's headache powders and assorted prescriptions which were handed over in discreet white bags with McPherson's and an emerald green mortar and pestle on the side. I could take it all except Braine's. The shop stank of lard and had black-spattered fly-paper dangling from all the light fittings and dogs going crazy sniffing up sawdust. Cora said they had buckets of blood and eyeballs through the back to make sausages and black puddings and that's why she wouldn't go. She didn't go just because she was Cora, but it was the kind of thing she said. I watched the butchers' hands, white and wrinkled from working with the cloy of meat all day, their cuticles rimmed crimson or bitten to the quick, and wondered how they stood it. In a good mood, they'd put in a couple of pork links with the rest and say, *Tell your mother that's a present from her boyfriend*. It was a joke, but it always made me blush. Sometimes Mr Braine gave out red lollipops with the change, but they had the taste of death about them and I waited till I was clear to slot them down the nearest drain. Free to choose like Cora, I'd have gone only to McPherson's for the soap displays and the sparkle of glass, Woolworths for threepenny books and the beach balls in the window. Free to choose, I'd have chosen the

Music Shop. It drew me though I couldn't play a note and never went inside. There was an awning outside to stand beneath if it was raining and plenty to see through the glass: gap-toothed pianos, red guitars, black clarinets peppered with silver-trimmed rifle holes, the sheets of Morse-code manuscript that could be read, by those that knew how, as tunes. The pianos were what caught me: the high polish on the wood, the way the keys splayed out like an invitation, blatant and white. The trombone, the only brass instrument in the window, looked merely loud, the oboe like something for printing out Braille. The pianos sat modestly at the back with a stool, a cunning suggestion that deeper acquaintance was not unwelcome. Wanting a piano was crazy. I knew that. It was looking for looking's sake, the enjoyment of a lust that hadn't a snowball's. I watched Vespa scooters and snappy little cars shoot by in the street with the same feeling. Some things out there that were only for Other People, but it didn't hurt to look. It was idle pleasure: *daydreaming, staring into space*. After enough of it, I'd hare with the brown bags full of shopping, keen to be back to the stuff I legitimately counted mine: Lego, a handful of books, the dolls, things to draw with, my own imagination. With Cora in bed and no other children likely to call or even appear in our cul-de-sac, these were the raw materials of Saturday afternoons.

By and large, I spent them as somebody else; Hiawatha with a doll's blanket hanging over the washing line to make a tent, Aladdin in a pair of sawn-off pyjamas and my mother's Sunday turban hat with a brooch on the front, a teacher with dolls ranged in rows on the kitchen floor. Story corner apart, teaching was mostly thrashing and rightly so: Mickey Mouse was a lousy speller, the Baby Doll was cheeky and Sindy, my sole glamour-puss, was rubbish at gym. Thrashing and drawing scores on their wrists with red ball-point *gave me no pleasure,* but it was *for their own good.* Between times, my mother dotted in and out of the kitchen making broth, reminding me Cora was still asleep. *If you can't do that quieter,* she'd say, looking down her nose severely, *you'll need to batter them outside.* There was grated carrot on the chopping board if I fancied it, chocolate biscuits in the cupboard. When I'd done with pretending, I stood on a kitchen chair to flake parsley into the stock, watching it darken and sink among the chunks of yellow vegetables. Everything ran softly, without undue excitement or rush. With Cora asleep, the steaminess and under-the-breath singing of the kitchen with just the two of us in it had no reason to break. There were other girls out there playing skipping ropes and going to the pictures and freewheeling about on bikes. I had seen clusters of girls with Chinese ropes outside the shops at the scheme end of town, screaming with pleasure as they jumped and raced and skinned their knees. But I hankered after none of it. *This* was what I wanted: the perfume of beeswax insinuating itself from the living room, the nasal bottle-brush of Coal-Tar and Co-op bleach, the illusion of cleanliness and safety that felt like being held. This was where I belonged: indoors, the washing machine chuntering, the necks of dishrags wrung in whispers and chamois cloth squealing. That Cora was uncon-scious yet we were alive and bright in the house made me ripple with content. Housework was comfort. It was an ordered and vital and necessary thing and I loved my mother for shoring it round me. Even if I'd never have used those words, I knew what love was, the importance of the moment. Staring into space stock-still in the corner of the kitchen, I drank it all in while it lasted. I knew I'd miss it when it was gone.

In the short term, that meant from around three; when something inside Cora went off like a factory clock. It drove her to leave the sheets behind in a shape of herself for my mother to deal with and head up the hallway, hunting for a lighter and a box of fags. It drove her round the light switches, switching, laying a trail of electric charge. It drove her to turn on a radio station she would not listen to, click on the immersion heater and birl the bath taps right up full. *I'm up*, she'd holler without needing to; *where's my coffee? I've places to go and people to meet. I've things to do, me.* As if we didn't know. As if, for a moment, anything earthly could get in her way.

There's no excuse, in this day and age, for an ugly woman.

Cora could talk and put on eyeliner at the same time.

You show me a woman who's ugly, she said, mouth gaping as she held the brush dead steady, one pinkie cocked, and I'll show you a woman who's a lazy bitch.

She blinked twice, checked her work, then turned full on to me. Her face was blanked out with pan-stick, even the lips, so she looked freshly dipped in orange wax. Against this backdrop, her teeth looked yellow, like a dog's. I knew they were false and wondered if they were sore.

Ta-da, she sang. Come on then, what do you think?

Good, I said. It wasn't true, but she had just kicked off. There was lots more to go. All I had to do was sit back on the end of her bed and shut up, and the whole thing would unfold like magic before my very eyes. She sat at the dressing table in an underskirt and bra to get done up, all black straps and cleavage, with red weals where the elastic dug in. The least I could do was be encouraging. I'd watched it enough to know the drill as well as she did. The pan-stick undercoat came first, a greasy tan crayon slicked up from a navy blue Max Factor case painted on in stripes then slapped around a lot to make it spread and settle. Everything else went on after this.

That's how come you call it foundation, right? It's the bit *underneath*.

Eye-shadow was next up and always green. I can't recall her in any other colour. Black hair, green eye-shadow: it was, she said, smearing it on with a fingertip, a natural law. The mascara lived in a box of its own with a tiny brush like the one that took animal hairs off coats. The trick was to spit on the black stuff and rub the brush in till the black went soft and the brush was clogged with it, like oozy inky jam. When it's thick, she said, not before. When you'd done that right, you were ready to apply, blinking your eyelid up and down while you held the brush steady in front of your lashes so it coated them, again, again. The more coats, the bigger the night out. The Bobby Jones Dance Hall was a three-coat event, requiring lots of fluttering, eye-rolling and occasional tears. I got to hand over toilet paper in case of emergency dabbing. After that, the liner, thin and black and flicked up at the sides like Maria Callas. It was complicated stuff, involving split-second timings and angles of the wrist to make the lines keen but Cora knew what she was doing. A little pencil only half the size of her thumb drew on the eyebrows. She only had half-eyebrows so the pencil had to be sharp, her hand steady. Sometimes my mother stormed by the door, not being helpful.

What do you expect if you pluck them to buggery? she said, charging up and down the hall in a pinny. You'll never get them back.

She meant the eyebrows. Cora knew but didn't care. The drawn ones were perfect arches and her own had been flat lines. Eyebrows done, she sat back, poking her tongue into one cheek as she checked the separate parts of herself in the mirror. There was always more. Powder on the sides of her nose, then 4711 behind the ears and on each wrist, rendered her ready for the frock.

Lipstick and hairspray *after*, she said. Frock *first*, lipstick *after*. You think about it.

Her best frocks were sleeveless with side zips, but the necks were intact circles that needed to be guided over her comb-back carefully then patted down into place before the zip was done up and the construction complete. Lipstick *after*. She had thought it all through: it made perfect sense.

Cora's bare skin always made me think of pork links and I was glad she never asked for help with the zips. But touching was not something our family did. I remained a voyeur, safe on the yellow bedspread, as she Hokey-Cokeyed her way into columns of cloth, arms first. She had four dresses, all patterned: green with lilac flowers, black with lotus blossom, purple with hydrangeas and navy with forsythia. The navy satin sprinkled with yellow was the best: cinched waist, corset-tight and low-cut with tiny puffed straps she pulled over her shoulders to look Italian. Her stockings, hooked double to a dangly ironmongery of suspenders, came next, followed by shoes, a handbag hardly worth the bother, elbow-length gloves and dress watch round the wrist and she was into the final lap. Putting lipstick on in gloves could not have been easy but that was how she did it, kissing her lips in and out to check she had covered all eventualities whatever she did with her mouth. Last thing was the beauty spot, with the licked tip of the eyebrow pencil: a full stop above her lip and another on the fat curve of her right breast where it rose, a full moon, over the edge of midnight satin.

Like Rome, Cora did not build in a day, but she was glorious to behold, a miracle of engineering and design from her cantilevered bra to her dead straight seams. She could have no idea how wonderful she looked, I thought, how wholly free, chucking a swing coat over her shoulders and bolting for the door, the bus to Ayr, the wide, wild world of the Bobby Jones Dance Hall.

You'll not be late? my mother shouted, Cora! You hear me? I'm saying you'll not be late! To the diminishing echo of her kitten-heels. Cora didn't even answer. I imagined everybody in the block heard, looked out of the window to catch a glimpse of a mysterious princess running down our dreary little six-house lane towards the glitter ball shadows and whatever they concealed, but not Cora. She kept going like the wicked Queen in Snow White, running to the dungeons despite herself, ignoring the bones beneath her feet, desperate to know the answers to fearful questions.

She'll be for it one day, my mother always said, checking the window when there was nothing left to see. Too bloody cheeky by half.

Who she was telling was anyone's guess.

First thing next morning was a man's voice.

I sat up, listening and realised it was Sandy. Sandy was in the house first thing on Sunday morning saying *It's not my fault* and *Honest to god it's the truth* over and over. Cora will be furious if he wakes her up, I thought, hiding back under the top sheet. He better watch his step. One of my mother's curlers, the kind like a leg bone only blue, was on the pillow where she had slept till not long ago. She was in there with him now, I realised, listening to him crying. It was what Sandy did. Cora dumped him and he came to our house and cried and my mother made him eggs and eventually he went away. Sometimes Cora spoke to him and sometimes she didn't. This was one of the mornings, it seemed, she didn't. I could picture the eggs from here now I listened harder, spitting and congealing in the frying pan. It wasn't a good picture. Suddenly Sandy roared blue murder. *I don't know where she is,* he howled, a huge sob rolling out with the words like a wave. Next thing, my mother appeared at the door in her dressing gown, her head decorated with pink and blue plastic under a covering of net. Despite the festive touch, she looked drawn, but she always did in the morning.

He'll be away in a minute, she said. It's Sandy.

We both waited, listening to see if he was staying put. He was.

He's been here since thon time, looking for her, but she's not here.

It turned out Cora didn't come home. They had some kind of argument and she'd just upped and left Sandy outside the Bobby Jones.

He says he waited all night to see if she'd come back, but she didn't. My mother was getting agitated. Now he's here and she's not and I'm stuck with him. It's not right, this, she said.

I could see that. Everything was inside out and nobody knew what to do. I pictured Sandy, distraught, roaming the streets of Ayr and calling her name and nothing happening, just the odd stray cat keeping out of his way.

He's drunk, she said, unnecessarily. You wait here. I'll try to get him to go away.

She was distracted, not annoyed, holding her dressing gown shut at the neck like a comforter. She'd pulled out some of the curlers at the front because there was a guest, and one fat curl escaped the netting in a perfect circle. Sandy cranked up again like a tractor, sudden and sputtery. *I love her*, he honked, desperate. *Honest tae god, it's torture.* We heard a row of awful, phlegmy sniffs. My mother rolled her eyes, sighed and went back through, pulling the bedroom door shut behind her.

By four o'clock Sandy was long gone, still sniffing. He had lifted me up the way he always did at the door, and snot had smudged on to my pyjama sleeve. He was still crying as he walked down the road, not caring who saw. Now there was just us two, me and my mother, both dressed for the usual Sunday except it wasn't. My mother did not choose a hat and go to church or fill an offering envelope. She stayed in her pinny, resigned, waiting. We stood at opposite ends of the living-room sofa, looking out at the rain making dimples on the pavement, gathering in the gutter.

I could bloody choke her, I could, my mother said. I canny be doing with this kind of upset. I've got work to do. And went back to the kitchen with her fists tight. I could hear her banging open windows, the paint seals shearing, banging them shut again for no reason. Being in there with her wasn't much of a temptation, so I stayed put, pressing my knee into the sofa arm, burying my tartan trews in palm leaves. The rain kept belting down. All I could see between the drops was Cora.

She'd had a sleeveless dress on, sling-back shoes. All that hair-spray. I couldn't stop imagining her, prone in a dirty puddle, mascara running in wavy lines while the rain fell on her open eyeballs, bouncing. I imagined one of her shoes missing, one stocking too. I forced myself not to imagine her neck, kept my brain fixed on her feet, their red-painted toenails scandalously on show.

Cora couldn't run. Even Sandy said it. Cora couldn't swim, and she couldn't run to save her life.

Looking out of the window wasn't helping. I found my coloured pencils, the good set in the red zip case, and drew daffodils for my spring project. I told myself I couldn't be doing with this upset. I had work to do. I wore the yellow pencil down to the wood and there was still no sign of Cora, so I found a sharpener and just kept going. It seemed the best thing.

She did come back.

Near tea-time with her hair lank and her face blotchy, all that careful make-up turned to crumbles and streaks. At the first door-click my mother belted down the hall with her *Where the hell have you been?* face on. But she didn't say it, maybe because Cora looked so rough. It was getting dark outside and the shadows on her face made her look tired, lined. Her gloves were missing. She stood in the open porch, flapping a hand at the raindrops on the shoulders of her good swing-coat, showing two broken nails.

Well? she said, looking at me as though I owed her an explanation. What are *you* looking at?

For godsake, my mother said, we've had Sandy round and everything.

Cora sighed. I've just been out to the dancing, OK? I stayed with a friend.

What friend?

Somebody I met.

Who? What bloody friend?

A friend, she said, flat. She took the coat off and one of her stockings was ripped at the knee, spidered on both sides, like she'd had a fall. Somebody from work.

My mother looked momentarily outraged, as if she might strike Cora with a thunderbolt, or at the very least the drying cloth in her hand. Not even I went for it. People at Cora's work didn't go to the Bobby Jones. They lived in Glasgow and had manicures. Cora was telling lies. I felt shocked and sorry for her at the same time. She must be in a terrible fix to be telling lies. Behind me, my mother rose to her full height, inflating as she went. I could hear her taking in the breath, filling more space than usual.

I've been worried sick! she said. She was trembling.

Well, you can stop, then, can't you? Cora said. I'm fine.

Is that it? Is that all you have to say? Is that bloody it?

Look. Cora sighed. It was a very deep sigh. She closed her eyes before she spoke. I'm back now. And I'm fine. Just leave it at that, eh? She opened her eyes and blinked. I'm fine. Hello, hen.

I said hello back and felt daft. It seemed not the right thing to be saying at all. My mother's face gave up as Cora folded the coat over her arm and went into her bedroom, closing the door quietly behind her.

I'm not having this again, my mother roared, rattling the

handle. You hear? But she was talking to a door and knew it. She hit it once, hard, then her eyes filled up.

I don't know, she said, turning away from the gloss sheen, its dogged lack of response. What did I do, eh? What did I do?

She looked at me, but I didn't know either. I could see myself being useless in the hall mirror, the back of my mother's head where the curls hadn't taken. She'd have been better off asking Cora. But not now. Even I knew that. Not now.

Given precedent, she could have stayed in her room for days. She didn't. She resurfaced briefly when the theme tune came on for *Sunday Night at the London Palladium*, wearing her dressing gown and her eyes puffy, her hair a state. My mother looked up from behind her glasses while the Tiller Girls high-kicked in the lens reflections, but Cora didn't come in. She just went to the bathroom and away again. We heard her running water till the routine ended and Norman Vaughan came on, a nondescript little man with a thumb fixation who made bad jokes at the orchestra who bantered back.

Bloody idiot, my mother said. She was eating a liquorice pipe. I wish they'd put something good on.

The water kept running. One bath a week each was the house limit, everyone on a different night. The immersion heater was too dear to waste on being clean just when you felt like it. It wasn't Cora's night, but it didn't matter.

A balancing act came on, mincing, and my mother went to make a cup of tea. We both knew it wasn't the tea she was after, not really. She was checking on Cora. I heard her mumbling at the bathroom door through the jazzy balancing music, being kept waiting. Some too-skinny girl in a tutu was chucking a ball in the air and catching it on her toes. It had to be a rotten job, being a balancing act. You gave your all in spangles and tights and nobody cared. I kept watching out of pity. Meantime, the mumbling was all at my mother's pitch. It was only when the telly stopped clapping and the next act was being introduced I heard Cora say anything back.

Aye OK, she said, her voice very low, almost broken. I could murder a cup of coffee. Ta.

Cora never said *thank you*, but the odd *ta* escaped her lips in times of high feeling. I heard my mother sniff and cut her losses the way she always did, her feet padding off to find the Nescafé jar. Whatever it was that happened would not be mentioned again. At least not till my mother found mileage in it, got desperate enough to rake. For now, however long now lasted, it was past. A crooner was on when my mother came back through, crooning. She put Cora's coffee next to her chair and settled down opposite, tilting toward the screen, hoping something better would come up soon. I remembered us watching somebody on telly once and my mother saying *He's dead, him, he died in a car crash*. I couldn't remember what the film was, only her saying it. *He died in a car crash*, and getting chills all over at watching somebody dead moving around, as though they had no idea. You wondered what their relatives thought, how they came to terms with the whole unseemly show.

Cora came in smelling of soap and headed for her chair. She

leaned in for the coffee and the lamp behind her head made her glow; skin, hair, fingertips all tinged with light. She hadn't washed her hair and it looked wiry, barely contained, but it sparkled at the tips like a black halo. She drank half the cup in one go, cradled its warmth in both hands, and flicked her eyes toward the telly.

Christ, she said, is this all we're getting?

And despite the bruise on her knee, the circles under her eyes, the awfulness of everything, she sat back where she belonged. She looked terrible and wonderful all at once, lighting up a fag and threading it between her fingers, completely unaware how close she had come to losing us. She drew in the smoke deeply, held it in her mouth. Not dead at all. It seemed impossible, there and then, to believe she ever would be.

Watch the bloody telly, she said. I did. I did.

12

Look at the state, Cora said, rubbing a lipstick smear off her teeth. She meant me. She was making herself lovely in the mirror and I was haring out with my satchel on squint. You think it would *try*.

It did. My hair was neat enough and my clothes were clean. But I was growing. My arms poked like asparagus tips out of the ends of my sleeves. The clothing grant for the new school year didn't cover more than shoes, my mother said, not if she bought shoes that didn't leak like council guttering at the first sign of rain, so she bought some grey wool and a pattern and set Cora knitting.

Cora had always knitted, watching telly and with two fags on the go at the same time, jammed deep into the roots of her middle left fingers. Nothing caught fire, no matter how delicate the fabric, and falling ash brushed off even baby shawls easier than it had any right. She knitted for work colleagues, boyfriends, neighbours with pregnant daughters and strangers who asked. She knitted matinee jackets and bootees budded with little wool roses and scarves and pixie hats with full-flush pom poms and bala-clavas with contrast trim. She fashioned tank-tops and guernseys and sailor tops with scallop collars in all-over lace. My mother got whole suits in four-ply, knee-length skirts on round needles and matching Fair Isle cardies with trees and birds and flower-petal shapes in matching bands round collars and cuffs. Once she knitted a whole shawl in two-ply that stretched over the sofa, right to the floor on all sides, light and weird as fog. Cora knitted like a champion, wool sliding over her fag-laced fingers like ticker-tape, and her next project was me.

I needed a skirt, a V-neck pullover, socks and a cardi with a school crest. The crest we could buy and sew on after, and she drew the line at socks – *I'm turning heels for nobody* – but the rest was mine before a fortnight was out. To crown this snappy new look, I argued my mother into buying me boy's sale-price grey suede Chelsea boots to kick off Primary Four. I thought they'd make me look like Elvis.

Jesus, Cora said, gurgling with laughter whilst casting on something lurex so her fingers looked electrified. Who *do* you look like in that get-up? Hoo. She wiped her eyes. It's frightening.

I didn't need a mirror to tell me. Getting older made it clearer. Even in a pigtail and skirt, I looked like Eddie Galloway. I looked, however much I wished it different, like *him*.

Mrs Tough died.

She was the big, breezy woman next door, pink and wholesome with silver-grey curls and a different floral apron every day.

Mrs Tough had smiled and shelled out biscuits as you passed by the door: Mr Tough was a shrivelled old stick who kicked kittens. Mr Tough never even said hello. But it was her that died.

Heart attack, the postman said. He snapped his fingers. Just like that.

Excess weight, Mrs McFarlane upstairs said, and her husband smiled. He couldn't help smiling because something happened to his face in the war.

You just don't take it in, my mother said. He's the one that looks as if he's on his last legs and she was in the pink. You can't believe it happening to *her*.

The coffin being shouldered out of their door and into the hearse made it real enough. Mrs Gregg, the wife of the pigeon fancier, ran round from the back gardens, her arms folded tight. Terrible, terrible, she said. The pitch of her voice was high and nervous. It was that way all the time. Today, with her chest so badly constricted, Mrs Gregg's voice was dog-whistle range.

Terrible terrible terrible, is it not, Mrs Galloway. Terrible, terrible.

To a high soprano chorus of a single word, we all watched Mrs Tough, the nicest of our neighbours, being shoved inside the back of the black car in a wooden box. She seemed to have packed away neatly, with so little fuss. The couple's deaf daughter had come from college in London and stood at the door in her beatnik clothes. Her name was Myrtle. She looked like Audrey Hepburn but it wasn't the time to say. Everybody in the block, everybody except Mr McFarlane with the smile, went to the funeral, and Mr

Tough didn't speak to any of them even there. There was no do, and only Myrtle brought flowers. After that, we hardly saw Mr Tough and didn't want to. He'd pass the window sometimes traipsing to the corner off-licence for paper-wrapped whisky, pyjama bottoms showing under his coat. All he did was remind my mother that his wife was gone. Pig, she said. She had been fond of Mrs Tough.

Despite herself, she was fetching and carrying for him in a matter of months. She bought his whisky so he didn't have to go over the door at all, and delivered it to his bedside where he checked the change to make sure he hadn't been done. Not long after that, she was changing his sheets, making him put on new pyjamas and bringing over his piss-stained stuff for our machine. Every so often she snapped, but never at him.

All he does is lie in bed, she said. I wish they'd take him away.

But of course they didn't, whoever *they* were. They never did anything you wanted.

He's accusing me of stealing his kitchen forks. What would I want your bloody forks for? I said. What would I do that for? You know what he did?

I didn't.

He shook his fist at me. Like this. She demonstrated, bunching her fingers hard. He'll not get anybody else to fetch and carry for him, that's for sure. Can you imagine? she said. She bunched her fist again, but it gave her no relief. Can you *imagine*?

He looked as if a strong puff of wind would knock him down last time I'd seen him. Godknew what he looked like now.

He's a mean-minded, lazy auld bastard and I hope he rots in hell. He used to beat her about. For nothing.

Cora's ears pricked up. That wee weasel next door? she said. Him?

Him. She had bruises. She showed me once. Didn't deny it when I asked.

Pig, Cora said. You should have got the police.

Her business, my mother said. Never interfere between husband and wife. Believe me, it's always a mistake.

There was a long silence.

Even his daughter hates him, she said. And I don't blame her. I don't blame her one bit for not leaving her life behind to come up here and look after *him*. She owes him damn all after what he did.

Jesus, said Cora. You never know what's going on right under your nose, eh?

Nobody mentioned dad. I tried to think about Mrs Tough instead, the way she'd slip me a sixpence after checking her husband wasn't looking, and realised it hadn't been a game. Giving me the sixpences was a secret and a risk. She looked over her shoulder and whispered *shhhh* because she was scared of him. Maybe he would have hit her for being nice to me. His house smelled like the filth under kitchen lino, and I decided in that instant I wasn't going in there again. Even if I was asked. Next time she asked me to take in his whisky I'd just not bother. I didn't like him anyway, his face a road-map of veins and those red, watery eyes. I thought about Mrs Tough waving at me through

her front window. I thought about Myrtle not able to hear things
and my chest choked up.

Why do you do it then? I asked. It was out before I knew. How
come you look after him when Myrtle doesn't have to?

The cheek in my own voice surprised me and Cora drew me a
look. My mother didn't even blink. Because nobody else will, she
said. Why do you think? You can't turn your back when he's next
door. He's dying in there.

Not fast enough, Cora said.

No, my mother said. But you don't just kid on it's not happening and walk away. Do you?

Cora coughed and rolled her eyes as though my mother was
crazy. My mother saw her doing it.

Well I just hope there's somebody there for me when I need it,
she said. It came like a bite, sudden and shocking. I've had it if it's
you two.

Cora cocked an eyebrow, smiled and reached for her lighter.
Christ, she said. She placed a fag carefully on her lip. What's
eating you?

———

Bad faith. Bad faith and smoky air, the kind that open windows
did not help. It haunted me, this exchange. I had no idea what she
thought might happen to her to need someone the way Mr Tough
needed her. He was dying. I wondered how you knew someone
was dying, how long it took; if she meant that me and Cora would

favourite niece? And Mrs Tough? How's Big Mrs Tough next door?

Fine, I said. Mrs Tough was far from fine but Rose wasn't hearing it from me. School was fine and the house was fine. Everything, always, was fine. Opening your mouth unwarily could cause all sorts. It was always better if things were A-OK and hunky-dory sure-thing perfectly fine.

Angus and Rose had never had children. They married late, my mother said. She pointed it out often. Your father's sister, she said, was never bonny. Rose was *your father's sister*, even after he died, or *Bloody Rose*. I learned only in my twenties they had tried to get custody of me after my father died, why the phrase *unfit mother* tripped from my mother's lips unbidden, as though she was a radio tuner for a distant channel every now and then when she saw them, why Angus was so seldom invited in. But she let me have my day trips, my walks in the woods gathering speedwell and clover, the gifts of rock I brought from sunny Largs, gifts she must have known that Rose had paid for. All the while I was buttering the lives of *my father's sister* and her late-in-the-day husband with lies, with things being *fine fine fine*, they were doing exactly the same. Quiet Angus and gullible Rose, with their kindly, childless, threatless lives had tried to acquire me like a teapot. I'd had no idea.

———

The Fair arrived down the shorefront and Angus was keen for me to go. Big lorries rolled up first with bits of hobby-horse and individual

waltzer coaches on the back, then trailers, then the vans and cara-
vans that settled in a ring only a stone's throw from the breakers
behind the high shore wall. They came every summer but I'd never
been. Rose said it was good fun but *common*. *Rough sorts* went. I pictured rough sorts and didn't want to go. Don't be daft, Angus said.
There's nothing to be scared of at the Fair. It's fun. Rose wouldn't
come – she had accounts to do – but Angus took me anyway and
held my hand all the way through. We threw little wooden balls at
coconuts, chucked horseshoes and poles and caught plastic fish with
a cane rod. We won nothing, but Angus got me candy floss which I
ate with my mouth and not my fingers. Nothing sticky happened at
all. It was fine.

   Three weeks later Cora took me to the same place and it wasn't
the same place at all. For a start, it was dark (only wee babies
went to the fair in the daytime, she said, *everybody* knew that), and
for seconds, it was loud. We could hear Helen Shapiro *Walking
Back to Happiness* from three streets away and the rides for bigger
boys and girls were in full swing. I followed her down the muddy
corridor of stall-backs with bits of Tommy Steele and Elvis roaring
round different corners trying not to care about the clash: the
important thing was the excitement. Cora was dressed to the
nines in a green and navy skirt and sailor top, pointy shoes and a
four-inch wide patent-leather belt with a horseshoe buckle. Her
black hair showed red and blue and green depending on which
bulbs were flashing round the Chair-o-planes, the way things
looked at Christmas when you held Quality Street wrappers in
front of your eyes.

Cmon, she said, smiling fit to split her lip, we're trying *everything*.

The wild lights and laughing strangers, the scents of sausages, sugar, cheap ketchup and hot toffee apples were dizzying. She opened her little red purse's brass frog-mouth and showed two folded, russet-coloured leaves inside. Ten bob notes.

We're spending the lot. Race you.

Where we raced first was the Dodgems. She drove. The idea was crashing, not dodging at all. Cora was keen to bump into as much as possible and I was glad when it was done so I could stop pretending it was thrilling. Cora, however, had charge of the money so we did the Dodgems three times.

Great fun, eh? she roared over the juke-box boom.

At the hobby-horses, I chose one painted in exactly the same flame and cream colours as the school spelling book, but Cora wouldn't come on, not even to sit on the tiger.

That's for wee tots, she said. I'm not getting on even if you are. You're on your own, chum.

She wouldn't wave as I went round either, so I stopped waving to her after a while. It was better to let Cora do things her way, keep things sweet.

Thank Christ that's by, she said when I got off. Right cmon. We're going to the Waltzers.

Waltzers had nothing to do with old-fashioned dancing. They were little chariots on a rising and falling deck, each spinning on its own turntable to Gerry and the Pacemakers. You sat inside your chosen chariot and after a slow start, the man came round and spun you hard as you sea-sicked up and down and *How do you do what you do to me?* hollered from the amps. We got three fast spins in a row from a skeletal boy in jeans and a scuffed leather jacket but Cora wouldn't scream. She laughed with her head tilted back, cheeky and cool, which only got us spun again till the rest of the fair was just poster-paint streaks. The boy liked a challenge and he liked Cora. That was why he was trying to make her scream, she said: boys liked it when girls screamed. But she didn't.

If he thinks he can scare me, he's another think coming, she said over her shoulder as we got off, loud enough for him to hear. Silly bugger, she roared, and laughed like an actress.

I was impressed, but hardly able to walk for dizziness. Cora was stone cold sober and walked a straight line with her hands on her hips to prove it. Nothing beats me, she said. I could stay on that thing all night and not turn a hair. She threw ping-pong balls into a round glass bowl and won me a prize, a sliver of orange-gold in a blue polythene bag, first go. The fish looked too big to be in there, just one third filled with water and nothing else, not even a pinch of food. It was my first pet, and I didn't know whether to be pleased or sorry. Cora had a fag and bought me popcorn, something else not to spill.

I don't eat stuff at fairs, she said. Hot dogs, jesus. She screwed the flat of her shoe on a cast-off dout till it died and pursed her lips to redistribute any displaced lipstick. Cmon, then. More stuff then we'll get chips on the way home.

We threw darts at playing cards and missed every time. Cora

tried the strong man machine, and we both got weighed. The machine said I SPEAK YOUR WEIGHT, but it didn't; it just rang the numbers up as though we were parcels of beef ham in Braine's. On the way home, the sky pitch black and the sea shushing away behind the flood wall, she bought us chips at The Golden Supper. They were fresh, the kind you ate drawing cold sea air in over the teeth to avoid burning the soft skin of the inside of your mouth. The view of Saltcoats from the middle of the railway bridge was noble and suffused with mist from our chewing. The last train was long gone and the station was quiet. You could see right over the shops to the pub where my Uncle Allan played the accordion, all the way down to Windmill Street and the pointy tips of the Fairground rides beyond. The bump and grind of mixed-up pop tunes was still there if you listened carefully, skirls of Frank Ifield yodelling above all the rest. *I remember you*. When the chips were done we screwed the news-paper wrappings to cannonballs and she wiped her hands on my cardigan.

Fair's fair, she said. I knitted it.

I was worried about the fish, still circling in his flimsy little bag. What happened when we got home? I had no idea what we could use as a fish bowl. I had no idea what he ate, how he was cared for, but getting him home seemed the right first step. I wanted to put him somewhere unburstable. Rather than say, I held up the bag, showed her the fish circling and gasping, looking less gold by the minute.

Christsake, she said. She sighed. It's just a fish. I looked at

her. Look, she said. We could pour it down the drain and go for
a walk, eh? See who we meet? The night is young and all that. I
looked at her harder and clutched the bag tight. Jesus, she said.
Cmon then. Just my luck to get stuck with you and a bloody
fish.

And she pulled away from the bridge with a great drag of her
heels against the metal walkway. All through my childhood, the
sound of steel-tipped stiletto against the metal tread of the railway
bridge made a background echo: women signalling their presence as they crossed, usually alone from the trains, at night. Like
chalk down a greasy blackboard, a howl from a trap. She made it
now on purpose, and started walking.

I had never got her to do anything she didn't want to before,
but it didn't feel triumphant. It felt awkward. It finished this
lovely night out with the wrong flavour. Somebody whistled as
we went past Massie's, but Cora looked oblivious. I thought for a
moment she hadn't heard. *Don't turn round,* she hissed. *Don't turn
round or I'll choke you.* Whoever it was shadowed us as far as the
corner shop on Springvale Street, where he whistled twice more.
Cora kept on walking, if anything even slower, expecting so strongly
for me to follow suit that that's exactly what I did. A moment later,
we heard the echo of his footsteps, fading away. Out here in the
dark, weaving past the side-alleys and culs-de-sac that led to our
house, a helpless fish to look after, I had followed my sister's lead
and found it not wanting. Angus might not believe in rough sorts,
but Cora had an instinctive grasp. I had absolute faith she knew
what she was doing.

My mother put the fish in a cleaned-out bowl from the coal shed. It was dead less than a week later, belly-up on the surface of the water when I came home from school. We had bought it some grainy powder the Pet Shop insisted was fish-food and a piece of plastic fern, but it hadn't helped. My mother turned huffy with sorrow.

Stupid thing to do, get the wean a fish. They die. You should never have got her the bloody thing.

It's just a fish, Cora said, put out. For crying out loud.

I buried it in secret and put a cross made out of twigs and bound with an elastic band on top. I would have made a head-stone only there was no name to put on it. I'd waited rather than pick one, just in case, thinking it would be sadder to see something with a name not needing it any more. It was a wasted precaution and sad anyway. *It's just a fish*. My wrists were poking out of the sleeves of my blazer again, my shoes felt pinched. I had the sensation, as my eyes filled up looking at the secret plot between the lupins, the twig cross tilting sideways already, that something, somewhere, was watching. It was laughing at me.

13

The door said MUSIC. Not a number, but a word meaning sounds. The classroom teacher would still give us BBC radio programmes where we got to sing along to strange little songs about cricket whilst clattering castanets, but the rest, this spanking new upper-case MUSIC, would come courtesy of a *specialist*. And the MUSIC specialist, complete with piano and the means to play it, was Miss Wigg.

Queuing up outside the MUSIC door for the first time with the rest of 5b, I fancied the room full of song books, a glamorous rosewood piano flashing its teeth from the corner, Miss Wigg leading us all in a rollicking chorus of – I didn't care what. So long as it rollicked. The piano was there all right, and the books. There were even posters on the walls of orchestral instruments and a blackboard with pale orange staves printed over it instead of simple blank sheets. Centre-stage, however, was the *sol-fa* chart. Officially, it was Mr Curwen's *sol-fa* modulator with foreign-sounding words in round-eyed lower case *doh-re-mee*-ing its way up a ladder to the top. This chart was Miss Wigg's starting point, her finishing point, her resource in times of trouble. And we learned it, my goodness yes, we learned. We grasped where relationships were, how to render the names into pitch and organise them like socks in a drawer. We did *exercises* of rising, falling and step-wise scales, following the tip of Miss Wigg's pointer, making hummocks and curlicues of our voices in varying degrees of close-enough. After a while, I realised something awful. Miss Wigg thought this stuff *was* music. *Sol-fa* wasn't a means to otherwise unknown tunes, the warm-up to singing till our chests were fit to burst: it was Miss Wigg's idea of teaching. George Crawford threw bits of screwed up paper at her to relieve the boredom and Alison Bean made noises like a duck. After a while, there was a general air of revolt during our half-hour a week and she conceded ten minutes at the end for tunes.

I remember *Merrily We Roll Along*, *Three Blind Mice* and *The Skye Boat Song* to *sol-fa*, then her favourites from *A Collection of Scots Songs for Unison Singing* (James Adamson ed.); no harmonies, no deviation, no ornamentation or sly personal frills. The class, instinctively aware they were being short-changed, became mutinous and so did I. If we'd had an open boat, we'd have set her adrift in it. Instead we made the refusals that small children do. We hissed and made catcalls and rustled in our chairs, but nothing deflected Miss Wigg from her chosen, deadly course. She *sol-fa*'d us into the ground. The word MUSIC on her door was a wizened black lie. What happened behind Miss Wigg's door wasn't MUSIC, it was walks on a choke chain with no prospect, ever, of a run in the park. And it wasn't music's fault. Not at all. It was the teacher's.

Miss Wigg was the first teacher I remember loathing. The very sight of her made my nerve-ends twitch. Her head was made of pin curls crossed inside kirbies, like a bronze-age hat. Her clothes were tweed and wool and her shoes had leather laces. Her lips, a set of painted-on cupid-bows in vampire red, gave her the look of a garish Queen Mother got up in her Balmoral togs, only Miss Wigg wore this lot every day, in much the way she wore her music. I began to suspect we sang the same tunes because they were all she could play: *Charlie Is My Darling, Will Ye No Come Back Again* and *Westering Home* in a dreary cycle. Miss Wigg, I suspected, didn't like children and didn't much like music either. She was merely sticking it out at the keyboard to pay for her single flat and the budgie whose picture she kept on the desk. Music was how she earned her living till she got home with a box of Trill for some real company. I pictured my mother siding with me, ganging up on Miss Wigg and her mission to make something so *good* so laceratingly awful. *That woman,* I pictured her saying, the way she sometimes did of Rose; *you don't know whether to laugh or cry.*

Miss Wigg's main effort was the school show, an end-of-term everlasting extravaganza where each middle and senior primary class had their moment to shine. The shining took place in the setting of a play with music. A few chosen individuals told the tale in words out front, and the rest of us, an amorphous choir, intoned moral commentary, atmosphere and linking sequences in song at the back. In most of the stories being kind or beautiful or clever won a reward: in *Rumpelstiltskin*, the weird one, the thing that won through for the heroine was cheating and a healthy dose of luck. Miss Wigg chose the actors and trained the choir of leftovers. One girl with blonde hair down to her thighs was always a princess, boys with glasses had a good shot at being shoe-makers and freckly faces made good elves. I was always a chorister. Miss Crossland, the very elderly lady who steered us through P5, thought I'd make a good showing as the princess's miserable sister, but Miss Wigg wasn't keen.

I can't afford to lose her from the choir, she said. You have to rely on someone to *actually sing*. Some of them just make noises, for heavensake. She's my mainstay, Miss Crossland. She's staying put.

That was as close as I came to putting on a costume and being in the spotlight. I was not even the bridesmaid, just one of Miss Wigg's back-row choristers all over again. That I'd failed to make the grade *because* I could sing was what stung. It wasn't fair. The dictionary said a mainstay was a rope on a ship, something strong that secured the mast and let it sail. It didn't sound that great. She meant *workhorse*, my sister said; ask her and see. But I didn't. It was all just a fancy way to say *no*.

In picture after picture of school shows, then, you'll find me at the rear; dowdy in my shirt and school tie, wedged behind fairies and woodland creatures, outshone by hats with bells and face-paint, knowing no one was ever going to sigh with pleasure because I had just come on.

You could have tried harder, my mother said, disappointed again. Alma was a badger this year. Our Kitty won't shut up about it.

Dignity was at stake here, my chance of ever wearing whiskers.
I made a mental note to try.

———

Maybe it was gratitude. Maybe because it was the only way I
could think to try harder. But I wrote Miss Crossland a play. It was
based on the Norman invasion of England and involved a cast of
thousands. The plot was instinctual: a boy warns his village about
the advance of enemy Norman sorts and nobody believes him; he
runs for help and finds the Saxon army in a nearby field and leads
them to rout the Normans in the nick of time; he's killed by mistake, shot through the head by one of his own side with a
poisoned arrow; cue finale with family realising all too late what
absolute bastards they had been to him all along and weeping
without hope of forgiveness. I thought it was heroic and heart-
rending, and I wanted to be the boy.

Miss Crossland smiled. The author, she explained, would *never*
be in their own play. The author stayed behind the scenes. But that
was all finished, I explained. I'd done the writing. It was all ready
to go. Miss Crossland smiled some more and said I didn't understand. If this play was to be performed in class – and she very
much hoped it would be – the work was *by no means* finished. The
author's job, she said, her eyes on a distant and more beautiful
landscape than the interior of room 5b, was not just writing, but
rewriting; working out not only what people said but *why they
said it*. The author's job was to tell people how they might move

and speak. Who else, after all, would know how it went? Battle scenes, she nodded, would be added last. They were called *choreography*. But no, whatever happened, I could not be my own hero. Writing, she said, was not about *me me me*. I had better, she said, get my thinking cap on.

I was appalled. It was like being sent to the back of the chorus all over again, only without the rest of the choir. I'd written it, and now I had all this other stuff as well. The cast would have all the fun and I had the hard work. And even if I did it all, even if I could fathom out how to do everything she said, I couldn't think of a reason why anyone would listen. I imagined standing on a chair and telling Donald McKie, Irene Waters and Alan Paxton to fire arrows at Brian Coultard, who, as the only child likely to be able to memorise it, would surely get the role of the boy for himself. I almost wept.

Miss Crossland, oblivious to my despair, encouraged the class to make costumes. Children turning balloons into *papier-mâché* helmets with nose-guards, and careful cutting out of swords and cloaks took over the classroom for days while I tried to come to terms with what I had done. I had inflicted this upon myself. When chain-mail hand-knitted from string and sprayed silver by the wearers' own mothers started coming in, I told Miss Crossland I couldn't cope. She'd have to take over or call the play off. I couldn't do all this. I had no idea how. Miss Crossland was in no mood.

You wrote it, she said accusingly. You think you'd know what comes next, surely?

No, I confessed. I had no idea. Neither had Miss Crossland, only she didn't have to say so. It dawned on me I was turning pink and wasn't sure if I was angry or embarrassed. Miss Crossland was not focused on my mental state. She was *very disappointed*. Trailing her eyes from me slowly, she called off the whole show. Children took their silver Norman shields home and sheathed their bow and arrow sets. I gathered up my hand-written sheets and we called a halt. Next day, we had sums and story time and the Normans were consigned to the past, leaving the sulphurous whiff of blame behind.

I had nightmares for days, but even then it wasn't done. Six months on, Miss Crossland told my mother at parents' night I lacked sticking-power. Cleverness was nothing, she said, without sticking-power. It needed to be drilled home. My lack of nerve had let *the whole class* down.

My mother looked apologetic and so did I. I had written another play but this didn't seem the right time to say, and in any case, Miss Crossland wasn't done.

Strength of character, she said. It comes from the home, you know. She looked my mother up and down. Children without a strong lead can go right off the rails if we're not careful.

We, she said *we*. I knew, however, it meant *me*. I had come first in my first exams but it didn't seem to matter as much as this. Who needed to be careful was *me*.

We breezed straight into the living room when we got home and my mother spilled the beans from a great height.

Well, she said, still unbuttoning her coat. I've heard some things tonight.

Cora didn't look up. My mother kept right on going.

The teacher says she's clever but she's got nerves. The teacher says she *starts* OK, but she's got no sticking power. She lets the *whole class down*. Cora, organising different-coloured wool strands under a cloud of exhaled smoke, shrugged.

The teacher says she's got to watch her step.

There you are, Cora says. It's got no pals except that fat lassie and that yokel with the haircut.

The teacher says she's needing some sense drilled into her or she could go off the rails. That was what she said: *off the rails*.

Cora snorted. It dawned on me there was something about this she was enjoying and it wasn't fair. I'd been brooding about Miss Crossland the whole walk home and that hadn't been fair either. I had written the play all right, but the teacher was the one who had turned it into something else. Now *friends* were getting lumped in there as well.

She canny be trusted, Cora said. That's basically what the teacher's telling you. That's how come she's got no friends. You think about it. She's got *no friends*.

That wasn't true. Friends, or people who might be, *came* all right: they just never came back because they weren't allowed in or I had the shopping to do or Cora roared at them because she was still asleep and they'd rung the bell. While I was thinking this, Cora served her ace.

And she neglected that bloody goldfish. Remember? I got her a goldfish and it died. She can be trusted with damn all.

I went to the bedroom, not caring I'd left without asking, and hid at the bottom of the wardrobe with my mother's navy courts, breathing in the musty perfume of worn clothes. From the wardrobe floor, I could see the dressing mirror, my reflection inside it. My school tie stripes stretched and wobbled through the water on my eyeballs, the ribbon in my hair, loose and straggling over one shoulder, shimmered like a live snake. At this angle my hair looked almost red, syrup-coloured, against the black blazer. Nobody liked him and nobody liked me either. It wasn't *fair*. My mouth silted with running salt water, dripping on to my blazer sleeve. The damn thing would have snail-trails in the morning. Even in the wardrobe, out of harm's way, I couldn't be trusted to keep my own nose clean.

Cora brought home an Italian called Silvio. He was a waiter at a proper restaurant, a fancy place her boss had taken her to in Glasgow. The only proper restaurant I could think of was the one in Lewis's in Argyle Street where we had ice-cream when we went Christmas shopping once. The ice-cream came in a cone-shaped glass with a long-handled spoon and a cherry and I didn't spill any. I was four and had worn white gloves, the way girls out-for-the-day did, and got every fingertip filthy on the train home. I could imagine why Cora liked him. Silvio had a sharkskin cloth suit, thin lapels and a neat string tie. His accent was so thick you could eat it with a spoon and he looked, my mother said, like Mario Lanza. He brought her a box of chocolates as a present – *for*

Cora lovely mama – and she all but swooned. When he patted his knee for me to sit on it, however, things tipped too far. It was the kind of thing people did with babies. Cora poked me till I did it, though, and I perched on his shiny knees and tried not to run while he stroked my hair and chucked me under the chin. I tried, but not enough. Cora was annoyed at me when he'd gone. She said I was a cold fish and a funny bugger and she'd never been so affronted in her life.

If he doesn't want to come back here, she said, it's *your* fault. I hold you responsible.

Silvio went out with Cora another twice and my mother got excited.

If she likes this chap, you never know, she said. It's maybe a chance for her, eh? Anyway, I've got my fingers crossed. Don't you say nothing.

That weekend, Cora thumped me for bringing back not just one but two forbidden books from the library. I don't know what possessed me. Maybe it was the picture on the cover, maybe the librarian had warned me off. For whatever reason, I brought them and got my just deserts.

Edna O'Bloody Brien, she said. I can't read this. She knows damn well. The book missed my ear by inches and I didn't duck. I drew her a look instead, one of those cool looks she did so well herself. This mistake was the more serious. Cora tanked up the hallway and belted me hard enough to set me sprawling against the bathroom door, where I ricocheted, fell, and cracked my face against the enamel lip of the bath. My nose bled like a tap. I hung

over the bath in time – we had a new pink bathmat – and kept my
shirt clean, but the towel was scarlet. While my mother called
Cora names in the background, I checked it wasn't broken. It
seemed fine. There was no need for a doctor, not even a plaster.

She's a bloody irritant, her, Cora roared. It wouldn't have been
so bad if she hadn't fell. Anyway, she *asks* for it.

Then, horribly, she burst into tears and went out in her slippers,
banging the glass door shut. My mother didn't know what to do
and started wringing her hands. I got the paint from the coal-
shed and touched in the chip on the door surround for something
to do. And my mother did a remarkable thing. She put her hand
on my shoulder and said she was sorry. Cora shouldn't do that,
she said. I'm sorry she hit you. When I said nothing back she
sighed and made herself a cup of tea. Next day I had a black eye
as broad as a plum and Cora looked as though she'd been crying
again. It was worse than being thumped. I kept my head down
and took the Edna O'Briens back but the library was shut. Having
gone that far, I strolled past the Music Shop and looked in at the
pianos, meshed behind a safety grille for the weekend. The same
two pianos had been there all year. Maybe nobody wanted them
either, but it didn't seem conceivable. One thing that had to be
sure of its welcome in the world was a piano. In the afternoon, I
threw out bread for the birds because it was frosty but Mr Gregg's
pigeons came and ate the lot.

Cora didn't go out that weekend and Silvio didn't show. She
was moody and silent. I had nightmares off and on about falling
through trapdoors, woke with my heart thumping.

Stop that, my mother said, turning in her sleep next to me. Lie at peace.

Eventually, Cora came clean. She and Silvio were no longer an item. She dumped him because it was getting too serious, she said. He was telling her what to wear. At any rate, he was gone. Any notions my mother had that she might have an Italian in the family or that Cora might turn her face to happiness, family life and a home in sunny Barga went with him. Cora was home every night and knitting like a machine.

He was a nice chap, that waiter, my mother said. She said it for years after, wistful and not letting go. They say Italians are good to their mothers.

The lousy school year wound down to a lousy finale. On the day of my tenth birthday, Mr Waverley belted the whole class for disruptive behaviour. Miss Crossland was taking a phone call in the office. William Shannon said she'd only gone out for a fag and Danny McFairlie made big, dramatic gestures of puffing out smoke, generating mild hysteria. It wasn't rowdy, but Mr Waverley must have been passing and opened the classroom door. He chose the same moment that someone inside flicked a ball of crushed paper, and the paper bounced, incongruously cheerful, off his chest and on to the polished floor. And Danny McFairlie, still high on his hilarious impression of ancient Miss Crossland inhaling, laughed.

Mr Waverley gave us three chances like in a Fairy Tale. Whoever did it should come forward now. Nobody did. Danny McFairlie, weeping, tried to deny he had laughed out of anything other than nerves and Mr Waverley banged his fist on the nearest desk and told him he didn't want to hear excuses. There was nothing but the headmaster breathing down his outsize nose and Danny snuffling like a puppy. Then, choosing his moment, Mr Waverley slipped the tawse out from under his jacket. He held it up to the light as though it was a diamond and told us to stand. As if there was no choice, we stood. When scraping of desks and chair legs had stopped, he told us to form a line around the inside space of the classroom. And one by one we raised our hands as instructed and let ourselves be thrashed. Once each, over the palms: a single, heavy, downward swing. Even George Crawford with the neck like a bull winced.

Ian Carr, a scared little boy with slicked-down hair, had the worst time. He pulled his hands away and had to repeat the ritual of raising them up three more times, becoming more frightened with each repetition. He dropped on his knees when the tawse finally made contact, tucking his hands beneath the armpits of his school jersey to deaden the sting. Ian Carr that wouldn't have said boo to a goose was belted twice. We watched him get back up off his knees to let it happen, Mr Waverley's Marcel waves tumbling out of their careful alignment with the force of the swing. I nearly copped it twice myself for dumb insolence. It was my only resistance then, but I was very good at it. I could melt his eyeballs, I fancied, with a look, if I really wanted to, but I lost my nerve when he looked back. Just like everybody else.

These were unsettling times. I had thought that growing up's consolation was that you could escape from the arbitrariness of things, that somehow one acquired more control. Now here I was in two numbers till I was ninety-nine and it wasn't true. Growing up was just more of the same, but taller. *Rumpelstiltskin* was right; what happened was all luck. There was no logic to any of it.

14

You're a big girl now, she said.

I was doing homework on the fireside rug, making circles bisect and colouring in the ellipses.

I'm saying you're a big girl. My mother looked over the top of her specs and stopped trying to thread the big darner, blue wool dangling from her fingers.

I've got a chance for full-time. What do you think? I looked up and didn't think anything. She licked her fingers and rolled the wool tip, had another go. You can do your homework or something till I'm back. OK? We'll get a bit more money if I work full-time. So maybe I should take it eh?

Jesus, Cora said, don't *ask* her – she's ten. Just tell her, for crying out loud. She'll be fine.

OK, my mother said. She'd managed the threading, was moving on to the careful placing of a button band. I'll get her a key, then. I could get a key cut.

Don't be daft, Cora said. She'll just lose it.

She could put it on a string or something.

Name of god, Cora sighed. She unleashed a fresh ball, tied a tight knot. That's the daftest idea I ever heard. You give her a key and she'll let people in. Either that or somebody will take it off her. She can wait in the fresh air. It's good for her. She'll be fine. Sure you will. Tell her you'll be fine.

You'll be fine, my mother said. She smiled limply, pushed her needle, punctured her thumb and had to get a plaster. She hurt herself, my mother. I noticed like it was the first time. Her hands had rough skin on the knuckles, a snail-tracery of healed wounds. I made a point of sharpening four HBs with a razor blade and not hurting myself once, a demonstration for anyone in any doubt. I was, and would be, perfectly fine.

As it turned out, I liked the change. After school was now out-doors and all mine. The house locked behind me, I took to sitting on the doorstep like a stray, reading, doing homework with a pencil. Except for the odd baby in a pram or a toddler that had mistakenly teetered along from the Springvale Street tenement lets, I was the only child in the street. I parked myself on my schoolbag for warmth and slid my hands inside my blazer sleeves to keep my knuckles from rusting if it was frosty. Our cul-de-sac was more or less secret: the only regulars were people who lived here and every last one of them was quiet. Birds sometimes landed near the empty floral borders, pecking at the stiff ground in the hope of luring worms. The cat that tottered along the back garden wall came to be stroked. Its coat was an old shag carpet, gritty with lack of hoovering, but the purring was cheerful. It made you warm just to listen. Hedgehogs appeared by the side gate, snuffling their way under leaves, but they were boiling with fleas and best left alone. If it rained there was the coal-shed, door open so the light cut the outline of the cobbler's lasts huddled in the corner. In with the smell of damp coal dross, the old navy-coloured doll's pram, there was peace. The pram had rusty little nut and screw joints to let the hood swing, like a Swiss watch. Guarding against spiders, touching nothing in case I got my blazer filthy, I listened to rain pot-shotting the corrugated roof for hours. When snow fell, my footprints were next after the arrowheads left by the pigeons. I pushed miniature snow-drifts off single blades of grass to watch them melt and fade down the sides of my fat, pink thumbs. On TV, snow always happened in tandem: there were other people to pelt, to slide with down street-long slicks of ice. Maybe the kids up the scheme did that kind of thing: then again, maybe the telly made it all up. Maybe lots of children played alone. Sometimes I wished there were other people to share it with, but mostly I didn't. Rubbing my face with cracked ice off a puddle to feel the circulation sting, pushing my fingers into the mud in the garden to make drinking pools for blackbirds, I found plenty to do. Cora was right. This was good for me. Whatever else went with being a big girl, I could cope with this bit no bother. I was perfectly at home locked out with the wild things, waiting.

A man turned up at the door with a record player. He pulled up outside in a car and strolled up the drive in a uniform, but he wasn't the police. He wasn't Sandy or Uncle Angus or Mr

McFarlane upstairs either. My mother opened the door and wasn't surprised.

Hello, Duncan, she said. She was smiling and trying not to. He almost kissed her on the cheek then he saw me and bustled into the living room instead, smiling under the skip of his hat. The big wooden box was under his arm: the full weight, one arm. Mum came in after him, dancing like Chubby Checker.

Record player, she said. You can sit plates on it when you've finished your tea. It's functional.

She tried to shuffle it into place across the carpet, puffing against her asthma, and the man looked shocked. He took over, shifting Cora's chair with his feet and slotting the box neatly into the last remaining yard of living-room space. It looked like a child's coffin with legs. Everyone was thrilled.

Stereo system, the man said. He took off his hat and winked at my mother. Very nice, he said. Very swish.

His temples were grey. My mother came over limp and grateful and I noticed she had lipstick on. Just as well we know someone with a bit of muscle, eh? she said. You can change a light bulb in the kitchen while you're here, she said. He didn't say no. He put the hat under his arm and tested a window catch, said they needed oiling. Both me and my mother smiled.

Watching him here in the living room, pressed for space even to turn around in, I grasped this was the kind of thing men did. They took up lots of space, but they were *handy*. I'd seen it on TV and now here it was for real right in front of my eyes. He knew about oiling hinges. He'd shifted the heavy record player and wasn't even pink from the effort. The house smelled of outside from his uniform, fresh like rain, and before he left, he'd put up a light bulb. I bet he wouldn't even need a ladder, the height he was. He'd just reach. Cora came in wearing her dressing gown with all the buttons done up for once and said *Hello you* as though she knew who Duncan was. She gazed at the record player to catch up with the rest of us then had a crack at turning the knobs. Until then, it hadn't occurred to me the box did anything much or needed testing to prove its worth. Cora, even straight out of bed, was thinking ahead. The speakers fuzzed and made alarming space-age noises, then something recognisable hiccupped through the crackles. Everyone tilted their heads like doctors listening to a heartbeat. It was the Beatles singing *Help!* Hooray! my mother said and started twisting and Cora turned the radio off, embar-rassed. My mother danced all the time to music on the telly, but I guessed it was the man being here. Dancing in front of *real people* was different.

Well, it works, she said, drawing an end to festivity. We all looked pleased. My mother dusted the wood suddenly with her sleeve then stood back. I suppose we'll have to buy records now.

We gazed at the record player and thought about the implica-tion of its name. It was true. We had to buy records.

Like everything else, my mother said. One thing leads to another. It's all money these days, eh?

At least you've got full-time, the man said. A wee bit extra for nice things, eh? He knew all about her. I liked the idea of *nice things*. I hadn't put work together with *nice things* before.

I get more caramel cake now, she said. I'll be losing my figure. She patted her hair and Cora rolled her eyes, but the man liked it. He liked my mother being pleased and laughed with real teeth. You could see the fillings. He laughed as though she had made a sparkling joke fit to tell all his friends then looked at his watch and said he had to scoot. He looked back and gave a cheery wave through the window of his car. I waved back and he looked me right in the eye and winked. He put the skipped hat back on, checked it was straight in the rear-view mirror, scratched stubble on his neck as he drove away. He had hairs on his arms, a heavy watch. A big, man's watch.

Our first record was a Cliff Richard single. It was my mother's fault. She bought it because she'd seen Mr Richard in *Summer Holiday* pretending to drive a bus and she thought Cliff had nice eyes. Cora thought he was a drip but we listened to it once. We also had a huge LP of a singer called Robert Goulet and played through a whole side, sitting rapt in the pauses while the needle arm went gently up and down like a boat at sea. Six songs at once took discipline but we persisted. Before long, we could be well behaved through Mario Lanza and Gordon MacRae, attending to the music and the words. These were songs after all. The words mattered very much. I say *we* but do not include Cora. Cora couldn't sit for five minutes without making remarks and mum said she took the magic out of everything, so *we* was me and mum when Cora was doing something else. Even then, we did not listen as an activity in its own right. She cleaned and dusted, listening at the same time, and I pretended to build things with Lego. We listened secretly, almost sideways, homing in on the voices without showing too much enthusiasm, as if we were afraid we'd be too rapt, too caught up, too carried away. Or at least, too afraid to show it. But I was rapt all right, goodness yes indeed. I was carried away halfway through castles and houses into dizziness and a vacant stare, the Lego pieces making only the merest cover for forbidden absorption. Mr Lanza was exciting and the high notes carried all the dangerous thrill of full-to-bursting balloons, but tenors were nothing to baritones. Mr Goulet and Mr MacRae had dark, manly voices that pitched and coiled in swooning downward spirals, that gripped then rumbled along the floorboards so the carpet rippled. Every song seemed a miracle: a man came off those big black plates and along a needle into the room. If the volume was loud, my mother said she felt as though the singers were hiding behind the curtains, ready to come out and share the joke. She plumped up cushions in case they did, let her head reach beyond normal things to fill with *moons, Junes* and *golden chances passing by*. Cora still had her own opinions.

It's OK, she'd say. But you canny imagine an *actual man* saying it. *If ever I would leave you*, for goodness sake. It's daft and soppy.

And my mother would turn the men and their voices off. Listening with Cora spoiling the mood was pointless. It wasn't that Cora didn't try. She brought home some borrowed Elvis from the office and gave it a spin, but she'd rather have gone to the pictures. *Blue Hawaii* with no Elvis to look at wasn't that great, she said. She wanted to *see*. As I recall, she didn't listen to the record player again except in passing till we got a Tom Jones LP, and that was a couple of years down the line. I, however, did. I even listened *alone*. On the odd occasion when Cora was out and mum went to Kitty's I could choose what I liked from the handful of discs and be private with the chaps, but it was never entirely comfortable. Even when you didn't have to hide your face or pretend not to be excited, listening was more than it seemed. You could ignore the radio or the TV without feeling rude: they were *background*. A record was different. You *chose*, which meant you made the invitation. You could no more ignore the singer than ignore a visit from Uncle Tommy. Only there was *nobody there*. So you listened inside your own head, drawn deeper and deeper in to show you were pleased they'd come, that they'd put on this private concert just for you. You had no option, alone with the music, but to *receive*. It needed nerve. Especially when you closed your eyes. More than once I started crying with no warning during *If I Loved You*, or the Serenade from *The Student Prince*. It happened without my say-so and if Cora had walked in while it had me in its grip, I'd have had to kill myself out of shame. So I rationed my listening, thought twice before plunging in. Then, as I'd learn to do years later with sex, would effect the blankest of faces in the hope I'd look as though I hadn't done it at all.

I wasn't stupid. I knew the words were soppy and that real men probably didn't say those things out loud. I knew the noises were the manipulations of machinery, a trick of the ear married to electricity, that whoever had created these lovely phrasings had been miles away or could even be dead now and that none of it was meant, specifically, for me. *But it felt like it was at the time*. It felt that these men were close enough to touch, their chests rising and falling with the breath it took to make noise as good as that. And with these living, breath-filled voices, they were telling me something. Even if I didn't know precisely what it was, the meaning of it was certainly *there* and huge. I had no explanations, no excuses; just a driven, clandestine desire to listen more; an equal fear that I should, in everyone's best interests, stop. My mother came home with a Liberace LP somebody at work had lent her, and I melted into a mortifying heap listening to a tricked-up *Revolutionary Study* and two Chopin preludes and was ready to agree with Cora. It was safer to watch. Thank god and three cheers for the telly.

Like a magic colouring pad and not a proper book, telly didn't ask much. It was pictures and the words spoken for you, a self-confessed show. You could watch it in slippers and pyjamas with a plate of toasted cheese on your knee, the fireside tongs with thistle tops in full view, and not worry. You could talk right through what was happening and nobody's nose was out of joint. You didn't invite the performers, they were there anyway, inside the box at their appointed hours, getting on with it. Telly was detached, and while it was true there was nobody like Elvis in the gorgeous stakes, we could watch other entertainers trying to be like him if they fancied. A talent competition and beauty parade in one, telly brought us men.

Our house welcomed crooners, comedians, actors and tap-dancing song and dance men. We liked movie stars and newsreaders and players of harmonicas and magicians and Sand-Dancers and men in tights. We liked stovepipe hats and costume dramas. We didn't say no to ventriloquists or quiz-show hosts or naturalists or arts pundits or even politicians though we drew the line at sport. Sport was sweaty and for the gaze of other men. We knew who wanted us, all right. In our front room of an evening, masculine beauty was openly celebrated with shining eyes and frenzied chewing of caramels.

My mother thrilled to Liberace and Russ Conway, men who had no need to look at a keyboard to master it, and who chose to smile with the spare time left over. Russ was British and Liberace was not. All glitter and cuffs and gold-flecked jackets and dickie-bows edged with fairy lights, he killed show-tunes with frills and tinkly filigree and was much too carried away by his own clothes, but in between, he played Chopin and Rachmaninov and Lecuona's *Malagueña*, and *that* was worth putting up with the rest. Who cared if Cora thought he was a big Jessie? Liberace, Jessie or not, made my mother, even in curlers and a housecoat, with her nails broken from scraping chipped school plates, feel faint with gorgeousness.

He's not a Jessie, she'd say pointedly, he's a gentleman. That's what a *gentleman* is, *gentle*. Bloody *gentle*. Don't lecture me about taste, you.

My mother's tastes were clear. Movies with mobsters, brawlers and hard-drinking cow-hands were switched off as soon as sighted. Football tunes were greeted by screaming and racing to the set with the power-button finger already erect. She liked warm men, men who made her laugh, and who sang and played and smiled with all their teeth on show; men who were smart and urbane and were game for flirtation, even if it was only a trick of the light, the ear and the cathode ray.

Cora's tipple was good-time boys with a mean lip. Dark was better than fair, and leather was an optional extra. Me? I was ten. What did I know? The odd glimpse of Cora's dancing partners, Daft Sandy and assorted greasy-quiffed individuals hanging about at cafés; Mr Tough not dying fast enough next door in bed; Mr Waverley with his belt and the school jannie for whom everything was too much trouble; a priest bouncing up and down at my granny's window and Mr Moore from the EU with his free bags of lentils for Harvest Home. A Santa with a stick-on beard and Cora's boss in Glasgow with a manicure. Snotty Dr Hart, old men wanting fags, the boozy crush at Massie's, the butcher, the baker, the candle-stick maker. Soviet-faced Uncle Jack and Uncle Allan with an accordion, and Uncle Angus with his airbrushed fannies in the garage and dad, godhelpus, dad. Where Duncan fit into all this I didn't want to think, but he was there and there was no denying it. *All* men were exotica. Our house rang with their insidious absences, their glorious show before, like dog-roses in summer, they disappeared leaving only a scent of dust behind.

That's that finished, Cora said, taking a long draw. Quick, change the channel before the football comes on then hop it.

She meant me on both counts.

I went through to the cold sheets, the single reading lamp on

my mother's side, and watched the ceiling, listening to the low
drone of live voices and telly in another room, trying to distin-
guish the two. My mother rattled the ventilation grille above the
fire every so often, dislodging soot. There was nothing going on
through there, just two women talking. My head was full of men:
Sammy Davis Junior to Des O'Connor, their stark tuxedos, their
bright, magnesium-flare smiles.

Miss Phillips went to hospital and we got a supply teacher. Miss
MacLean was twenty-two, with dyed black hair in a page-boy
cut and lots of mascara. She was perfectly normal, apart from her
age, till Friday, when she gave us dancing. She kicked us off with
a twist herself to set the ball rolling, then taught us how to Pony.
At the end of half an hour, we could Bunny-Hop and Hitch-Hike
as well. It was so good, she said, we'd have it again on her last
day, one week later. She showed us one more dance, the Swim,
and told us to practise. For her last day, she said, we'd all Swim
together. By the time Friday came around, I could Swim like a
thing possessed, toss my hair out of its pigtail and shake my hips
like a greyhound after a rag. I'd hidden in the coal-shed to get
that good but it was worth it. Miss MacLean was so impressed,
she got me up to do it for the class while Danny McFairlie put on
his best black soul voice and sang *The Clapping Song*.

Woo, Miss MacLean said. Steady on. There's a girl with a
wicked streak trying to get out.

Trendy for the first time in my life, I fell in love with Ena MacLean. I imagine a lot of us did. When the session was over and she'd given us a boiled sweetie each to calm down, three of us, all girls, followed her to the bus stop, soaking up a last look of her black-fringed eyes. When the bus came, I bit off a lock of my hair as a gift.

I'm just a stand-in, she said, holding on to the bus pole. Miss Phillips will be back on Monday and I'll be somewhere else. She's your real teacher. You see and be good to her.

We looked at her, not sure what to say. We had wanted something wild, not this disavowal. It felt too grown-up too suddenly and I felt daft for giving her chewed hair. The bus revved up. To get rid of us as much as anything else, she hollered as it drew away.

I predict you'll all be chasing boys in a fortnight, she said. You'll have forgotten all about me when the boys kick in. Good luck, she said. You'll need it.

We watched her wave as the bus turned the corner, laughing. What she left behind, apart from the love-struck trio, was a new sense of the possible. We wanted fun with lessons. We wanted to be spoken to as though we had ideas. We wanted participation and we wanted it now. Miss Phillips, an upstanding spinster who genuinely liked children and enjoyed her work, liked the change in us as Miss MacLean had said she would. Miss Wigg did not. Her popularity hit a fresh low. The class all but refused to sing *Marianina*, a jolly song about a girl who turned waves into foam, and George Crawford said Jesus Christ loud enough for everybody to hear.

Miss Wigg called in Mr Waverley, who threatened us with the belt then stood in for the rest of the lesson, watching. Miss Wigg's apparent level of enthusiasm shot up in the Head's presence but none of us trusted it. She was just sucking up.

Who would like to play the piano? Miss Wigg beamed. She creased her lipstick moue into a smile. We can all be musicians today, not just me! Nobody spoke. Someone may even have yawned. Come along, she said. Who would like to play? Aware Mr Waverley would turn nasty if no one volunteered, I put my hand up to half-mast but she hauled out timid little Margery Thom instead and showed her where middle C was, then shooed her back to her seat with a triangle. The rest of us were thrown sleigh bells on strings and the instruction to jingle with a BBC calypso recording while Miss Wigg swayed her tweed-covered hips off-beat and tried to look as though she was having the time of her life. It was nothing like a normal lesson, but Mr Waverley didn't know. He simply watched, now and then caressing the tawse on his shoulder as though it was a pet. I thought about Miss MacLean telling us boys would kick in. I observed Mr Waverley preening his length of leather and Miss Wigg simpering across at him ignored and pretending not to be. And out of the blue, I was furious. I rattled my jingle hard when she pointed at our group, and hoped she saw. *I* would like to play the piano, I thought. This girl with a wicked streak trying to get out. Let me at the damn piano. My eyes were watering. *Me*.

Rose heard we had a record player and asked me how I liked it. I liked it fine. Did I want to sing my favourite song? she said. I didn't. Turned shy, have we? she said, her eyebrows arching. Angus, come quick! She thinks she's too big for a sing-song! It'll be boyfriends next! Angus winced. It's a joke, she said, tugging at my cardigan sleeve. Don't look so affronted.

To cheer things up, she suggested we had a crack at the sewing machine in their spare room. There comes a time, she said, for all girls to learn how to sew. You never know when you might need a party frock, she leered. Do you?

The machine was all levers, hooks and metal prongs. Watch, she said, sucking a length of purple thread through twenty different holes, it's easier than it looks. She guided a piece of canvas under the presser foot, turned it, brought it back again to make two rows of stitching. One foot rocked back and forth on the treadle to sink and lift the needle, and the stitches were almost even. That afternoon, I made a bag and Rose sewed a popper on it. When it was finished, there wasn't a thing I could think to put in a square canvas bag with only a popper to hold it shut and it must have showed.

Give it to mum for Mother's Day, Rose said. She'll like it because you made it. Everybody likes something hand-made.

I imagined giving Cora something hand-made for her birthday but pressed on regardless. There was a red satin ribbon in the off-cuts box, and Rose fished it out to thread through the trim little holes along the top for finishing. It looked just the same only with a red line.

There, Rose said. She put it in a brown paper bag and gave me a flower from the garden to go with it. She only had the one in bloom and it seemed a kind thing, to pick your only flower for someone else. I felt mean for not liking the little bag and tried to see it through her eyes. There, she said. Lovely surprise. *Surprise*. The word always brought me out in bumps.

My mother wasn't that great with surprises either.

What do you do with this? she asked when I handed it over, blushing. She opened and closed the popper for clues. What's it for?

I made it, I said. It wasn't strictly true and explained nothing. It's for *you*.

Is it for hankies or something?

Money, I said. If I didn't say something, it might show the whole thing was Rose's idea. It's for loose change. I wasn't entirely sure what *loose change* was, but it made the bag sound useful, as though it stopped unruly pennies from rioting in secret. It stops your money being a mess, I said.

I've got a purse, she said, genuinely puzzled. I tried to look unruffled but the disappointment showed. Tell you what, she said, if I ever have enough money not to fit in my purse, I'll put it in here. She shook the bag as though it might rattle, then said thank you the way she did to the boy round the road who wasn't all there. I wished I had made her a drawing.

Mothers on the TV get breakfast in bed, she said absently. I bet Alma gets breakfast for Marie this morning. I bet her boy mows the lawn. Some people get the works eh?

I went into the kitchen to put the flower in a milk bottle with water to perk it up. It was a narcissus with only a little trumpet in the middle, not like a daff. Prettier. It occurred to me looking at it, I could have put MUM on the bag in chain-stitch to make it more personal, but it was too late now. She put the flower on the kitchen window-sill and the bag in the drawer with the spoons and the Sellotape. It was time for *Family Favourites*. They had a special edition for Mother's Day with some not-very-good crooner singing *M is for the million things she gave me, O means only that she's growing old*. When it got to *R means right, and right she'll always be*, she said well that's a load of tripe anyway, but we listened on. She even sang the last line. *Put them all together they spell MOTHER, a word that means the world to me*. Cora hated *Family Favourites*, but it was Mother's Day so my mother could get what she liked. Besides, Cora wasn't up. We were just putting the radio off when she staggered into the living room in her nightie, holding something up in one hand.

Look, she said. Look at this thing.

It was the machine-sewed bag, waving in the air like a scalp. What's that supposed to be?

I told her it was a Mother's Day present and she belted me round the head with a limp magazine.

You're supposed to spend money, she said. Not *make stuff* at your age. It's Mother's Day for christsake. It's a present for your *mother*. She scratched her ear, yawning; she stretched. You need to grow up, you. I'll get ice-cream later, she said. That's a decent present.

She slithered off in a good mood to put lots of bubbles in a bath and stir them up with the taps on full pelt. While she was in there, I sat in her chair, poking a knitting needle into my wrist till it grazed and seeped blood in a beaded line, then went for a chocolate biscuit. Cora forgot all about the ice-cream. Instead, my mother hauled out a big box of hard-centres and we ate them watching TV.

Who gave you those? Cora asked, a Russian caramel teetering on her lower lip. My mother winked and laughed. Secret Admirer, Cora said. She made a hooting noise. Mum's got a boyfriend, Cora crooned, haha. A Secret Bloody Admirer.

I was about to ask who it *really* was that had given her chocolates, suspecting Kitty, but Tom Jones chose that moment to stride on to the London Palladium stage waving a microphone and nobody wanted to miss it. Whatever – whoever – it was, we all had sugar and the much put-upon stitching of Mr Jones's trousers for company. All else was beside the point. Besides mum didn't have a boyfriend. The idea was absurd. I sneaked a look at her while the Welsh Voice slung his hips from side to side and noticed she was smiling, but only at the inside of the chocolate box. Light shone on her specs as she rustled among the nut clusters. *Boyfriend*, I thought. That'll be the day.

Sandy showed up for Cora.

Proverbial Bad Penny, he said round the corner of the door. He grinned, shifting a plate sideways with his tongue to let us

see he had three new teeth. Should take you dancing, Mrs G,
never mind the lovely daughter eh? You're looking very nice
tonight.

My mother called him a Daft Article, but she checked how she
looked in the mirror.

How's my wee yin? He rubbed his chin on my face to let me
feel the stubble, and I felt nauseous from the distillery smell.
Fine, I said. There was no other answer. I was always fine. He
poked the record player a bit with his fingers and said it was
nice. Yous can open your own dance hall with that, eh? What's
your favourite record? I showed him the Liberace and he pretended to faint. He's a Jessie, he said. You canny like that stuff!
It's terrible! I showed him the Mario Lanza and he reeled like an
actor. Wow, he said. He's too auld. Young things like you are
supposed to like the Beatles eh? The stuff for cool cats. You'll
never catch the boyfriends like your big sister listening to they
auld men.

He was teasing, but I felt stupid, like a little girl. He'd said to
pick a record, a favourite *record*, and we didn't have the Beatles
or I'd have said them. Who didn't like the Beatles for heavensake? I bet he thought I was a freak. I was on the verge of diving
into my show-stopping versions of Ena MacLean's dances in
the hope my Swim would knock his socks off when Cora came
through, which was just as well. I didn't even sing in the house
any more never mind *dance*. I'd never have lived it down. But
Cora showed in the nick of time, wrapped like a movie star in
her new astrakhan-collar coat from C & A and saved me. Sandy

dropped the teasing to check she had gloves. He paid attention to nothing else when Cora hove into view and I had always thought it was the clothes. Now I wasn't so sure. It was her eyes he looked at. They headed off together for the bus, her red nails and long white fingers vivid against the arm of his dark coat as they walked down the path and on to the pavement. I heard her ask when he was going to get a car as they passed the window and he laughed as though she was a real card. He laughed all the way to the end of the cul-de-sac. My mother poked her head under the blind to see what was so funny but they'd gone. Ah well, she said, here's hoping she makes a go of it this time. She held up a candlestick, checked the tarnish on the brass. Tell you the truth, she said, I can't think of anybody else who'd have her.

I couldn't imagine Cora and Sandy *making a go*. Sandy was dependably daft as a brush and I guessed that was what Cora liked about him. She had chased off Silvio, and if mum pushing her made her chase off Sandy by pushing, I'd miss him. Anyway, she was still married to a man in Glasgow so far as I knew. Mum was crazy or desperate if she thought Cora and Sandy would ever walk down the aisle. They were just friends. I said so and she looked at me.

Just friends? she said. That'll be the day that Cora's keen on *just friends*. Well I tell you what – if she thinks I'm here looking after her for ever she's got another think coming. She needs to grow up and settle down.

There was a short pause while we both recovered from the

surprise. Then she coughed and looked at me. What I'm meaning is that Sandy's all right. Her voice was softer now, gentle. I just want her to be happy. You never know – he might just help her steer her life around.

Sandy that couldn't drive a car. Daft Sandy. If I hadn't felt so sorry for my mother, the hopelessness of her dreams, I would have laughed out loud.

———

It was about this time I met Donna. Donna was blonde and blue-eyed and lived on the other side of the wire mesh that ran along my granny's path. My mother knew her already from the Kyleshill dinner queue. Their back green was a wilderness of reed and weeds, clumps of clover and rye grass, but she picked daisies in it and looked over now and then. Donna wasn't allowed to talk to people, but her mother watched me from an upstairs window, her pale knuckles clutching the side of a curtain, and flicked her fingers to give permission.

You never see that woman, my granny said. Bloody *Phantom*.

Shhh, mother, my mum would say. That's not a nice name for the lassie's mother. That's her *mother*.

It was true though. Donna's mother was a mirage that slipped out of, never into, view. I knew she was thin, thin enough to pass for a sci-fi alien or slip between cracks in masonry, and pale enough for her to be known as *The Phantom*. My granny called her *that red-heided whooer*, but that was the kind of thing my granny said. She called all sorts of people *a whooer*. People's mothers were just people's mothers. You might as well wonder about the private business of a rock.

We didn't do much to begin with, mostly made plasticine animals on my granny's step, skipping or noughts and crosses with chalk squares on the front pavement. We talked. After a while, I saw Donna every weekend if she was allowed and sometimes she met me at my school on a Friday. Cora took to calling her *your little friend* in a twee tone of voice and I supposed, after a cautious interval, she was. There had been Colin and Ian before, but both of them melted. Alma was a relative and people at school didn't count. Donna was – I rolled the word about my mouth like a cough drop – my *friend*.

She had opinions and ideas and could recite the plot-lines of TV programmes. She could mime whole *Thunderbirds* plots, the two of us walking up and down Guthrie Brae on imaginary strings being Virgil, Scott, Brains and Mr Tracey. We mouth-to-mouthed the same bottle of home-made pop and sat under the street lights when it got to that time of night, blowing dandelion clocks to guess the hour. We did not discuss families, classmates or what we'd like to be when we grew up. We had no interest in growing up. We discussed puppet-based drama, education, current affairs and the natural world. We told jokes and played games and made sugar water out of sherbet and puddles. We made pretend butcher shops out of plasticine and weeds and put the hairy seeds or rosehips down each other's jumpers. We gathered petals from the park and mashed them in a jar with a

fork and made perfume fit only for throwing away. We walked
along the bridge in the wildest of storms, daring the waves to get
us like they did a boy from Glasgow who died one summer,
swept out to sea by its giant hand, and shivered at the horror of
what surrounded us every day. We chucked bouncy balls at my
granny's side wall under the night-filter of sodium lights, repeating *Mrs Red when to bed and in the morning she was dead* till our
fingers turned blue. It was a race against sunset, the moment
when Donna would be called in by a woman you never saw but
who had, according to legend, red hair. Bright, wild, natural red
hair.

———

All week, Miss Phillips had been getting us to draw pencil por-
traits during Art time. On Friday last thing, she raked out some
thumb-tacks and pinned them up on the wall. It wasn't a competition, she said: it was a gallery. We sat on top of our desks to
admire the view when it was done.

Well then, she said, Where should we start?

First up was a lollipop face and we all knew it had to be Alan
Paxton's. Alan's pencil skills weren't all they could be.

I like this one, Miss Phillips said. It has humour. We marvelled
at her tact. I looked over to see if Alan was pleased but he had no
idea it was his drawing we were talking about. His attention skills
weren't too great either.

This one now, she said, pointing a few drawings along, the one with the missing tooth here. It's someone's wee brother. Am I right?

We saw him up there at the gates all the time. Esther's mum brought him when she collected Esther. It was a good picture. We were all enjoying this. This one was exactly like someone she knew, this one with the hat had to be someone's next-door neighbour on holiday, this one looked like a film star. We had the sun on the backs of our necks, the knowledge that the bell for end of lessons was not far off and the weekend was ahead. I was desperate for her to pick my drawing before it was too late. We had had a rocky moment the week before when I broke a fresh stick of chalk by accident when she'd just taken it out of the packet. If she said something nice, it would show there were no hard feelings. She did Margaret Hastie's and Brian Coultard's – they had drawn their fathers – and Jeannie Chapman's, a picture of herself with ringlets and hair clips all in place. Margery Thom had drawn her dog and George Crawford had done his grandpa being angry. Time was nearly up. I was putting my pencil back in its case when she picked one I recognised.

Now this one, she said, I get the feeling she's just had bad news. Is the old lady sad?

Nobody answered. Miss Phillips checked for a raised hand while I stared at the picture, trying to see it through a teacher's eyes. I had sketched the portrait as she watched television and hoped I'd made her lovely. I had put in the grey hair because it was there, and the frown lines between the eyes. They weren't quite right yet, but it was a reasonable likeness, right down to the wing-tipped specs, the twin reflections of TVs inside them.

Whose is this? Miss Phillips chimed, impatient for a confession. I had to tell her. The sad old lady was mine.

Is it your grandmother? she said.

No, I said. I swallowed hard. No. It's my mother.

Somebody sniggered and I blushed. Well, said Miss Phillips. I'm sure she looks younger in real life.

Her mother's ancient, Margaret Hastie said. I've seen her.

That'll do, Miss Phillips said. That's rude.

Margaret Hastie did not look abashed but at least she shut up. Miss Phillips nodded. I wanted to say my granny had a glass eye and really was ancient, that my mother looked nothing like her. But Miss Phillips hadn't the time. The bell was due to ring, and she wanted to end on a high.

Now this – she stretched a long arm and pointed – this lovely clown! It makes you smile just looking at it. It's Suzanne's, isn't it?

It was, it was. Suzanne sat next to me and I had watched her do it and thought it childish. Suzanne came from a pretty bungalow a stone's throw from the school and her mum was a skinny lady with specs who kissed her at the school gates and didn't care who saw. Everything in the picture showed it.

You're a ray of sunshine, Suzy, Miss Phillips said. Suzanne, and her portrait, beamed.

The thing about my mother being ancient plagued me all the way over the railway bridge and down Springvale Road. It wrestled, fighting to make me unhappy for no reason I could pin down. If it was true, it made her or me deficient in some way; if untrue, Margaret Hastie would need to be brought to book for the insult and my mother might conceivably have a boyfriend after all. However you looked at it, it was terrible. Back home, things were no less confusing. The door was open and the record player man, the man who lifted heavy things with one arm, was perched on the living-room sofa. Hello, he said, slightly sheepish. He put out his hand. Remember me? Duncan, I said. Unaccountably, he looked thrilled to bits.

My mother was in the kitchen putting biscuits on a plate, fussing with a milk jug. Half-day, she said. Surprise. There was a box of chocolates on the draining board, still sealed, a big pair of workman's leather gloves. She had lipstick on the apples of her cheeks and smelled nice when she moved to turn the tap. Duncan was an old friend, she said. They had met up in town, fancy that. I trailed her down the hall with the biscuits, irritated. She didn't notice. His children had gone to the same school as Cora, she said, but they were all grown up now, wasn't it funny.

Oh yes, Duncan smiled. I'm a granddad. His big waxed-cotton pockets creaked as he brought out a huge handful of paperclips. They were a present from the fire-station, he said. I'd be surprised what they had in there. If I wanted 5B pencils or insulating tape, he was the very man.

I sat on the rug trying to be less grumpy and making a spy gadget with the paperclips while they had tea and chatted about dull stuff: who'd got married, who'd moved house, the weather and old times. It was soft – no sudden shifts of tone or mood, just talk. He told my mother she looked nice in that dress and she said *oh for goodness sake, it's just an old thing* and patted her hair. Me and your mum go way back, he said, talking to me as if it mattered to join me in. I remember you in a pram and look at you now. You're a big girl.

I sat up and looked at him then, tried to take it in. He was someone who went back further than me. I suddenly wanted to ask if he'd known my father but didn't. Duncan's hat was on our window-sill, I realised. He was in our house and perfectly at ease. Not only that, but my mother looked animated. She looked radiant. Umpteen times, horsing about with old clothes in the back bedroom, she had held up an old frock in front of her reflection and said *I was good-looking once. I had the best legs in Saltcoats*. And looking at her now I could see it. It wasn't Cora's kind of good-looking; it was another kind, one that took longer to register, but there all the same. It didn't come off with the make-up. She looked like the Queen, I thought, but older. One streak of white coiled back into the curls that framed her face like an exclamation of surprise. Maybe Margaret Hastie was right. Maybe my own mother was an old lady, already half way to one hundred. With a sudden shock I remembered Cora saying *Secret Admirer*. Duncan's hair was grey with a bald patch. He had white hairs in his nose, but it was him. There were chocolates in the kitchen now, next to his working gloves. It was him all right. I didn't know whether to be embarrassed or not be bothered, and settled for feeling the former whilst affecting the latter. The words *Secret Admirer* whispering in my head made me feel dirty-minded and small. Even so,

I watched them, the way she led him to the door and Duncan held her shoulders, smiling and not smiling at the same time. He kissed the air above my mother's temple and I studied his reaching towards her face, the way the kiss was made by his mouth yet did not connect. By the time I got to the window to wave, Duncan was off down Wellpark Road, a man going back to work. It was his ladders and engines, I remembered. That was what he did. His work was fighting fires. My face, I knew it, was burning.

————

When Donna came over in the evening and chucked stones at the window for me to come out, I was almost settled. We walked up by Carlo's and the phone box at the top of Springvale Road and I asked her if she'd ever drawn a picture of her mother. She said no, she couldn't draw to save her life. I asked her what she'd do if somebody said her mother was ancient if they saw a picture of her and she said she'd punch their lights in. I told her about Margaret Hastie and she looked thoughtful.

Is she big?

No, I said.

Well, she said, punch her lights in. She made spacecraft noises and whirled in circles. I'll do it if you like. You can't have people saying things about your mother. It's not right. I said I didn't feel up to the punching thing. OK, Donna said, pragmatic. Bite her.

I'd been trying for a quiet chat and solutions to life's problems, but Donna wasn't in the right mood. Trying to let it drop, I asked

Donna if a man that might be her mum's boyfriend ever came round her house and she said no. She said no like I'd asked her if she ever strangled kittens with a skipping rope. Whoever told me that was telling a rotten, rotten lie. They were – here her voice broke – a bloody liar.

I said sorry but she left me at Carlo's and headed off to Guthrie Brae crying. Some days you had no idea what you stumbled into.

15

You better have done all your homework, my mother shouted.

I always had.

You better not be late.

I never was.

You better not get into any trouble.

This last was Cora. She liked the last word.

I knew everything they'd say before they said it, hardly listened any more. I was already running as Cora started muttering I was out with that tinker's lassie all the time, over the wall by the time she opined I'd be found dead up a close one day and she wasn't taking the blame. By the time my mother was into a round of *Shut up, you*, setting their evening on track, I'd be in another street entirely, heading for Donna's. Keeping running, in the clear.

I wasn't allowed in Donna's house and she didn't come all that much to mine. We met most often at street-corners, bridges, lamp-posts, the street sides of garden privet hedges, parks. Wherever we met, waste-grounds were where we went, havens of abandoned bramble patches and poppy fields left over from building sites, islands on the concrete that had been let go to rack and

gorgeous ruin. We allowed ourselves to believe that we had discovered them. Like explorers cracking virgin territory, these lands
were ours to claim. We thought of making flags but they'd have
drawn unwanted attention. Instead, we charted their names and
locations in code in an old school jotter and kept it safe in a plastic bag in a clump of bindweed, alongside other treasures lost or
discarded in clumps of long grass and under stones. We hoarded
buttons and slices of broken china plate, spokes from an umbrella
and broken garden shears, ribbons blown from the hair of hapless
little girls. *One day*, Donna howled into the rain, turning her face
up to be drenched, *all this will be yours!* Screaming with laughter,
running like ferrets for the shelter of scrawny sycamores. We were
near as dammit eleven and crazy with freedom and this was our
task in life. No more embarrassing questions about mothers or
men. I couldn't think what had possessed me. We were fine just
the way we were.

Then it stopped. No warning, no clues: Donna just stopped
showing. After nearly a week I knocked at her front door, but
nothing happened, not even a creak on the stairs. My mother,
watching out for her from behind the serving hatches, said she
hadn't been to school. My granny had the idea that Donna had
been taken away because her big brother wasn't right in the head.
It was the first I'd heard tell of a brother at all. My own mother
was shocked.

O for godsake, mother, she said, don't tell her things like that,
that's a terrible thing to say.

He makes models, my granny said. He's up in that room with

wee tubes of glue all the time and disny go to work. He keeps razor blades in his overall pockets. Everybody knows he's off his rocker.

Her voice was rising and my mother sent me outside to play. It wasn't much of a distraction. Outside my granny's was side-on to Donna's house, the empty clothes-line, my granny protesting at the top of her vocal range inside. *It's the truth*. The bits of brocade cloth tied up at the windows did not move. Nobody showed.

The woman in the shop at the end of our road said Donna's mother was in a sanatorium, but nothing about a brother. My mother said not to go in that shop again because people who said terrible things like that were poisonous old bats. Nobody else had any better ideas about where she was, though. For all I knew, she had fallen off the edge of the world.

For godknew how many miserable days, I went to the places me and Donna had gone together on my own, but they looked barren, the magic melted into the dry soil. I found broken bottle glass and squashed beer cans, sopping wet toddlers' mitts blown here by gales or carried by strays. Spiders clung darkly in unidentifiable bushes and thorns caught my clothes when I ran, horrified, home.

Donna finally turned up at the streetlamp outside our house, waving so I'd see. She had on a light summer dress with no sleeves and my mother had three goes at giving her a cardigan before she took it as a loan. She swithered at the door, but asked Donna nothing. Not even one question. Neither did I. What she did do was give me sixpence and tell us to go for a walk.

Whatever we did thereafter, we skirted all discussion of families, school, our hopes for the future. We weighed each other up for silence and did not disappoint. I had my friend back. Not entire, but back, and she looked like she'd bolt if I pushed my luck, so I didn't. We spent the sixpence on sweeties, walked along the shorefront, poked about with crab claws under rocks. Whatever we did was less important than the fact of us doing it together. When I left her at the wire fencing round her back green, the sun was setting and dark coming down. She'd not be coming out as much, she said. Not for a wee while. I fancied I saw her mother's hand, skeletal, ruffling the curtains of the upstairs window before it disappeared.

Over the next few weeks, visits to the waste-grounds fell into neglect. Going alone, I thought the treasures looked like junk. I wondered now and then if I should shift the jotter with its maps and drawings back to my house, but Cora would find it. I imagined her turning the pages over in her hands one by one and asking what *this* was supposed to be. So I left it where it was and they built flats on top of where it had been six years later and the flats have no gardens. *Que sera.*

Lonely for company, I turned to something else. *The Observer's Book of British Wild Flowers* was the first real book I bought for myself, acquired with saved pocket-money and a final two bob bit from Uncle Angus. Beautiful in itself, the book was little enough to fit in a pocket, and had small hard covers with a Briar Rose on the front. The pages were sewn into the spine: you could see the white, waxed thread that held the whole show together if you opened it wide. Back home, my mother looked down through her red-winged bifocals and turfed over a page or two.

It's weeds, she said. She looked at the front, back again. Did you buy a book about weeds?

If she read the introduction, I explained loftily, she'd find that wild flowers were not weeds. Weeds were flowers growing in inconvenient places. This wasn't, for goodness sake, a compendium of daft fairy stories or a wee girl's Christmas annual; this was a *real book*. It was facts and pictures and stuff about nature. I could win a Wild Flower Recognition Prize or something like that with these facts. It was an underhand appeal, but it worked. She looked impressed. I could even, I explained, win badges at the Brownies.

You're not in the Brownies, my mother said.

No, I said, rolling my eyes, but I could win badges *if I was*.

You could have got that in the library and not wasted your money, Cora said. That's a stupid sort of book to pay money for.

Well. My mother shrugged. It's her money. I suppose she can do what she likes.

The book irritated Cora enough for her to go out the back door and smoke a whole fistful of Embassy Regals. If she wanted to be huffy it was up to her. I got to sit in the living room alone and read.

The first plant inside was Meadow Rue, every petal in place, every frond and runner delicate as the horns on a garden snail. Campion was the pink thing with playing-card shape petals. Gorse was a clutch of mustard yellow balloons; Tufted Vetch, a clump of exclamation marks livid as bruised arms. We had Meadow Thistle in the flat patch of abandoned land behind the garden wall, Birds Foot Trefoil and Speedwell in the gaps between slabs, Common Catsear round the corner from the sweetie shop, and Coltsfoot with its silver dragon-tooth leaves in the cracks on the back wall. I could look on the shore for Sea Campion and Thrift if I wanted, haul Ragwort up by the roots out the back door. Like sunglasses, the book let things emerge from blinding igno-rance. I marked pages to show Donna when she turned up again and copied some of the pictures into a fancy drawing book Rose had bought me. The whole thing was pleasure.

I had the book nearly a month and as near as dammit memo-rised when it went missing in the school changing rooms. It wasn't even Sports Day, just something new called Outdoor Activities, mostly races and running in circles round the fence. I came last in the Dash and last in the Egg and Spoon. I didn't even finish the Sack Race because I fell. Miss Phillips blew a whistle and said it might be better if I didn't become an Olympic athlete after all, and thought she was smart. I had grass stains on my hands on the walk back to the school building, one pigtail loose and the other unravelling, but at least it was over. Except it wasn't. The book was gone.

I had put it under my jumper and skirt and on top of my shoes, the filling in a sandwich, but it wasn't there any more.

Not under the bench, not under anyone else's stuff, not in my bag either, just gone. Miss Phillips was sorry and helped me look but we found nothing. Mr Waverley came all the way up the stairs to our room and asked the class if they'd seen it, but no one had. Mr Waverley turned from the class to me, looked down the twin barrels of his nose and suggested I only *thought* I'd brought the book to school. Was it possible that this book was still safe at home? I shook my head and started to speak, but he cut me off. Was it possible, in that case, he said, pinking up, that since Miss Phillips could not find it and nobody but you seems even to have *seen* it, that the book did not exist? Brian Coultard started grinning and I felt stupid. Mr Waverley turned to Miss Phillips like he was a normal person, and not someone who had just called me a liar in front of the whole class. And one of them, one of the people who surrounded me now, had my book. I scanned the eyes, looking for guilt or triumph – either would have told me something – but whoever it was wasn't giving much away.

You, Mr Waverley said suddenly, look after things better in future. Your parents will not be pleased if that's how careless you are.

He swept his bits of paper together, the bits of paper he always carried and which I suspected were always the same bits of paper, unchanging, less important than they looked, and left the class in a flurry of dust-motes. I peered into the place he had left behind and hated him. He had told me to look after a book he did not believe existed so he was an idiot and I hated him till I seethed.

Reckless, I stabbed Robert Patterson's rubber and wrote ARSE on it in pen when he wasn't looking.

By the time I was walking home, however, self-blame had kicked in. I had no idea how to look after stuff. I lost things. Things lost me. People lost me. I was useless. I wondered if I should go to the police station and imagined a policeman, kindly and concerned, saying *What's wrong with you then little girl?*, leaning forward to catch my every word, but I couldn't hold it long. I had no idea where the station was, apart from anything else. They might ask for a reward for the finder and I didn't have one. They might even laugh. Policemen didn't look for lost books. Godknew who did, but it wasn't policemen. The whole thing was a nasty, dead-end mess.

I said nothing at home. Cora was out. I went round for Donna but she didn't show. There were no distractions from loss. My book was gone and there was no hope of buying another. Even if I'd had the money there were no more in Rankin's. I would never be able to own up I'd lost the damn thing either. I couldn't face Cora crowing, my mother looking sad and wise and saying exactly what Mr Waverley said she would: *look after your things better*. The only way out was jumping in the Galloway Burn, but I knew I wouldn't do that either. I had to face the fact that I was useless.

Stalling for time, I went down the shorefront to the pagodas and watched the seagulls. When it got darker and too cold, I walked back past the memorial statue to the fallen of the First World War – GIBSON, GIBSON, GILL, GILLIES, GRAHAM,

GRIER, GRUBB, not one with the same name as me – then through the stretch of open ground called the Glebe, past its two shut tennis courts, the putting green, the path to Springvale Street and its adjoining Crescent. There wasn't a soul on the road. By the time I hit the narrow lane between the two sets of tenement backs, the street lamps were making the grass a sickly grey and the sky was completely black. Some people were watching telly with the lights off, bathing their front rooms in flickery blue, like aquariums. I was nearly home when the man appeared.

Not even a man to begin with, only a shape and a voice, pitching out of a blind close-mouth at the side of the lane, and asking for a light. I could see already he wasn't holding a cigarette, and was hovering too near the opening he'd come from. He didn't move for a moment, and neither did I. Neither of us spoke. It didn't feel right and it didn't feel good. The best thing, I knew from Cora, was just to keep walking, but as I tried to put space between us, curving away from where he stood, he reached an arm, missed, and reached again. This time, he got my shoulder. I felt it tug, the whole grab of grey wool V-neck bunching away from my skin and into his fist, hauling me sideways. He stumbled me against the wall, pinning my breastbone with his forearm to make me stay in one place. I could feel cold moss pressing against my school shirt-sleeve, my neck brushing the elbow of his jacket. I had enough visibility to see he'd backed us into the shadows, a place where overlooking windows would not see, enough alertness to notice his aftershave. Lots of aftershave. It was not what I expected and I looked up, wanting to see his face, who it was that did this kind of thing. There were his eyes, part of a mouth. A voice. I was coming with him. He sounded strained but the words were clear enough. You're coming with me.

Instinctively, I stiffened. I didn't fight, I didn't speak: I just did what I was good at and turned rigid as concrete. Refusing down to the bone, I locked my eyes on his, hard, and tried to hurt him just by looking. There wasn't much light, but the sheen on his eyes was bright. He looked young, certainly in his teens. His eyebrows were heavy, his mouth a plain slit. He shoved my shoulder one more time, reaching with the other hand for my grey skirt waistband, then looked back. That was what I wanted. I couldn't fight. But I wanted us to meet, eye to eye; for him to know and understand that I was taking in every detail, observing his face so I'd never forget. The arm that pinned my chest buckled slightly, but I didn't seize the opportunity. It wasn't in me. I didn't run. He did.

Maybe it was the school tie. Maybe he realised I was ten and that wasn't what he was after. Maybe it really was how I looked at him, making my eyes small, mean. But he dropped me like an empty wrapper and ran.

I moved into the light as his footfalls faded, tracking every one to make sure they kept going. The sound said he had run down Springvale Street to the corner shop then on to the train station, then nothing. I waited where I was till there wasn't even the echo left, steadying my breathing, keeping my ears keen. The close-mouth was just a black space with washing poles on one side. Skin crawling, but in no rush, none at all, I started walking and kept going the hundred yards or so to home, eyes on the road slabs. And walked straight into a wall of waxed cotton. Scared enough to jump, I looked up and it was Duncan. Duncan's waxed-jacket coat arms bracing mine, his face startled.

Steady, he said. You'll get into bother, not looking where you're going. He was smiling, uncertain. Are you all right?

Yes. I nodded, teeth chattering like matches in a box. Of course I was. I was always fine.

He was just round to see mum, he said. She wasn't feeling so good. And he brought me some drawing paper to draw flowers.

She says you've a lovely book, he said. You like flowers, eh?

I said nothing. He held on to my shoulders and I wondered if he could feel me shaking under the layers of wool and cotton.

Well, he said. He had to run or he'd be late. He looked again. Are you all right?

Behind him, I could see my mother was watching at the window, her face drawn. She waved once, at Duncan, trying to look more like herself, then came to open the door for me.

You're late, she said. That wee lassie's not allowed out late. Don't you get her into trouble.

She meant Donna. She thought I had been out with Donna.

No, I said, I won't.

Her nose was red and the rims of her eyes pink. You'll be wanting your bed then, she said, smiling a smile that wasn't. Maybe she had a headache. She got migraines off and on. Maybe this was one of those times.

Yes, I said. I'm tired.

Her shoulders dropped. On you go then, she said. Early night.

I'll be through in a minute. She sighed deep enough to swim in. It's time we both had an early night.

I lay in bed listening to the sound of running water from the bathroom, wondering how to say anything at all. I didn't look after stuff and I couldn't fight for toffee. Telling anyone else wouldn't help. I fell asleep eventually. I know, because my mother getting out of bed woke me up. The bedside clock said after two in green painted letters, the hands shiny in the half-dark, and light was coming in from the kitchen. Her pillows were on the floor. I called her name and she told me to get to sleep. There was nothing to worry about. I should get to sleep.

Next thing I heard was Sandy greeting. *What did I do this time? What did I do?* His voice came through two walls. *Shut up,* Cora roared, *just shut the hell up. This is not about you.* Listening to them fighting, the morning fishing through the fibreglass curtains, I remembered the book was gone. It was eight a.m. I held both hands up and stared at the fingers, the shapes they made as they spread and closed again. Sandy was weeping in the kitchen, Cora yelling from her room as she left for work – *You let the bugger in, you deal with him.* My mother shouted back. It was time she had a bit of help around here, she said. Some of us had lives of our own to deal with, not just mopping up after other people, mopping up after other people's mistakes. It sounded limp, unsure. Then she was crying too. I could hear everything, but kept my attention on my fingers, stretching them wide till it seemed the skin between might split and bleed and trying, somehow, to let the whole thing go.

Some things last for ever and some things just feel as if they might. Which is which is immaterial – they shift sides, play games, refuse to settle – but you get by. That was what I believed. Whatever your luck, in some shape or other, you got by.

I believed we were lucky people. Things happened to us all the time. I had a notion, gleaned from books and lessons and being inside my own skin that *being lucky* wasn't about winning at bingo or getting an extra bag of salt in a packet of crisps. That was accidents. *Being lucky* meant *things happened in your life*. We were kissed by busy-ness, the requirement to rise to occasions and think on our feet. Your life and your luck were the self-same thing and they carried on regardless, irrespective of your hopes, wishes, desires. All you had to do was last through whatever came towards you, good or bad. All you had to do was hold on tight.

I was only eleven. What did I know? I had no idea that life could be wrong-footed; that your luck might be sidestepped or simply left behind. All you had to do was refuse to greet it. All you had to do was let go.

You're a big girl now, she said. Take the key.

I was only going out to the pictures and wouldn't be late, but she insisted. She was wearing a yellow floral housecoat and no curlers and took the key out of the blossom-pattern pocket, shiny as though it had been recently cut.

Cora's out, she said. I'm not asking, I'm telling. Take it.

Maybe her eyes looked sore, maybe her wedding ring was off. I don't remember.

Donna turned up late outside the Countess and we missed the beginning. It didn't matter. It was *Carry on Screaming*, and keeping on top of what was happening wasn't the point. It had a comedy vampire and werewolves and Joan Simms being dipped in wax to turn her into a shop dummy and lots of jokes about *big ones*. There were breasts with steam coming off them and a woman with a pet werewolf called *Thing*, and we could laugh as much as we liked even if the jokes weren't funny because the cinema was nearly empty. It was first house. The second showing was one we avoided because it was full of young couples being embarrassing, but first house was fine. I didn't understand why breasts were funny, but Charles Hawtrey, a skinny little actor specialising in twits, played Dan Dann the Lavatory Man, and I wanted to watch the whole show again on his account. When Pearl and Dean rolled out their adverts for the second showing, I wouldn't budge. Donna was agitated. When I stayed put during the music and opening scene, all mist and owls hooting, she called in an usherette and got me ejected. Second house needed the seats, the usherette said, flashing her torch: I was just being greedy. The place was still full of empty rows, but I didn't argue. Donna had made her point. She wanted to go home.

Walking Donna back was a promise to my mother. To get out at all, she said, Donna had to say someone would take her home or her mother would worry. If she was leaving, so was I. That was the price of company. That I walked home alone bothered no one much. Maybe I seemed capable.

We strolled out of the Countess past Veronica's shop, still strung with bright-coloured buckets and fishing nets late in the year, then past the chippie to Dockhead Street. After that, it was over the hill to the Labour Club and across the Steel Bridge to the cast-up of shells and sand from some forgotten storm, the shore pitch black but for the ships' lights out at sea. You could see the Heads of Ayr from the beach, Donna said, that's what the glitter was. We watched it till drizzle started up and it rubbed out, like a mistake. Apart from that we didn't speak much. I was too annoyed about her hauling me out of the film to say goodbye properly, and did not wait till she went inside. I may have hoped to hurt her feelings. My granny's door was shut as I went past, her window tightly curtained. I was wearing a blue wool jumper with the sleeves shrunk past my wrists, nylon trousers in an Argyll check, flat school lace-ups. I watched them pacing, one foot after another, the bows on my arches bouncing all the way home.

Turning into the street, I knew something was wrong. The brocade winter curtains hung like ghosts up to dry, unlit from behind. Our lights were never off. Even at night, one was left on sentry in the living room. Not tonight. Cora's bedroom curtains were drawn too, the room lifeless behind, as though everyone was asleep. It was just after nine o'clock. I wondered if maybe they'd gone out to a party. Only we never went to parties. There was nothing for it but to approach the door.

It seemed crazy to ring the bell of my own house, but I did it anyway. The paint was chipped in the right hand side, below the bell press, where I'd picked it with the screwdriver and not made it good again. No one answered. I knocked this time, listening. It was my house and not my house, foreign and unlived-in, like the house in the movie. I rustled in my pocket for the key, the one my mother had insisted I take, and put it in the lock. It didn't turn. There was no need. The door was open. Wherever they were, no one had clicked the latch. Behind the glass interior door the hall-way was a tunnel of echoing dark. I pressed the panel, heard the ball-catch click and release. My own voice, when I found it, was frightening.

Hello, I said. *Hello*.

Nothing happened. Looking up the hallway, facing a mirror reflecting nothing, it occurred I had the wrong house; that my being here was not a dream, but a mistake, a terrible error of judgement. Maybe we had moved and other people were listen-ing to me behind these shut doors. Maybe I was surrounded by strangers. I stood very still for what felt like a long, creaky time. It was cold from the open door, and my ankle, when I let my weight rest square on both feet, admitting I was really here, clicked. That click was the first sound. Then I heard something else. A noise like shuffling over carpet. And sighing: one distinct, deep sigh.

Cora was standing behind me in a nightdress, mascara running in cracks from the corners of her eyes and into her hair. Her eyes were open but she didn't speak. Scared to death, I thudded sharply against the wall, stumbled over my own feet and ran. I heard a voice call out behind me, but I was in no mood to hear. Whatever it was she had to say I didn't want to know alone. I wanted someone else.

My feet took me to the corner of Countess and Vernon Streets and the Keys Bar, where I stopped and looked up at the pub sign, two fat keys like crossbones without the skull. For a whole second I had no idea what I was doing here. Then it struck. That's what she had been shouting. Get Allan. Get Uncle Allan. I knew my mother's brother played accordion in the Keys, and that knowledge, buried, had served me up at the right door. Facing that door now, however, I could go no further. I watched half a dozen men breeze past, gusting the warmth and the sickly beer-sawdust smell outside, and peered past them into the thick yellow light beyond. It was no good. The doors swung hard back into place, not letting me see. Panicked, I touched the long brass handles to open them for myself, but someone stopped me, spreading his hand over mine and lifting them away. You canny go in there, he said. It's a pub. The truth of it made my eyes start to run, and I heard my voice, taut as catgut, asking anyone who might be listening if he knew my Uncle Allan. Nobody answered. One man brushed past me and went straight on in, the doors snapping like a turtle bite behind him. Excuse me, I said, not able for this. *Excuse me*, jesus. I couldn't remember his real name, the one adult men would call him, only *Uncle Allan*. If somebody, finally, hadn't asked me who I was looking for, he would never have known I was there. But someone did. Allan, I said. He played the accordion and his sister was Beth Galloway. The man went inside and left me with my nose running. I heard a shout inside, and Uncle Allan came out in a flurry with the accordion still sprawled on his chest, his breath turning to cloud in the night air. His face fell when he saw me. I don't know who he'd been expecting, but not me. All I managed to say was his name.

After that, everything was fast. I know we went back to the house with two other men, that Cora was in the living room, barefoot with her hair wild, and that Allan went into the back bedroom alone. Cora had been there already and wouldn't go again. I stayed on the front step while people I did not know went in and came back out again, one of them jingling change in his pocket. I stayed there while my mother was carried out on a stretcher, possibly a sheet. I could see Cora through the window, folding a piece of paper in her hands over and over till Allan came and took it off her. He looked once, then crushed it in one hand, eyes still moving over the empty space where the paper had been moments before. There were blue lights and people, the sound of unfamiliar voices tuning in and out like a radio, and closer to, Cora, weeping. And every so often, Uncle Allan shaking her shoulders between the hiccups and saying *how long, how long has she been like that?* In a very short time indeed, all the noises started drifting into each other and fading out, washing back into nothing much against a bigger, more frightening noise altogether. Like helicopter blades veering closer, like water, rushing, like drowning.

No one addressed me directly but I had good ears. I listened.

She had taken pills. She had gone into the bathroom cabinet, the one I had put on the wall, and taken all her asthma pills and some migraine medicine and other things with a cup of tea. Her face had turned blue. But they'd done something at the hospital and she would be coming home. She was being looked after now. She had written a note but keeping a thing like that wasn't healthy so it had gone in the fireplace like a note to Santa. It was best just to keep it quiet: no need to tell the school or anyone else, so for now it was just the wee one and Cora. It was not a place for a wean, a hospital. It was too upsetting, so it was best not to visit. It would be better for both of them to wait till she was home. Kitty wasn't well just now but Marie would come over now and then, make sure everything was all right. Not Rose. You didn't want *his side* knowing anything if they didn't have to. It was all upsetting just now but we would look back and laugh one day. If Allan hadn't come, well, it was best not to think about it. You just hope nobody saw anything. Beth wasn't the type to want anybody worrying. You didn't know whether to send flowers, did you?

I remember Allan saying we would be all right. We were both big girls. We'd be perfectly fine.

Just me and Cora then. Big girls together. It would not have been professional to simply stay off work so Cora took holiday time, kept herself legitimate and above board. The school were told I had a tummy bug. It sounded cute, like something in a

Disney film – *a tummy bug*. Marie came once or twice between
shifts on the buses and looking after her own two kids. Marie
was a dutiful daughter, sunny by nature, and she loved her Aunty
Beth. She said it often. *I'd do anything for my Aunty Beth.*

The witch in the corner shop asked if my granny was all right
and I pretended I didn't hear. It was my granny, wasn't it? she
said. Her husband handed me change. It's her granny all right, he
said. It's the other lassie that's her mother. As though I wasn't
there. A couple of days later, when they asked if my mother lost a
baby, I decided we didn't need milk that bad and gave up. Some
folk, I told myself, didn't know what they didn't know.

———

Being alone with Cora was all right. Even the pace of her knitting
slowed. She tried to make soup by melting an Oxo cube with
onions and lentils, but the lentils didn't cook and she poured the
lot over the McFarlanes' back wall. After that we had chips from
Piacentini's and tins of two fruits in syrup. The house was calm,
like after a noisy party. Nobody yelled. I was frightened in the
double bed by myself, but I slept. I never asked Cora why she was
in a nightdress so early that night, why the door was open; if she
knew what had happened and simply didn't want to. I didn't
want to conjecture about anything and facts would not have
helped. I kept the key I'd been given and let myself in after school
with it without complaining, and switched on every light in the
living room, the hallway, the kitchen to make the place bright.

Cora came in to a house blazing, lively with electricity. Neither of us knew how to make beds so I slept sheetless. But I knew how to clear a grate and fold the ashes away in newspaper, then light a fire with paper twists and kindling. I had practical skills and Cora appreciated that. It's nice, she said. I like a fire.

Where my mother was, I had no idea. Hospital brought to mind only the place I had last seen my father, and I hadn't known where that was either. We did not mention her much, save to note she wouldn't be long.

After a while she came back with a little vanity bag Marie had packed for her and wearing her nightie under her coat.

I wasn't well, she said. It won't happen again.

That was it. Her face was the wrong colour and her eyes were dull, but she made the beds. Somebody left a big bunch of bright pink gladioli on the doorstep and she said it was Allan, but it wasn't. Allan wouldn't have bought a bunch of flowers if it saved his life. They sat in their paper, uncared for, till I tipped the plastic bulrushes out of our only vase and gave them some water. That was when she cried. Not much, but she cried.

For a time, I went up the hallway with my arms outstretched, feeling round the corner for the light switches. I did not barge. I was biddable and breezy and walked with the lightest of treads. I made no demands, asked no questions, cultivated an expression of vacuous content. I looked for plausible reasons to follow my mother into the kitchen, and sat near her when she made me toasted cheese or her last-thing-at-night cup of tea. Anxious, I listened to the half-worded mumbles that came through the wall at night or watched her through the crack of the living-room door but there was never much to see. One night, talking late, my mother said *we're getting it, whether you like it or not* and the words stuck. She didn't often draw a bottom line and this time, she did: she was getting something of her own choosing and Cora could fly a kite. I didn't wonder what it was – the thing itself was beside the point – what mattered was that she wanted *something*. That she said so with her voice strong and clear, that she wanted it whatever anyone said, embraced me. It made me bury my face in the pillow and howl.

———

Not that long after, my mother found Mr Tough. She went in with the whisky and he was out of bed, stone cold and half his face blue. She didn't need to call a doctor to confirm what she already knew, just to get him to call Myrtle. Myrtle came the next day and gave my mother a crystal fruit bowl that had been lying empty on his window-sill for years as a thank you. She held her hand and mouthed the words because we didn't know sign language. My mother smiled a lot which didn't seem right, but there was no way to say anything back.

We'll get new neighbours now, she said when she came in. More bloody trouble. Poor lassie. She's on her own now.

We missed the hearse arriving. Nobody wanted to see it much or send him off, but I caught a glimpse of Myrtle putting sheets in the bin while I was in the back bedroom, hiding. I stayed in there, trying not to hear the bumps and thumps coming from Mr Tough's bedroom as men in suits moved around, doing what they had to do. My mother came in and sat beside me, making a dip and shifting me towards her weight, but we didn't touch. She didn't say anything for a long time and the sounds from next door got louder. I swear I heard a hinge, creaking. Eventually, without looking up, she spoke.

You'll never have to look after me, she said. She was shivering, winter ferns already feathering their way through the single-pane windows. When I'm ready to go, I'll go.

I had no doubt she was telling the truth. That was what scared me. Even so, it seemed reasonable. There was no good argument against and besides, it was information, not invitation to comment. It was kind information and I tried to treasure it. I did not lift my head and we exchanged no glances but she knew I'd heard. Eventually, she got up and fiddled with the curtains, though there was no more light to let in. The whole of the back of the house was in shadow.

Myrtle's digging up his tatties now, she said. She shook her head. Funny what you do eh? She put her hand to her mouth. Almost imperceptibly, she smiled. I think she waved.

16

Are you sure?

The hairdresser levelled her eyes on me in the mirror, raised my pigtail in one hand. I mean, really sure?

Sure she's sure, Cora said. You don't want your hair that old-fashioned way. You want it short, eh? Modern.

The hairdresser snapped a bubble, shifted her gum from one cheek to the other. Well?

I had never had a haircut before, not a real one, not one that wasn't just an aunty with the kitchen scissors or mum trying to tidy it up. This was the real deal; a salon full of sprays and big dome driers and eye-nipping peroxide. Even if it was only a tiny room at the top of two flights of stairs and the dresser was doing a favour for Cora, it felt special, grown up and full of promise. I might emerge a swan from under these rats' tails given half a chance. Cora had been telling me for ages that a pigtail was stupid. It was silly wee girl hair and nobody wanted to look like a silly wee girl if they could help it. I was fed up with losing ribbons and elastic bands, the screaming knots that tore teeth out of combs. Also bats loved hiding in it. I had seen it in a film and the idea made me lose sleep. The salon had pictures of Twiggy and Lulu, short-bobbed and cool as rocket lollies on the red-painted walls.

Cmon, Cora said, are you a man or a mouse?

There was an answer implied and I gave it. The hairdresser shrugged at the queerness of folk and opened the scissors wide. It took four big bites of the shears, cold metal tipping my neck with every bite, then my head dropped towards the sink as the weight lifted. It was a sensation of head-spinning lightness.

More, Cora said. Shape it a bit, eh? And remember she wants short.

By the time the dresser was done, the floor was thick as a shag-pile rug and my ears felt conspicuous. It was short. It was very short. Spring was not well advanced and even here in the salon, my ears felt chill, as though someone was blowing on them from behind. Men must feel like that all the time, I thought. Then it hit me. Flat-chested in my after-school jumper, the person facing me in the mirror had to admit to her new face. I looked like a boy.

Takes a long time, hair like that, the dresser said, holding up the severed pigtail next to my new face. I wouldny have done it.

Nah, Cora said. It's old-fashioned, long hair. This is better. For godsake, you canny have long hair all your life.

Cora's was shoulder length, blue-black and, for the first time I remembered, longer than mine. My neck prickled and tingled with cold, but I went home feeling modern, the pigtail safe in my back pocket. Boy*ish*, that was the word. I didn't look like a boy, I was boy*ish*. Gamine. It was all the rage. Keen for reassurance, I charged into the living room to show myself off to my mother and hear her exclaim in delight. She had her back to me, stooping over the embers in the grate trying to get the damn thing to light. The room stank of sparked matches.

Look, I squeaked, running on the spot. Look!

She turned from the fireplace, still in her hat from being outside, and I saw the teeth. They looked huge, these teeth, as though they'd been made for a llama and she was trying to stop them taking over her whole mouth.

We've got a piano, she said, stumbling over consonants. I've got new teeth.

Ta-da, Cora sang, traipsing in behind me. Jesus. What in christ's name happened to your face?

My mother dropped the fire tongs. Finally, she had noticed what was different about me.

Oh my god, she said, her face falling as best it could. What have you done to her hair?

It's here, I said, chirpy, and brought it out from behind my back so it dangled, writhing like a prize rat. The lady let me have it.

It was the closest I'd ever seen her come to passing out.

There was a bit of commotion in no particular order and Cora took the huff. She went to her room, complaining she could never do nothing right around here and I made my mother tea. It wasn't very good tea, the colour of magnolia paint with loose leaves floating in it, but she tried it anyway, manipulating her lips over the new teeth with mixed success. And we looked at each other, our new faces to the world.

I suppose it's all right. Her eyes were shiny with the sun on her specs. She touched my fringe. It'll grow on me.

No, I said, it'll grow on *me*.

It took a moment, but she did laugh. She had to put the teeth in a glass to let me know the piano would be coming in a week, though. They took a while, she said, to settle in. She meant the teeth. I'd know all about it when it was my turn.

That was it. No big announcements: we were, in our own way, modest people. The day I acquired a piano, what stole all the thunder was teething gel, the inevitability of dental disease and a rope of dead hair. Lying in bed at night, the scraping sounds of my new hairdo whispering in my ears as I turned on the pillow, I remembered a piano knew our address. I did not wonder what it looked like for fear of building too much hope, spoiling too much surprise: I focused on the fact. The sheets were warm. Cora had gone to bed early, probably reading, and my mother was singing, shaping wordless tunes over her red-raw gums in the kitchen. It was a good feeling, this separateness, each split from the others, thinking different thoughts. Till mum came through to bed, at least, and I pretended to be asleep so I could listen to her breathing. It dawned on me that this was a good time and to enjoy it while it lasted. This was happiness, even. I could take to it fine.

It wasn't till there was a van outside, two big men with shoulders like packing cases and something very heavy edging out of the van doors, that it started to be real. The piano, wrapped in canvas and webbing with folded brown blanket at the corners, inched down two little wooden planks they'd sloped between the van interior and the pavement, creaking and dipping the boards as it came. Two boys I had never seen before rolled up on bikes and watched. They leaned on their handlebars, grinning, anticipating the tightrope act to come.

That's no a piano, is it? a man asked, on his way over the waste-ground wall, smiling and shaking his head as though it was the wildest thing imaginable. Cora waved from her bedroom window to the piano men, an affected wave like a lady about to be cut in half only minus the feathers. She even put on lipstick. We were a side-show: the piano was the star.

The difficulties of manoeuvring something so unmanoeuvrable into the flat were obvious now it was outside and keen to get in. First, there was the narrowness of the front door, then the glass door beyond. Inside the hallway, it would need to be turned sharply, edged into Cora's bedroom to straighten, then out again to cross the hall and head for the living room. Any disasters wait-ing to happen bypassed their chance. After half an hour, the canvas package thumped heavily into the living room, echoing from the recesses of its guts, but whole. The piano was a brute. It looked delicate on TV with Liberace's candelabra on top, but here it showed its truer colours. This was something made of cast iron and whole trees that could give a small elephant a run for its money in a tug-of-war, and we would never be able to shift it, not for anything, once the men had gone. So it was staying, ours, incontrovertibly and for ever. The idea was dazzling.

Unwrapped, it turned out to be a smart upright made of chestnut wood, so highly polished that Cora could use it as a mirror if she took the notion. The word LEHMANN showed in brass on the lid, and there were brass page holders and a strip of red felt muzzling the hinges behind the eighty-eight ivory slats. Like a cow in a bathroom, it dominated the space but it fit nonetheless, backed against the wall we had once shared with Mr Tough, jammed between the window and Cora's chair. Our walls were thin – we heard telly from both upstairs flats if ours wasn't loud enough to drown them out – but nobody had moved in next door yet, so we reckoned that place was OK. Cora stood up and played *Some Enchanted Evening* with lots of black notes and thick, spread-out chords. I had no idea she had that inside her. It was astounding.

She had lessons, my mother said. She had a piano in her time so she better not start. You hear me, Cora? You got everything money could buy.

It needs tuned, Cora said. She looked mean suddenly and I thought for a moment the day would go wrong the way even the best days sometimes did. You'll need to fork out for a tuner before I touch the bloody thing again.

My mother looked crestfallen momentarily, then sat on the sofa back and played *Chopsticks* instead. She got up rubbing her back. That's something else I forgot about, she said. We need a stool.

A teacher, Cora said. Don't forget the teacher. You needny think I'm teaching her.

I'll put you in touch with somebody if you like, said the hauler. A tuner as well. It's all expense eh?

I touched the keys without making any noise at all, just running one finger as far as the red felt edging, back again, making sure they were mine.

Music, my mother said. We'll need to buy sheet music.

Cora laughed and lit a fag. I told you, she coughed. Don't say you weren't warned.

The neighbours came round to ask if they could see and made cooing noises. It was a nice thing to have, they said, a piano. Duncan called in and put *Tiger Rag* on the record player, rushing to the keyboard to move his fingers about and pretend it was him and not the record playing the tune. An old man I had never seen before came up from a house at the end of the road with a big stack of sheet music. He had played when he was young, he said; just dance band and popular medleys, the odd bit of Beethoven. He'd seen the piano coming and thought he'd offer the music to someone who would bring it back to life one day. We let him in to see it and he called me *maestro*, but his fingers were crippled, bent back like fish, and he couldn't play. Young people, he said. It's in their hands now, isn't it? People liked a piano, my mother said. It brought out the best in them. Cora said nothing. That night, dizzy

with excitement and my new-found ability to bring out the best in
people simply by owning something, I asked. Things cost money
and we didn't have any. How had it been paid for? It's second-hand,
she said. I pushed. Even second-hand, pianos cost money. Maybe
I wanted to be sure of keeping the piano without fear someone
would come and take it back. She swithered for a moment and
told me straight. Who paid for the piano, inadvertently and with
no willingness on his part, was dad.

There was money left after the sale of the Cabinette. No one
had expected it, given the fire damage, but a couple of hundred
pounds had come through when he was sick. Since there was no
will, it should have gone to his wife. Then Rose turned up with a
bit of paper he'd scribbled out while he was dying in her spare-
room bed. *Everything in trust for my youngest daughter*, it said.
Nothing for mum, nothing for Cora. Just me.

Two hundred pounds, she said, before funeral expenses. The
injustice of it suddenly shot through her like adrenaline. We were
staying in an attic with one bed, but he had to be the Big Shot. *My
youngest daughter*. Who did he think was paying for *his youngest
daughter* at the time? Not bloody him, anyway.

It had never struck home before that just living cost money.
Things cost money, any fool knew that, but I hadn't grasped, at least
not so clearly, that I was one of those things. *I* cost money simply by
being and she was the one who'd been dumped with it. All this
time, I'd thought that was what *mother* meant: someone with the
weight of *looking after* on her shoulders. That *he* should have done
something had never occurred. Now it did, and it was startling.

Mr Big Shot, she said. She poked the fire, sending sparks on to the rug. He left money for Rose's electricity bill, all right. But nothing for a roof over your head. That's the sort of man your father was. Full of bloody surprises.

It was the *everything in trust*, then, that had bought the piano. Lawyers were supposed to keep it till I was eighteen, but that was a lifetime away, she said, and money whittled to nothing if you just let it sit. So she made up her mind before they spent it on their own fees to get it for me now.

I told them it was for your education, she said. They said they wouldn't pay for singing lessons, only an instrument. So there we are. Piano.

I looked at it behind her, thought about dad writing his note. I didn't know if he had really wanted me to get the money or whether he'd just wanted to keep it off his wife.

They asked Rose, she said, rolling her tongue inside her cheek. They wouldn't take my word. They asked Rose if she thought it was *a suitable use of funds*. Rose with her electricity bill money.

She almost laughed. Then her eyes focused beyond me to somewhere else.

They make you fight for every bloody thing you've got, she said slowly. I waited till she was ready, but there was no more. Eventually she smiled, thinly, asked if I liked the piano. Yes, I said, I did. I *loved* the piano. It was less true than it had been, but true enough.

Don't tell your sister what I just said. She looked at me. It's just private. It's between you and me.

She was telling me something important. Even if I wasn't sure why it was a secret, that's what it would be. I crossed the room and ran my fingers over the high-gloss varnish, refusing to see the cloudy reflection of my own face. My hair was short now, my jaw too thin for comfort. The last thing I wanted to see was the image of dad, looking back.

On Sunday, Rose asked if I'd had any surprises. I knew right away she was angling for me to talk about the piano. She was pretending not to know we had it but I wasn't keen to play games and resented Rose being coy. I chose to let her in on a different secret, took down my anorak hood and released the haircut.

O my god, she said. Her teeth almost fell out.

Later, I hid the pigtail, brought for emergencies, in the cutlery drawer and it scared the living daylights out of her when she reached in for forks. Angus laughed too. We laughed till our eyes watered; we rolled on the floor. Surprise! I hooted, knowing more than I should. I hoped she caught the fury that was burning my chest. Surprise! Life was full of them.

Miss Millar lived round the road from my granny's. Her flat smelled of cream horns, furniture wax and ancient dust. The paper notice pinned to her door that read PIANO TEACHER had curled at the edges and turned beige. There was a plaque with a piano above the ancient box of an instrument, ceramic

pianos on the mantelpiece, and lessons lasted half an hour, timed
on an alarm clock with numerals painted like piano keys. Miss
Millar was keen on her work. Even after the first session, dots
and dashes began turning into tunes: one hand, then two, then
chords and scales. Her teaching books had pictures to colour and
songs about elves. She said it was because I was *a late-starter*.
Lots of people sent tots to her, she said, little ones whose feet
didn't even touch the floor. It didn't put me off. Hoping for great
things, my mother bought a piano copy of a *My Fair Lady* medley
with Audrey Hepburn on the cover, but Miss Millar only laughed
at it.

That's much too difficult just now, she explained. People don't
realise. You don't just put music on the stand and out it comes. It
takes years of practice – day after day.

She asked if I practised hard and I said yes. Every day? I said
yes, but it wasn't true. I wasn't allowed to play when Cora came
in after work and weekends were out because Cora was sleeping
or watching the telly. In the evenings, our walls being thin, my
mother worried the neighbours would be disturbed. But I played
after school without being told. Unless Cora was off work because
of a bank holiday. Even so, I reckoned it was fair to say every day
because that's what it would have been if there had been a chance.
I loved to play. Hearing the notes coming good, a melody rising
out of individual plonks, each acquiring their correct allocation of
timing as the fingers learned how to move, was all delight. *My
Fair Lady*, however, was terrifying. It was stuffed with flats and
sharps and eight-note chords, signs and signals that looked like

semaphore. You had to have a twisted mind, I reckoned, to write music that congested, and turned back to *Chipmunk Parade* with a mix of relief and anti-climax. Learning piano was going to mean sticking with pixies and woodland mammals for a much longer time than my mother had expected and I was afraid she'd get fed up waiting for the tunes she liked and stop paying for lessons. Miss Millar did her best, and became so tragically irritated if I made mistakes, I was keen to work hard. Within a month I was turning out ditties about marionettes and garden swings with promises of greater things to come. Every week, I left her envelope on the mantelpiece, and she didn't count the money till I was gone. Miss Millar had dignity.

And where will you be this time next year? she'd ask as I went down the cold concrete stairs of her block to the security door, its crush of broken glass and cat pee. I'll be like Liberace, Miss Millar, I'd say. I'll be playing Chopin.

She did not haul me up for being precious; she was thrilled. Hahaha, she laughed, you just might!

It was our routine. In the year and a half I spent with Miss Millar, I saw no mazurkas, not even so much as a polka. The *Blue Peter* tune and Souza marches were our apogee. Maybe she didn't give me hard stuff because I wasn't as good as she pretended. Or maybe she didn't know any. I stepped up practice and had a go one Saturday morning with the soft pedal on, hoping it would be quiet enough to get away with. Cora got out of bed and set fire to the edge of the page with a lighter. It didn't stay lit for long, but the varnish marked and the page carried a scorch mark for the rest of its life. I didn't try again. She said it was my fingers next time and I had the feeling she meant it.

———

Donna didn't think much of the piano and wouldn't let me talk about it, even when I tried to curry favour by saying the lessons were stupid and that I was no good.

You'll be thinking you're special next, she said and tried to teach me backgammon with a set she had suddenly started to carry under one arm, but I had no aptitude. Next time my mother tried to give her a jumper, she turned it down. She was getting huffy and awkward and brushing her hair back under an Alice band and couldn't eat Smarties these days without rubbing them on her face to look like lipstick. More than once, her mouth blotted out with red sugar, she told me my hair was horrible: it made me look like *a boy*. Even if I did, it wasn't the kind of thing you said to your friends. Donna was a pig. I took up with another girl the year below me called Lena Ledbetter. She lived in Springvale Street, and was an only child with an only dad who made nice soup out of potatoes. We taught ourselves dance routines to the radio in odd moments, pretending to be on TV. We made costumes out of old clothes and staged our own adverts on the stairs, pretending to be sticks of Wrigley's Spearmint Gum and McKellar Watt sausages. Her dad just laughed. Younger pals, I discovered, played whatever you told them to. Even so, I missed Donna and wouldn't admit it. We were last year at primary and she'd be disappearing before long. I didn't know if it bothered me. We'd all be shifting on whether it did or not.

Where's Donna these days? my mother said. I liked Donna.

I noticed the tense of the verb. We were doing grammar with Miss Phillips and tenses were so easy I smiled doing homework. This tense shook me. Donna in the past was not something I had seen coming. Covering up, I lied and said Donna had a part-time job at Dreever's newsagent round the road from Guthrie Brae. It was a stupid thing to say.

Tell her to get you a job as well, she said. You can pay for your own lessons. Can you play that *On the Street Where You Live* yet? I don't think you're even trying.

Duncan showed up cheerful and brought me three sheets of card and a roll of wire. I tried to look pleased but I didn't make *Man from UNCLE* radios any more.

Oh well, he said, and gave my mother a box of chocolate-coated nuts and she smiled and made tea. She knew how to accept a gift, I thought. I had to learn grace. I had to learn better trying. Grasping straws, I had another look at the medley but it was no go. It still had five flats and chords for more fingers than I could manage at one go. The pages looked like ant wars, a mess of legs and bodies and gaping holes. I knew she would have liked me to play it for her birthday, that it would have been better than a present, but I couldn't manage. Looking at it, I couldn't even think straight. Instead, I practised the hardest thing I knew, a simple arrangement of the *Sugar Plum Fairy* tune from one of Miss Millar's pixie-infested books. It was a classic, Miss Millar said.

She'd know that one. In addition, I'd buy her something knock-
out. With saved money, slipped shillings from Angus and the sale
of three boxes of Lego to people at school, I had nearly sixteen
bob. Sixteen bob was a fortune. I told Cora I was going to the
shops and she sat upright in her chair.

Get her something good, she said, suddenly in cahoots. Not
cheap perfume from Woolworth's or anything like that. She could
do with something nice. Here – she gave me two shillings. Put
that in with whatever you've got.

Touched by the money, I told her, not sure it was the right thing
to do, that I was playing a special tune as well.

What tune? she said.

I didn't mention the *My Fair Lady* stuff. I couldn't play it anyway.
I told her the thing I had picked was something really famous.

What *really famous* thing would that be? she said. She jerked her
head back at the piano, meaning I should play. Let's hear it. I sat
at the keys wondering if it was a trick. Hurry up, she said. I've not
got all day.

Mum wasn't in. I could have said it would break the surprise if
she had been, made some kind of appeal. But she wasn't. So I settled my fingers and played. It wasn't as even as I'd have liked
because I was uncomfortable – she came up behind me as I
worked – but there weren't too many wrong notes in the left hand
and the tune was intact.

That's it, I said, anxious. It's short.

She looked at the keyboard then looked at me. I looked at my
hands.

Aye OK, she said. She shrugged. But that's not a present. That's just you playing the piano.

I know, I said. But she asked. I suspected giving this away was a mistake, but it was out now. I repeated it to dig myself in nice and deep. She asked me to play something. It's extra.

Cora nodded very slowly and went back to her chair. Asked eh? she said, raising her needles and casting round for matches. Some of us must think we're pretty special.

I swithered about giving her the two shillings back, not sure I was allowed to keep it any more, but she told me to put on the TV. It was afternoon races from Epsom. I waited to see if there were any more instructions and changing channels. She didn't look up.

The shops weren't easy. There was nothing very good in the racks of LPs I could afford, and chocolates didn't seem special enough. Then I saw the box. Right in the middle of the window, a big pale green box of TURTLE OIL LUXURY TOILETRIES with pictures of clouds and little flowering shrubs. Under the cellophane, there was soap and talcum powder, perfect cubes of bath-salt wrapped in shiny emerald paper and a tiny bottle of *eau de cologne* with a cherub on the front. It was fifteen shillings. I pored over it so much, wondering if this was the right thing, the assistant came outside in her white coat, and asked if she could help. She seemed to mean it, so I asked what she thought. I needed to know this was the best present anyone could get. She wrapped it for me in purple paper with ribbons, no charge.

She'll love it, she said, sighing. Wish someone would buy it for me. That's special all right.

It took me the rest of the afternoon to show it to Cora. She was in her room listening to the radio. I could hear it through the door. Eventually, I knocked, knocked again and she let me in. The gift was all wrapped up so I tore the edge to let her see. I knew what she thought before she opened her mouth, but the slap took me by surprise. It was sudden even for Cora. Was that my idea of a special present? she said. Talcum powder and soap? That's *special?* She grabbed my fringe and pulled my head down towards the bedspread, tugging at the hair with every sentence. There were a lot of sentences, all half-whispered. I didn't need to catch them all to know what they said. I was selfish and thoughtless and lazy and all the other stuff I'd already heard before. It was a disgrace after all the money my mother spent on me. What was new was the abruptness, an edge of uncontrolled craziness underneath. And the word *snob*. The sentence *you and your fancy ideas* sprung out at me as my eyes watered. It had something to do with the piano. How, I didn't know, but it had.

Just chuck it straight in the bin and tell mum you couldn't be bothered, she said. It shows nothing but what a little snob you are. She was shaking. Godknew where you get these attitudes from, she said. Selfish, selfish, selfish. You think everything's about *you*.

I waited dead still, my hair tangled into her hand, not sure what either of us did next. Then she leaned forward and whispered, calmer, almost as if she was tired. Take the damn thing back. Don't get a credit note or an exchange. She sighed. Just get the money back. She bounced my nose off the iron bed end for emphasis, then let the hair go and sat chewing her nails beside me. I didn't look up or over. I didn't clear the hair out of my eyes. They were watering and nippy, best not on show. Blind, I reached for the package and inched off the yellow spread.

I'll play you cards when you come back, she said, almost to no one. Now clear off. Get out of my room.

Outside on the doorstep with the half-opened box beside me, I wondered if I should sneak back in for Sellotape to fix the wrapping. But I didn't chance it. My mother was in the kitchen, and hadn't heard a thing. And the game of cards had thrown me. I was more than usually confused. Whatever was going on here was about more than soap. I felt the weight of the box in my hand, pictured how nice it had looked in the window with its perfectly drawn flowers and pale blue sky. The little angel on the perfume had looked the model of authentic love. And special, very special. Now, my idea that mum would open it and know right away that she was special too seemed babyish. The whole thing was a ridiculous mistake. A wall of unhappiness rose in me so suddenly I felt sick. I would never learn this, never make it stop. Maybe I deserved it. But these thoughts were scarier than Cora and I pushed them away. Instead, I slotted Cora's two separate shillings, unspent, under her bedroom door and checked my nose wasn't bleeding. It was runny, but fine. I thought about getting a tissue but she might come out and catch more evidence of my *fancy ideas* so I used my sleeve instead. There was a pain in my head and a useless gift in my hands. Damage to undo.

The man wouldn't give me my money, only a credit note. I didn't have a receipt. I took it, defeated. All they had in here were toiletries. They were, as I was now acutely aware, no use to anybody. As I was leaving, the blonde girl came outside with me and handed me a ten bob note and five silver coins.

Bugger him, she said. She took the credit note. You keep your money. She breathed in deep and looked at me. I'm sorry she didn't like it, she said. It's a nice present, maybe just not her kind of thing, eh?

I didn't go home till it was dark and my face was back to rights. I hid down the shore wall, inside one of the little concrete towers where a harbour might have been if Saltcoats had had one. In the end, I got her gloves from Duncan's, the place we bought my school ties. Kitty got her gloves every Christmas so they were a good bet. Plain, ordinary, common-or-garden stretch gloves in black, no bows or poppers. Not special but safe. I wrapped them nicely, and jettisoned the *Sugar Plum Fairy* as too big a risk. If she didn't know I'd planned on playing it for her, she wouldn't miss it. Anyway, she'd only have said it wasn't Lerner and Lowe.

School should have been exciting. We'd be moving on before too long, finishing the last of primary before launching into proper Secondary Education. This was a last chance for the primary specialists to throw caution to the winds with wild-flower pressing competitions and recognition of signs of spring, with Enid Blyton

stories on Friday afternoons and carolling, unbroken voices reading poems aloud before it was all too late. That we had had our
day of things like nature study, toads on the table and the ever-
intriguing wormery and moss collection, was only just occurring.
Instead, there was fretting about the Quali. The Qualifying Exam
was a test to see who would be allowed to pass on to the proper
school and get Latin and who would be stranded at Jack's Road
with Cooking and Technical Drawing. Everyone had to sit it. In
preparation, our lessons changed shape. They revolved around
rotes, tables, tedious little tests. Grammar was dreary – how
many adverbial clauses of time, place, manner or condition did
anyone need to be able to underline in a given text – and Miss
Phillips fed us up on sums that didn't even have proper numbers.
I wasn't against algebra, *per se*, but it went on for pages. Gym
split us into sex groups and we got to watch the boys with their
nipples on show running about outside doing something mysterious called *training* while we got rounders. *Training* looked like
rounders but with more fighting. Girls were allowed to wear
funny little skirts over their navy knickers but my mother said
they were a waste of money. Some girls in class acquired trainer
bras and I thought it likely that would be a waste of money too,
when the time came. I got taller, moodier, more shiftless. I toyed
with faking illness to get rid of school even for a day but hadn't
the nerve to carry it through. In class, I took to yawning and
turning pages of my book to see the next one during reading
periods knowing it was disallowed. I carved the word JOHN for
John Lennon on my desk and drew a face on Brian Coultard's

jotter. Miss Phillips said she was surprised. She was disappointed. She didn't know what had got into me and I should
pull myself together. When I reached home, I put music on and
cried so hard my face hurt. All alone in the house, crying. I didn't
know what had got into me either.

Rose bought a length of orange material and a pattern for a shift
dress. Shift dresses were all the rage, she said; just above the knee
and falling sleek on either side of the body with a line across the
chest. Models had no bust these days. It was the *in thing*.

Perfect for young things, she said, and winked. She meant no
bust. Also, it would go with the short hair. Short was all the rage
as well. I'd be groovy, she said, a real cool cat. All the boys at
school would say wow.

I was a lot less embarrassed when she cut out the trendy chat
and showed me how to open up the pattern and spread the bits
on the floor, then pin the jigsaw pieces on to the cloth. We were
covered in frayed orange fluff by the time the shearing stopped,
but she kept smiling, determined to show me how easy it all was.

If you can make your own clothes, she said, you'll be well
dressed for life. Think how surprised mum will be when you go
home in a nice new dress.

It didn't look like a new dress. It looked like a school nativity
garment that had had a run-in with a lawnmower. But I watched
while she ran lengths of cotton under the presser foot and rocked

her feet on the treadle. It was clever, I thought, the thinking that had gone into such a machine, but not as clever as a piano. I would have chosen the piano every time. Rose held every seam up for my approval, pointing out where the stitches had turned out uneven. Then she held up what we had made and turned it right sides out. The turning made a transformation. This was almost the real thing, ready to try on. It shook over my hair with a flurry of orange dust and thread-ends, snug at the neck and shoulders. The zip would go *here*, she said, poking her finger into my side. All we had to do was pin the hem.

Right, she said, kneeling in front of me with a mouthful of pins, stand up straight and I'll measure.

I stood up so straight I didn't see it coming. Rose reached with her tape and pressed it bang in the middle of one of my nipples. She was pushing hard so the tape didn't slip, but all I knew was a bloom of pain, a strange, nerve-ending burn that spread right down to my knees. By the time she'd finished hemming, I was ready to throw up but I hadn't said a word. I couldn't say *breast* or *chest* or even *ouch*. Angus brought me an orange squash in the middle of it all, while I was in my knickers and vest and at the point of fainting, popping in like it was no big deal. We'll need to get you stockings for this lot, Rose said. Maybe a wee suspender belt and you'll be the belle of the ball. And I was suddenly, within an inch of noticeably, furious. I didn't want to be the belle of anything. I didn't want any more of these terrible moods and pain and embarrassing things happening at all but I couldn't think how to make them stop. The varnish of *being fine* was getting thinner, less dependable. I was turning into a moody cow like Aunty Kitty. If I didn't get a grip, I'd be a cheeky bitch like Cora before I knew what had happened. I wouldn't trust me to behave at all.

That night, I paraded the dress in the living room holding my back concave to deflect attention. My mother asked if there was something wrong with my back.

Nah, Cora said. She's hiding a bust, aren't you?

I didn't know what to say, but it didn't matter. My mother liked the dress. The new dentures had settled in now. If they had changed her face, I couldn't remember what she had looked like before. This was her face now, mended.

You look modern, she said, nice. Your hair's growing. I liked the idea of being *nice*. She looked as if she meant it. We'll be getting you a bra next. She smiled at me with her freshly adapted, clean and even teeth till I almost did it back. Then Cora dropped fag ash on a matinee jacket and said I looked like an orange lolly so I sneaked off to bed. My chest still throbbed where Rose had squashed it, and my appetite hadn't been right all day. Things were becoming harder to control, anticipate, avoid. Twiggy was the woman of the moment and here I was with a fresh growth of hair and breasts. Nobody wanted breasts in this day and age. With my luck what came up under my jumper would be like Cora's and huge. Gangly, my ankles and wrists poking from my pyjamas like puppet extremities, I checked myself in the mirror by the light of the bedside lamp. Bits of me were stretching, growing wilder as I watched. Even my jaw was changing. Daring myself,

I lifted my pyjama top and stared at the blue-white and barely discernible swellings beneath, the little snub-nosed button tops. Like kangaroo pouches, waiting to fill. This was no respecter of persons, this change. It was ruthless, relentless and not done yet. All on my own facing the dead certainty of the unguessable, I was blushing.

17

It was already the second half of the year, dark laying claim to the evenings earlier every day, and the word *holiday* was being bandied about with intent. It had never happened before and I wasn't sure I liked it. Angus and Rose fancied a trip to Blackpool. I could take the orange frock, Rose said. All the best young ladies had special clothes to go away in, and the shift dress could be mine. There were amusements and a beach in Blackpool, she said. I'd like it. There were donkeys on the beach and arcade machines. We would have a *lovely* time, all four of us.

The fourth was my mother. Angus would drive, Rose would choose a nice little B and B and we'd go to the Pleasure Beach together.

If you go she'll go: simple as that. Rose spoke as though I couldn't refuse. We'll pay for the petrol and everything.

Even so, they waited for my decision. I'd rather they said they were taking me whether I wanted it or not. The responsibility of being the centre of it all like this, of pushing my mother into it too, was all a bit tacky. Why Rose wanted to take my mother anywhere escaped me: why my mother would accept a holiday with a woman who'd taken her to court would have escaped me further still if I'd known. The bit I liked the sound of was the donkeys. But if I said yes I'd be to blame if the whole thing went cock-eyed.

Mum hadn't shown much enthusiasm. Rose was paying for me, she said, but even so. How would we pass the time? I toyed with telling her about the donkeys and didn't. It would sound like I was keen. Duncan, come for a visit between shifts with a fresh consignment of biros and rubber bands in his pockets, took me to one side at the doorstep as he was leaving.

Holiday in the offing, he said. I shrugged. Nice for your mum, he said. She'll get her breakfast cooked for her. I shrugged. It'll get her back to her old self, maybe. After the last wee while and everything. She's not been right since she came back from that hospital. She could do with the break.

It took a moment to think what he meant. Then it clicked. He knew the secret. He knew about the pills and the ambulance and everything that went with it. And if he knew, Rose and Angus knew it too, which was why they were doing this. They wanted to take *her* away, not me. The relief of working this out was momentary, because it also meant more people than I thought knew my mother had tried to finish herself off. They knew me and Cora were rubbish daughters, not able to look after a goldfish never mind their own mother. Duncan was waiting. I was turning mental somersaults and keeping him on hold when he had his work to go to. I must look spoiled and petty, I thought, not wanting to go. I couldn't look him in the eye.

Tell her you'll go, he said. You be nice.

Be nice. That was what I had to be. He tilted my cheek so I had to lift my face. I focused on his ear. Regardless, he slipped a pound note into my hand.

Have a go on the Ghost Train for me, eh?

He curled my hand around the money, held it tight shut. I couldn't quite manage the smiling back but I tried hard. Nice was going to win through if it killed me.

———

Blackpool was for ever away, but we took grapes. My mother did *Silver Threads* but Rose joined in and since Rose couldn't hold a tune to save her life, I started a game of I-Spy. I was too old for I-Spy, but the need was pressing. Mum caught my eye and smiled. We were sharing something, even if it was only that Rose was a rotten singer. It was a good start.

We had a big rigmarole finding a car park, but the address was easy enough and the rooms were small but neat. My mother dusted the dresser top with her sleeve anyway, shifted a little lady with a basket ornament to one side to see if she left a ring on the wood.

I don't like strange beds, she said. You never know who's died on these sheets.

In the morning, I found one of the towels in the bathroom had a hole in and folded it so no one could see. I washed the soap after I'd used it and settled it back in its dainty pink cradle on the sink surround so mum wouldn't have to face it being slimy. We ate only the toast for breakfast, except Angus, who polished off everyone else's eggs and black pudding as well as his own.

Angus likes his food, Rose said. As if we didn't know.

Out along the prom, we saw Kiss-Me-Quick hats hanging by their red cord chinstraps and rubber swim rings with spots. We counted striped awnings and deck-chairs up for hire, and laughed out loud at giant red candy dummies and candy floss spirals bluer than blue-rinsed hair. There were lots of little Blackpool towers for sale, some that looked as though they would break if you stared too hard, and postcards of red-faced men holding cucumbers and bunches of bananas, or looking down women's jumpers while squeezing melons. I didn't mind at all about the crowds, the litter and the endless spill of children squealing. I liked it because Rose and Angus did, and every time my mother laughed, I felt almost sure she liked it too. Away from home, my mother had time on her hands. She could sit staring into space if she wanted, smile unconsciously at other people's children building castles on the cold sand, shivering in their trunks and summer cardies. She said the B and B was the first place she ever stayed she didn't have to clean and Rose laughed and said it was nothing fancy. We were all here together and that was what mattered. I wished I could think of something nice like that to say, but Rose had already said it and once was enough. My mother walked side by side with Rose while I hung back with Angus, keeping an eye. There was a flavour of best-behaviour about it all, but it was genial. As we drifted along the Pleasure Beach, by the stalls with jewellery and temple bells that fitted on the ends of your fingers and alloy cow-bells on strings, we passed, I imagined, for normal. It was 1967, a bright afternoon and *Hey Mr Tambourine Man* was playing over a tinny tannoy. A poster advertised that Jimi Hendrix had been and gone at the Odeon, and Frankie Howerd was yet to come to the Winter Gardens. I bought a paper daisy for my hair from a stall. Rose sang along with *Puppet on a String* blaring from a radio as she walked on the sands barefoot, her legs risen with varicose veins, and Angus looked at her as though she was a thing of beauty, the light of his life. Even my mother laughed.

I huvny been to Blackpool for years, she said. She breathed in the seaweed, laughing and choking on the ozone drifts. Last time I was here your dad was still alive. She didn't say she'd been with him, but the mention suggested she might. She didn't call him Bloody Eddie or *your father*. She let herself be. It's nice, she said. I feel – she smiled at me, eye to eye – refreshed.

The B and B was in Cocker Street. I remember being embarrassed by the name, afraid we'd have to ask directions. We went back for afternoon tea and to wash our hands and use the toilets. You couldn't trust anywhere else, my mother said. Soap in cafés gave you diseases. The afternoon was for the Pleasure Beach alone. Angus came with me on the Ghost Train to see if I would scream, but it wasn't in my nature. On the Log Flume, Rose's top set popped out but she caught them. I did the Big Dipper by myself, and didn't scream there either. I wouldn't do the Tunnel of Love because it was soppy. Everything else was a triumph. My mother came on none of the rides despite teasing, coaxing and bribery. She watched. She wore a headscarf and a camel coat and looked like the Queen at Balmoral. Her powder gave her face a dandelion-clock glow and she wore her best lipstick and her wedding ring. We took no pictures because we had no camera, but Rose paid a man to take a snap of Beth when she wasn't looking and said we could collect it next morning. The famous illuminations were still being strung on their frames, ready to light up after we'd gone, but we walked out at night anyway, enjoying the sound of the sea. It was distant now, far receded down the sand, but you could hear it rubbing its hands in the gaps between records from the kiosks along the front. Halfway back to the B and B we found the Pyramids Egyptian Café and went inside for egg and chips, Bovril and cream crackers. Angus told me the Bovril came from camels. I inhaled the steam, thinking it was the life, and Rose and my mother, on the other side of the Formica table, glowed from the early chill outside. Nobody fought. There was a picture of Tutankhamun behind the counter on one side, and a picture of Manchester City on the other. And I was Cleopatra, scented with Nile water, eating the food of the gods. I liked holidays, I thought, cupping the mug in my hands to warm my fingers. Next time, I'd bring gloves.

———

My mother was already up when I woke, lying beside me and looking out of the window. We hadn't closed the curtains.

Look, she said. You can see the Tower from here. It's famous, that, and here we are looking at it.

She dressed in the landing toilet and let me do the same.

Home today, she said. Hooray.

Hooray, I said, not sure what was so great about it. Hooray. I bought two cowbells on red cords, a Kiss-Me-Slowly hat for Cora and a dummy-shaped lollipop to take home. Angus bought me a plate with the Tower painted on it and told me they had a Tower just like it in Paris. If I kept the plate, he said, I would remember he'd been the one who told me when I finally saw it for myself. I'd see Paris one day, he said and I looked at him as though he was crazy. I recalled Duncan encouraging me to be nice and pretended I thought it might be true instead. Rose collected the snap of my mother from the Pleasure Beach kiosk and gave it to her as a gift.

There, she said. That's a lovely reminder of a lovely time.

She almost kissed her on the cheek but didn't. My mother took the photo and did her polite smile, then put it in her bag. She didn't look at it. Nobody pressed.

On the way back, Rose and Angus got out of the Hillman to stretch their legs near a newspaper shop. Rose's voice came back as they went inside, the word *toilet* three times. My mother shook her head and sighed a deep, long sigh.

What are they like, she said, to no one in particular. Mutt and bloody Jeff. I'll be glad when we get back, see Cora's been behaving herself. I bet the house is upside down. You all right?

I was all right. I was always all right. Since I was wearing my orange frock, I aimed for *nice* but she was looking out of the window at an empty Carlisle Street, a stray dog and a phone box.

Cora came to meet us at the door. She even spoke to Rose. Angus brought our bags but didn't come in, despite the invitation. They had to get back. Sure Cora hadn't been eating properly, my mother went straight to the kitchen and made chips. I was too full of grapes to want any, but I sat in while they ate. Cora wore her cowboy hat with the kissing message on the front, the chinstrap dangling like jowls. It suited her. She looked as if she could wear one all the time. She looked up at me and winked, a chip halfway to her mouth.

You pick this for me? she asked. I nodded. Some kid, eh? she said. Put on the telly on your way out.

The news and highlights from Doncaster. As though we'd never been away. My mother tipped out the suitcases and announced she had washing to do.

On you go, she said, keen to get on. You've been stuck in a car all day. Away out and play.

I had thought we would sit for a while, talk about the things we had seen and done, tell Cora about the Pleasure Gardens. Mum was home, though. The telly was on and the holiday finished. Things wheeled to a stop so suddenly, you could forget they'd happened at all if you didn't make an effort to remember. I thought about asking to see the photograph in my mother's bag, hold on to the feeling of being in Blackpool before it washed away entirely, but the moment didn't seem right. I left it behind me and went outside. The top step was cold, but a good place to watch the evening gather and thicken, sucking up the scent of damp earth. The roses were still in good shape – Queen Mother, Princess, Ena Sharples, Iceberg – and Michaelmas daisies and lupins were filling out under the window. When darkness fell, the scent of night stock would drift like a warm satin scarf from the beds beneath the windows.

Shut that bloody door, Cora shouted. I'm warning you. It's freezing in here.

Riled enough, almost, to get out of her chair. But she was missing it. I was out here breathing in the coming night and she was inside, the same place she'd been all weekend. Some things passed her by completely.

———

I took round the cowbell I had bought for Donna before it turned pitch, but she wasn't in. I rang the bell twice and looked up at the window from the street in case she was really in and playing hard to get, but there was nothing. It was only when I gave up and turned to go that the door to their house opened, and a thin, thin woman drifted out and across the thick tangle of grass that made their back green. She looked luminous with the reflected street light and I saw she really did have red hair. So red it was scarlet.

Hello, hen, she said. I know who you are.

I was so surprised I didn't say anything back, but the woman didn't seem to expect much. She just started gathering her towels off the line.

Donna's away, she said, not even turning in my direction. She's away to England, hen. She's away to live in a place called Kent now. She was folding a big green towel over her knee, pressing it into a flat square. She looked at me fleetingly, checking I was listening, then headed off. She'll not be back, she said over her shoulder. She's away.

The door closed soundlessly behind her after she'd gone and I stood for a moment, taking it in. The cowbell made a bump in my trews pocket so I took it out and wondered what to do. It said STRAWBERRY FIELDS FOREVER with a clumsy engraving of a daisy. I guessed I could post it, but DONNA HART, KENT was unlikely to get there. And besides, the gift hadn't been the point. I just wanted to see her. Maybe she was staying with a relative, maybe she'd shifted school. Maybe anything, really. Nobody ever explained the details. I'd hear a lot of ideas from Granny McBride, I had no doubt, but what was true would remain a mystery. It wasn't for me to know. Sometimes people disappeared. That bit at least was no surprise.

On the way back home over Guthrie Brae by the auto-spares and the billboard hoarding, I realised I had not one photo of Donna and never would. She might have come round to see me to say goodbye and only Cora had been in. I'd never know. And it made no difference now. I imagined invisible waves, like radar, radiating from my head as I walked, carrying messages. I imagined Donna sitting up in a bedroom in England, sensing the waves as they tumbled through her window and into her head, glowing with the power of their good wishes. She would know it was me, missing her. I hoped wherever she was, she knew I wished her well.

———

Just before my twelfth birthday, the air thick with possible snow, I came first equal in the mid-term class exams. First equal had no shine. There were no real strictures placed on how I spent my time in school, just that I didn't get into trouble and that I repeat my done-and-dusted trick of coming first in exams. That was all I had to do: keep my nose clean and beat other people hollow. On the way home with a report card that said I'd reneged on half my contract, I stood for a moment on the railway bridge and scanned the road that led into Ardrossan. There were big houses down there, the plantation park and benches for people to sit on in summer. It was the road I'd be taking to the academy next year, not now, but I stood on top of the bridge, catching my blazer on the hawthorns till my fingers frosted up, admiring the view.

My mother handed the card to Cora without saying a word. Cora looked over it once, taking in the information like it was betting odds. She was pleased and not pleased at the same time. I could see it.

Well, she said, and raised her eyes over the rim to focus into mine. Turn up for the books.

You're always first, though, my mother said, as though I'd

forgotten the rules. What happened? I said I didn't know. Was it hard questions? She didn't know what happened in exams any more. I suspected it was gym that had done it. For the first time we had been graded for cartwheels and forward rolls, but telling her that wasn't going to help. I had no explanation worth hearing.

Cora looked at me, almost playful. I know what happened. Was it a boy? The question was unexpected. She sighed and crossed her cable needles while I tried to work out what she was driving at before I rushed in. This first equal person? she said, enunciating clearly. Was it a boy?

It was. It was Brian Coultard.

There you are then, Cora said. She threw the report card up in its brown paper cover so it fluttered against my shoulder like a bat with lousy radar. I told you. She's let some boy be first equal. Cora looked smug. I said it was only a matter of time.

My mother slumped, pulling the crocheted antimacassar off the seat back. Oh, pet. *Pet* for crying out loud. She never said *pet*. Her eyebrows made tragic slopes. What did you do that for?

Cora snorted. What do you think? She's sucking up to some boy, trying to make him think he's the big cheese.

She'll do better next time, though, won't you? my mother said, sifting me into the third person for safety. The idea I might have control over the quirks of exam marking was cheering her up. Maybe it's a blip.

Hoo, Cora said. This is just the start. I know how it goes from here.

Shut up, you, my mother said, gathering her dander. She's nothing like you.

Oh is she not? Cora said. She put her knitting down, always a bad sign.

No, she bloody isn't. She's not man-daft for a start. She's not going to do what you did or anything like. She's got more sense.

Cora laughed to show she didn't care what anybody thought. It showed she cared very much. Aye right. You think she's so bloody special. Well, just you wait. Just you watch. And if I'm man-daft where did I learn it?

You learned nothing from *me*, my mother said. Her voice was cracking. You just keep your mouth shut. You've no respect for nothing, you, least of all your own weans.

Cora's face was a picture. All her features fell open. You dare, she said. You dare tell me *I've* got no respect? Me that brings in keep money when she does damn all, except start bloody arguments?

She's eleven, my mother said. Of course she doesny pay keep money. You're nearly thirty for christsake.

She's nearly twelve, Cora said. She could get a paper-round. But she's Saint Theresa of the Bloody Roses all of a sudden and *I'm* the Bad Girl. I've dealt with my troubles. My mother snorted. I have! Cora said. It's *her* you should be hauling up. She's done nothing but hold you back, for crying out loud. You've said so yourself.

You shut up, my mother said, desperate. Her cheeks were crimson. What *you've* done is nothing like her. Just stop dragging her into it right now.

You've said it often enough, Cora lashed back. At least I knew what to do with what I didn't want. Well, hell mend you for casting her up at me. Cora's eyes were blazing, the tip of her cigarette teetering with ash on the chair arm. She's let some boy trip her up in an exam and *I know why*, don't think I don't.

She's nothing of the kind! My mother's voice split, on the top end of an octave. Her eyes were brimming.

She's everything of the kind! Cora said. Chip off the old block. Ask her if she chases boys. Go on.

My mother caught her breath. So did I.

On you go, Cora said, a striker with the ball back, taking her time. On you go, *ask*.

No she doesny, my mother said, struggling against panic. Sure you don't? She looked at me, waiting.

No, I said, flatly. I had tried for outrage but it wouldn't come. None of what was going on around me made sense, and now I was in the middle. No, I said again, looking as angry as I could muster against an increasingly terrifying level of alarm. *Of course* I didn't let boys chase me.

But I did, I did. I sat there on the rug telling terrible lies with the pair of them on either side, fighting about things that had nothing to do with me and lied like a trouper. I *had* chased boys and what's more I had caught them. I had chased two poor souls up and down the central staircase at break and lunch times with two other girls for Kiss, Cuddle or Torture, reckless with excitement, and when both boys chose torture, I kissed them anyway. Kissing was the best torture I could think up, I reasoned, that was why.

But it wasn't really. I kissed them *because I wanted to*. I kissed them because my nervous system went on fire when I chased them, the rush as strong as a whole box of sugar mice, and it made me wilful, wild, someone I hardly knew. What's more, I did a *lot* of chasing and a *lot* of kissing and Robert Paterson, who resembled a potato with freckles, said he'd tell if I didn't stop. Now, in the middle of whatever was happening between my mother and my sister, I wondered if he had. I wondered if he had shopped me to Mr Waverley and Mr Waverley, in turn, had told Cora. I imagined Cora bringing pictures out of her knitting bag that showed me mouth-locked to Robert Paterson's face. I wondered if it could get any worse and I knew it could. If the past five minutes had meant anything at all, they meant this wasn't the worst by a long chalk. Worse still was what happened next. Chasing boys and letting them sidle up to you in exams and lying your face off was *only the beginning*. Something terrible, so terrible no one would name it, followed on. It had something to do with being *man-daft* and it possibly had something to do with children and it had happened to Cora. It sounded as though it had happened to my mother as well, and now they were fighting about it happening to me. I didn't even know what it was. The closest I got was grasping that you were good at school, then it melted because of boys and your life fell apart.

Watching their faces as they hurled half-understood insults at each other, the feeling of being *in the way* while most of it raged over my head was letting something else dawn as well. This wasn't about me. This fearful argument out of – out of as near as dammit *nothing*, now I thought about it – these lacerating spats that reared out of nowhere at all, were in some way connected but not, at least not that much, to me. This was about Cora and mum; mum and Cora doing something they'd done since Cora left Glasgow behind and turned up at the attic with her single suitcase and her make-up bag. Longer, even than that. *Weans*, my mother said. As though there had been more than one baby Cora had left behind. *If I'm man-daft, where did I learn it?* I've dealt with my troubles. My *troubles*. It was always the same in our house. Nothing you knew was solid.

With an awful sinking of heart, I saw the road before me veer sharply off the straight and narrow to a dust-dry rail siding, strewn with a tumbleweed of missed chances and buffalo skulls. On the one hand, boys were leading me to hell on a handcart: on the other, a runaway train was bearing down at full pelt that hardly saw I was there. Everything I did was kindling. My ears were dinning, thinking it. Meanwhile, my mother, hiding terrible secrets, was still looking at me. She was a picture of apprehension and disappointment. Opposite sat Cora, her smile spreading like chip fat. Knowing the odds here were fearful, I spoke. I heard myself doing it.

No, I said. Of course I didn't let boys chase me. *No*.

I felt the word LIAR rising in scarlet on my forehead.

No? Cora said. She looked at me, reading everything. Say *no* one more time when it's a bare-faced lie and I'll break your bloody arm.

I burst into tears.

It was weak. Maybe it was the end of the tether, the feeling of having my mind read when I didn't know what was in it myself. Maybe it was fear. Maybe it was the eggshells and the tiptoeing and the shifting sands. But crying was beyond the pale. It was not on the cards and I was doing it. I keeled over like a tree on to the fireside rug and bawled. Nobody did anything but watch for whole, silent seconds till I stopped out of sheer embarrassment. Slowly, Cora struck a match.

Oh for christsake. I heard the draw, the silent crackle of the tobacco strands, catching. Get. Up.

I sat up sniffing, trying not to look at anybody.

Who cares? Who cares about you or your stupid report card? The match burned down so far it seared the tip of the nail on her index finger, spoiling the neat point she had filed there. Bloody Drama Queen, she said. As much use as piss in a kettle.

Here, my mother said. She was worried and reached for her purse. I knew what she was about to do. She was going to send me for something sweet. That would soothe the whole thing over till it happened another time. Here, she said. She curled money inside my hand and rather than let it fall, I held on. Away you go and get us ice-cream.

I'm sure she thought she was saying more, but none of it was out loud. Cora lit another match. The living room smelled of phosphorus.

On you go, my mother said.

My nose was swollen, I could feel it throbbing as I turned and headed for the glass door. That slight resistance under my fingers as the door rose on the crest of the ball catch, clicked to let the world know the hard bit was done.

Three cones, my mother shouted, tentative.

And raspberry sauce, Cora roared. Don't bother coming back without the raspberry.

I caught the word *useless*, the sound of a match-head grating off sand before the glass closed behind me.

———

Carlo in the shop saw something was wrong, but he didn't draw attention. I remembered to take the change, asked for a paper to keep the ice-cream safe. I was perfectly polite but it took effort. At least it was calmer when I got back, out of breath from rushing so the cones didn't melt. I put mine on to a saucer, trying to look busy while my mother waited, fussing.

You not coming? she said. Her face was white. Don't sit in here by yourself.

All right, I said. I just need a minute.

She shifted the treats in her hands. I said my stomach hurt, I'd be through in a minute. I had homework and a sore head. I'd be right through.

I remember breathing out, closing my eyes, breathing in. It was red behind my eyelids, streaked with gold from light behind the curtain. On this canvas, I pictured the roll of uneven grass just outside, the sail-rigs of washing lines that led to our eight by eight plot full of broken stems and claggy puddles. Five months of the year it was just brown porridge but in summer, we had rhubarb, its leaves the size of Hiroshima mushrooms, fat buds of cabbage and leggy tattie shaws. You sank a fork into the earth and up they came, tiny skulls clinging to a tracery of nerves, smelling of newness and decay at the same time. Mr Gregg's pigeons would be on top of the shed with their wings tucked up, nodding like women in a knitting bee. The pictures made themselves, dissolved and made themselves afresh. It has hard to hold for any length of time, though. The McFarlanes' telly was playing the tune to some kind of comedy upstairs and I could hear a man's voice, laughing. This was a street where people lived quiet and kept their gardens neat. We had flowers and vegetables and fed the birds our cast-off bread. When something crackled on the other side of the kitchen I opened my eyes slowly and there was Cora, watching me.

Are you going to eat this or not? She nodded at the saucer of ice-cream. It wasn't much more than a thick, white puddle now. No, I said. I may have sighed. I'm not hungry any more. No thank you.

Your mother paid for that, she said.

I knew. But I was tired now. I don't want it, I said.

She stared down at the plate. You don't want it, she said. Don't think this report card thing is finished, cos it's not.

No, I said, I didn't think so. She looked at me intently, her eye make-up not quite as neat as it should have been. My mother shouted from the living room – *Cora, tell her there's a wildlife thing on, tell her to come through* – but she barely blinked. She wiped her mouth, picked up the saucer and brought it closer. You have it so bloody easy, she said. Her face was steady, almost sad. You don't know you're born.

Then, with no change of expression, she bit into the molten ice-cream, hauled the neck of my jumper close to her face and kissed me. I felt her tongue push and the cold mess slither from her mouth to mine, swilling to the back of my throat before I registered what was happening. Then she pressed her fingers against my neck, just at the bump, to make me swallow. When she pulled back, her face was smeared and she wiped it on my school top. That done, she stood back and poured what was left on the plate, red sauce and all, across my jumper like the mark of Herod.

Always remember, she said, in a tiny voice like bells, Jesus and Cora love you. Her eyes were bright, bright blue. We love you very much.

When she started laughing, that thick-as-paint laugh she saved for really good jokes, I stood up and ran. She shouted after me but I didn't hear the words. I kept going.

Opposite Carlo's and the start of Argyll Street was a sharp bend in the road where the cars had bounced up on to the pavement and worn the kerb away, and beside the broken kerb, near the tracks of stray tyres, was a call-box. It was the only call-box for miles and stank of dog and fag ash, but something took me there, led me to open the door and press myself inside. The little glass squares that made the box were sweaty from the breath of strangers and the iron frames, flaking red paint, were cold enough to burn. The only part of me that wouldn't be a blur from the other side would be my legs, just enough to mark ownership. A piece of torn plastic next to the phone had some indecipherable instructions for how to use the box, a picture of a taxi and an advert. The advert was only one word and I had to rub my eyes to see it through the waves, but it was a good word. DESPAIR it said, DESPAIR and a number. My mother's change, still warm in my pocket, unfolded in my hand. I looked from machine to number, number to machine, feeding in the digits one big turn of the dial at a time.

Samaritans, a woman said. I almost dropped the receiver. She didn't know and just kept going. Who's there?

I said nothing. She waited.

Who's there? Is there someone there?

I was trying, but nothing was coming out. I cleared my throat and managed a moaning noise.

Are you there? she said. I can hear someone there. Are you all right?

Yes, I said. It was a silly, squeaky voice that said it, like a wee girl through helium. I'm fine.

And what's your name?

I managed *Jan*, coughed, then tried again. *Janice*, I said. The oddness of allowing my own name to pass over my lips. *My name's Janice.*

You sound young, she said. What age are you, Janice?

And it occurred to me I was eleven. I was eleven turning twelve years old and talking to a stranger whose number I had found in a dirty call-box. She could have been anyone. So could I.

Hello, she said. Are you there?

I said nothing.

What made you call the Samaritans?

I didn't know. The little notice with the word DESPAIR seemed no reason at all. The whole thing was crazy.

My name is Janice, I said. Then I howled. It was a noise like a cat in the middle of the night and there was no stopping it. Through the awful noise I was making all by myself, I heard the lady with the gentle voice call someone else's name and put her hand over the mouthpiece making a noise like falling underwater. Maybe people my age weren't allowed to do this. Maybe this was a waste of her time and I'd get into trouble for being a nuisance call. Maybe there was someone desperate to speak and I was blocking the line. The words wouldn't come. They wouldn't even start. So I hung up. Outside, a car juddered against the pieces of kerbstone and kept going as though nothing had happened. I waited to see what would happen next but the street was quiet, not a soul on the road. For no good reason, I made cracks in two of the glass squares in the box, kicking hard with the sides of my good school shoes. Then I rubbed my face till it hurt, hit my head off the iron edge of the call-box door and waded my way back to Carlo's and looked east, down the length of Wellpark Road. At the end of it, tucked out of sight, was our house. It had been built by an architect, my mother said, a Foreigner with Big Ideas. That was who had them. That house was where I lived, where we all lived. I couldn't get away so it had to be and now I had to go back. My mother needed me. I was watching out for her because I'd promised and because someone had to. You don't get everything in this life and you don't just leave people. It mattered to think about that and go home.

I never got to see the photo Rose paid to have taken of my mother in Blackpool, but I remember her being there. I can picture the fuzzy edge of her lipstick, feathered by the sea breeze, the down on her jaw. I can summon up the sickly smell of hot dogs and pop-corn and cheap red sauce, Rose singing; the plastic smell of the car. Some things you remember whole anyway. Photos aren't everything. They serve for when memory refuses; grey filler for the gaps. They don't prove much save that you were there, but it's something. You were there.

This is a picture I don't remember, but I'm in it all the same.

It's a girl on the front step in tartan trews with stirrup straps, a home-knitted cardi with too-short sleeves and wild boy hair need-ing cut. Cold concrete presses beneath her thighs. She's squinting up at whoever is taking the shot, not smiling, exactly, but open-eyed and keen. There are only six more months of Jack's Road School left to run. She knows that too. She has no idea what the future will be like, only that it's coming and there's no escape. She has no idea that by Christmas, her stammer will be back, she will steal her first lipstick, and her granny's flat will burn down to the bedsprings leaving a rosary and a glass eye behind; no idea that music is set to open in her life like a bunch of fat, blown roses. But what she knows, she knows for sure.

She knows her name is Janice, that nobody chose it. She knows that some people die and that some people make mistakes and that there's no changing it, no appeal. She knows it's nobody's fault that she's a sensitive plant with a memory like a packet of razor blades, but it's not hers either. You get what you get and that's your hand, the same for everyone. It's fixed. The cards would never change, not now, but with luck, they might be shuffled, cut, turned to best advantage. Inventiveness counts for something. She's biding her time, waiting to play.